Seeming and Being in Plato's Rhetorical Theory

SEEMING & BEING
in Plato's Rhetorical Theory

Robin Reames

The University of Chicago Press
Chicago and London

The University of Chicago Press, Chicago 60637
The University of Chicago Press, Ltd., London

Published 2018
Printed in the United States of America

27 26 25 24 23 22 21 20 19 18   1 2 3 4 5

ISBN-13: 978-0-226-56701-3 (cloth)
ISBN-13: 978-0-226-56715-0 (e-book)
DOI: https://doi.org/10.7208/chicago/9780226567150.001.0001

Library of Congress Cataloging-in-Publication Data

Names: Reames, Robin, author.
Title: Seeming and being in Plato's rhetorical theory / Robin Reames.
Description: Chicago ; London : The University of Chicago Press, 2018. | Includes bibliographical references and index.
Identifiers: LCCN 2017054843 | ISBN 9780226567013 (cloth : alk. paper) | ISBN 9780226567150 (e-book)
Subjects: LCSH: Rhetoric—Philosophy. | Philosophy, Ancient. | Plato. | Sophists (Greek philosophy)
Classification: LCC PN173.R43 2018 | DDC 808.0092—dc23
LC record available at https://lccn.loc.gov/2017054843

♾ This paper meets the requirements of ANSI/NISO Z39.48-1992 (Permanence of Paper).

In memory of my father

What is so perilous, then, in the fact that people speak, and the fact that their speech proliferates? Where is the danger in that?

—MICHEL FOUCAULT

Contents

Preface *xi*

Introduction
Literacy, Dramatic Form, Metaphysics: Rereading Plato's Rhetoric *1*

- Orality, Literacy, and Rhetorical Beginnings *3*
- Martin Heidegger and the Critique of Metaphysics in the West *7*
- Literary-Dramatic Interpretations of Plato *11*
- Sophists and Sophistry in Plato *13*
- Plan of the Book *16*

1 **The "Cosmetics" of Sophistry: Seeming and Being in the *Gorgias*** *21*

- The *Gorgias* Dialogue and the Role of the Analogy *24*
- The Problem of the Double *Mu* *30*
- The *Kommi* in *Kommôtikê*: Athenians and Luxury *32*
- War: The Historic Context and the Thematic Unity of the *Gorgias* *38*
- Conclusion *43*

2 **The Oral Poet and the Literate Sophist: Divine Madness and Rhetorical Inoculation in the *Phaedrus*** *47*

- Rhetorical Disunity in the *Phaedrus* *49*

- The Speeches in Contrast *54*
- The Palinode as Epic: Themes, Formulae, Symbols *60*
- Writing and Rhetoric *67*
- Conclusion *72*

3 Heraclitean Opposition and Parmenidean Contradiction: Pre-Socratic Ontology and Protagorean Sophistry in the *Cratylus*, the *Theaetetus*, and the *Euthydemus* *77*

- Heraclitean Etymologies and Protagorean Relativism in the *Cratylus* *79*
- The "Man-Measure" Doctrine and Heraclitean Flux in the *Theaetetus* *86*
- The "Impossibility of Contradiction" and Parmenidean Nonbeing in the *Euthydemus* *93*
- Conclusion *96*

4 Sophistry without Measure, Dialectic without Rhetoric: The Interpretive Dispute in the *Protagoras* *99*

- Antilogic, Eristic, Dialectic, and the *Protagoras* *101*
- Socrates versus Protagoras: Simonides's Poem in Its Dialectical Context *104*
- Socratic Sophistry, Eristic, and Antilogic in the Interpretation of Simonides *111*
- Conclusion *118*

5 The Rhetoric of *Mimêsis*: Sophistic Imitation and Seeming in the *Republic* *123*

- *Mimêsis* as Language *127*
- *Mimêsis* as Falseness *133*
- The Dubious Metaphysics of *Mimêsis* *137*
- Conclusion *147*

6 Imitators of Truth: The Rhetorical Theories of *Onoma* and *Rhêma* in the *Sophist* and the *Cratylus* *149*

- The Stranger's Method of Division and the Sophist's Heracliteanism *151*
- Louis Bassett and the Problem of *Onoma* and *Rhêma* *154*

- *Onoma*, *Rhêma*, and the *Logos* of *Mimêsis* *158*
- *Onoma* and *Rhêma*, *Logos* and *Mimêsis* in the *Sophist* *161*
- Conclusion *167*

Epilogue The Past and Future of Plato's Rhetorical Theory *169*

Notes *175*
Bibliography *205*
Index *225*

Preface

This book was born, as many are, out of a passing curiosity. In an undergraduate course on rhetoric that I taught at the University of Illinois at Chicago, we were reading the *Gorgias* dialogue. One day in class, my students and I were breaking down the elaborate analogy in which Socrates compares rhetoric to cookery and sophistry to what is commonly translated as "cosmetics." I had taught both the dialogue and the analogy numerous times before, but for some reason, on that particular day, the term *cosmetics* struck me as odd. It seemed out of place in the analogy, and the root in Greek was unrecognizable to me. Upon further investigation, I discovered that the term in question was anomalous and idiosyncratic, and that its translation as "cosmetics" was anything but straightforward. My pursuit of a better translation for the term ultimately led to this longer project. I am grateful to the students in that course for letting me teach them about Plato's *Gorgias*, and in so doing, setting me on a course that would begin unlock so many of Plato's texts, which up until that time I now believe I had been reading entirely wrongly. That simple question inducted me into the prismlike puzzle of Plato's thought, and converted me from a reluctant reader to an acolyte.

I consulted numerous translations of the dialogues while writing this book. I have tried to prioritize those that remain conservatively faithful to

Greek syntax and word choice, and are at the same time fluid and readable for a modern reader. In both of these regards, the translations of Mary Jane Levett, Robin Waterfield, and Tom Griffith have been excellent resources. In some cases I have modified translations where I felt the translator's choices were either somewhat too loose or somewhat too turgid. When the original Greek is intended to sound archaic, I have deliberately used earlier, more formal English translations. Where I cite the dialogues, I provide both the Stephanus pagination and the translator's last name, followed by the page number in that edition; and where I cite fragments of ancient texts, I cite the Diels-Kranz (DK) number. I hope the readers will find this helpful, should they wish to look something up for themselves, and not too distracting visually. For this reason, the texts of the dialogues are listed in the bibliography according to the translator's last name. I have noted each place where I adjust or amend a translation. Primary sources that are referenced but not quoted are not included in the bibliography. There are a number of secondary sources that guided my reading or led me to other sources but are not explicitly cited in the text. They are included in the bibliography.

Because, as I explain in the introduction, one of the aims of this book is to offer an interpretation that is not overreliant on or presumptive about the metaphysical underpinnings of Plato's thought, I have chosen to transliterate as opposed to translate several terms that I feel carry far too much metaphysical baggage, or whose meaning is too broad and varied to be translated in one way only. For example, *psychê*, *logos*, and *eidos*, commonly translated respectively as "soul," "reason," and "Form," presume to varying degrees the preexistence of a transcendent metaphysics that Plato left in his wake but that did not exist fully formed at the time of his writing. I do not believe we have suitable terms in English that correspond with these Greek concepts. My own sense is that *psychê* meant something along the lines of "human life–perception–force"; *logos* meant "speech," but not in any sense that is captured by the English word "speech"; and *eidos* meant "figure-concept." Similarly, *technê*, commonly translated as "art," meant "way of skilled making or doing," and *mimêsis* meant many things to Plato, from "impersonating," to "emulating," to "imitating," to "representing." Translating these terms in the above ways, however, would obscure rather than clarify the ideas, so I have opted to leave the terms transliterated. I include various other Greek words and phrases where I think they may be important for readers of Greek.

A project like this is never a solitary endeavor, and many people have offered invaluable help and encouragement along the way. I am grateful first and foremost to my partner and interlocutor par excellence, Drew Dalton, for encouraging me to pursue this project when it was only an idle question, and for discussing these ideas with me at various stages along the way. Ed Schiappa, Marina McCoy, and Jerry Graff generously shared their time in reading early drafts of chapters and in some cases the entire manuscript, and offered superb advice and feedback. The anonymous reviewers for *Philosophy and Rhetoric* and Gerard Hauser provided critical guidance on what would become the first chapter. Several colleagues—Thomas Rickert, Connie Meinwald, Ralph Cintron, Nasser Mufti, Tarini Bedi, Tatjana Gajic, Bob Somol, Cynthia Blair, Susan Levine, and Michael Schandorf—very helpfully and generously participated in a stimulating conversation regarding the second chapter. Heartfelt thanks for their copious and thoughtful feedback. Several colleagues offered encouragement and interest in the project along the way; special thanks to Jerry Murphy, Sean O'Rourke, Sir Brian Vickers, Carol Poster, Bob Sullivan, Brian Gogan, and many others.

I would also like to thank my colleagues and dean at the University of Illinois at Chicago, who have been an exquisite web of inspiration and support: Dean Astrida Tantillo, Walter Benn Michaels, Lisa Freeman, Mary Beth Rose, Mark Canuel, Anna Kornbluh, Jennifer Ashton, Jeffrey Gore, and Nanno Marinatos—my deepest thanks to you all. To the graduate students who participated in a seminar on rhetoric and aesthetics, our conversations were highly productive and covered many of the themes that would become the content of this book. I am grateful to my mentor and former professor, Paul Hopper, who very helpfully introduced me to the work of Louis Bassett.

Thanks also are due to the intrepid editorial team at the University of Chicago Press, Susan Bielstein and James Toftness, who made this publication possible; and to Andrew Osborne and Johanna Rosenbohm, who offered superb copyediting assistance in the final stages of the project. All remaining errors are, of course, my own.

I am particularly appreciative of my colleagues, college, university, Dean Tantillo, and the UIC Humanities Institute, its committee, and its directors, Susan Levine and Linda Vavra, for facilitating the Humanities Institute fellowship (2015/16) and research awards (2015, 2016, and 2017), which gave me the time and funds to complete this project. Gratitude is also due to the librarians and support staff at the Daley Library, University of Illinois at Chicago; the Bodleian Library; the British Library; and Trinity College

Library at Cambridge University, without whose service and collections my scholarship would be far less robust.

And finally, I am grateful to my daughter, Thea, who daily prods me never to be boring; and to my parents for teaching me the value of hard work.

Aspects of the book were explored as conference papers at the biennial meetings of the International Society for the History of Rhetoric and the Rhetoric Society of America from 2013 to 2017. An early version of the first chapter appeared as “Seeming and Being in the ‘Cosmetics’ of Sophistry: The Infamous Analogy of Plato’s *Gorgias*,” *Philosophy and Rhetoric* 49, no. 1 (2015): 74–97. It is used with permission from the Penn State University Press.

« INTRODUCTION »

Literacy, Dramatic Form, Metaphysics

Rereading Plato's Rhetoric

Language represents the world, or so we are told. Although language may be in the world, it is not of the world. Rather, we have been led to believe that it is held at a remove from nature, from entropy, from the flux of *phusis*, and the arrow of time. This remove is maintained by the essential signifying power of language, so the story goes, predicated on an eternal logic, or a universal grammar, if not a symbolic system of differentiation. According to this logic, this grammar, this system, language and the statements it composes are true when they represent the world rightly and false when they represent it wrongly. So foundational is this belief about language that it allows only meager room for critique or question—surely the fact that language represents the world is not a modifiable belief. It could not merely be a matter of historical and contingent development. "Certainly, as a proposition, the division between true and false is neither arbitrary, nor modifiable, nor institutional, nor violent" (Foucault 1972, 218).

Indeed, this representational view of language is all these things: modifiable, historical, contingent, arbitrary, and institutional. It is, in fact, a theory of language that was invented by Plato, who introduced for the first time in his *Sophist* dialogue the idea of language-as-statement and of statements being either true or false, where truth and falsity rest on a distinction between being and seeming, or reality and appearance. It was not creation ex nihilo, to be sure, but it nevertheless constituted a permanent break between what language had been and what it would become.

That Plato is the inventor of this irrevocable and now ubiquitous idea of language has been generally acknowledged.[1] Until now, however, it has not been established *how* Plato created it out of his rhetorical theory.[2] The aim of this book is to show how the ideas of language-as-statement and true and false discourse emerged as a by-product of Plato's invention of rhetorical theory, weapons forged for battle with the sophists.

A robust appreciation of how Plato developed the assertion necessarily requires a significant revision to the standard view of rhetoric in Plato. This view is summarized as follows: Plato was rhetoric's most ardent critic. He held it in contempt or extreme distrust, believing it to be a sham art, a threat to true philosophy, and an inferior method to dialectic. It deals with belief and not knowledge; with appearance and seeming, not reality; with what is plausible rather than what is true. It is a knack, not an art; and a form of deception, trickery, and persuasion. Hence rhetoric is *mere* rhetoric—the lesser counterpart of philosophy, useful only for speaking to ignorant masses for whom more rational methods are ineffectual. He may have offered marginal and grudging allowance for it in the *Phaedrus* dialogue, but only as an ideal that sacrifices practical effectiveness. This view—which is nearly ubiquitous in the general summaries of the history of rhetoric—has undergone very little revision in the past century, despite seismic changes in Plato scholarship as a whole. To illuminate how Plato invented the concept of the statement, this book challenges this standard interpretation. I suggest that Plato has Socrates invent rhetorical theory even as he has him seem to disparage rhetoric, and this rhetorical theory, created over the course of several dialogues, capacitates his theory of language-as-statement. This is displayed most clearly and compellingly in his theories of *mimêsis*, *onoma*, and *rhêma*, developed in the *Republic*, *Cratylus*, and *Sophist* dialogues. These dialogues, and the rhetorical theories they package, provide an antidote to the poetic power, overwhelming influence, and epistemic peril of the sophists' words, displayed in the *Gorgias*, *Phaedrus*, *Protagoras*, and *Euthydemus* dialogues.

Through this analysis, I aim to fill what I believe is a longstanding gap in Plato scholarship and in scholarship in the history of rhetoric. Namely, scholarship that considers the role and status of rhetoric and rhetorical theory in Plato's dialogues has been inadequately revised in light of three key developments in twentieth- and twenty-first-century Plato scholarship and philosophy. These developments include (1) the rise and subsequent marginalization of so-called "orality and literacy" theory, (2) the not-uncontroversial critique of Platonist metaphysics initiated by Martin Heidegger, and (3) the influence of literary or dramatic readings of the dialogues. While each of these movements, which I describe below, has left a permanent mark—for the better—on how we read and understand Plato's work as a whole, these interpretive transformations have not yet synthetically redefined the dominant view of how Plato represents rhetoric and uses rhetorical theory within the dialogues. Indeed, as David D. Corey has claimed, "with few exceptions, the revolution in Platonic interpretation that has occurred gradually over the past century and enriched our understanding of Plato's thinking and his purposes has not made its way to the banks of sophistic scholarship" (2015, 11); and the same may be said of rhetorical scholarship. In the following three sections, I provide an overview of these three movements, which inform the methodological assumptions behind each analysis offered in this study. While these movements will be familiar to Plato scholars, historians of rhetoric, and philosophers, they are nevertheless not without their critics. I offer these summaries both as a justification of each as well as a rationale for their integration as a unified method for interpreting Plato's dialogues.

Orality, Literacy, and Rhetorical Beginnings

For a time in the mid-twentieth century, the work of the so-called Toronto school ignited a major revolution in how Plato was understood and read. Following the studies of Milman Parry and Albert Lord, who hypothesized that the methods of oral composition still in use in the early part of the twentieth century by itinerant Balkan bards might offer an answer to "the Homeric question," there emerged a new understanding about the fundamental differences between oral and literate language and thought. Based on the findings published in Lord's *Singer of Tales* (1960), which was the culmination of Parry's unpublished research, the *Odyssey* and the *Iliad* came to be read as a repository for Greek oral ways of speaking and thinking, defined primarily by memorable formulaicity containing concrete (as opposed to abstract) vocabulary, which was committed to writing only sometime during the eighth century BCE. On the basis of these findings—with the accompanying scholarship that suggests that Greek culture was entirely oral up until the mid-eighth century BCE, and that the rise of literacy in Greece both coincided with and prompted the rise of pre-Socratic philosophy—Eric Havelock wrote his masterwork *Preface to Plato*, published in 1963, and suggested that much of Plato's thought can be explained by the fact that he was living in the midst of the Greek literate revolution. In that revolution, the development and spread of writing technology made it possible to replace a concrete vocabulary and its attendant thought system with a new taxonomy of abstract terms and concepts. The abstract forms of thought that would become Western rationality were born.[3] Havelock's work, along with that of his colleague at the University of Toronto Harold Innis, influenced Marshall McLuhan's predictions about mass media in the 1960s and '70s, and by extension laid the groundwork for the great synthetic study by McLuhan's student Walter Ong, *Orality and Literacy* (1982). Ong applied these findings more broadly to oral and literate cultures writ large and suggested key distinctions between oral and literate ways of thinking; he also predicted the advent of a "secondary orality," given what seemed to be the implosive trajectory of what McLuhan ([1964] 2003) famously called "electric technology."

It was these later developments in the movement that ultimately determined the fate of orality and literacy theory, a field of investigation that has fallen out of fashion in the last thirty years. Not only did the rise of digital (as opposed to "electric") media radically shift the trajectory away from a "secondary orality," making the projections of Ong and McLuhan seem outdated and incorrect, the "great divide" between oral and literate cultures—which, in its fullest articulation by Ong, associated the former with concrete thought and a lack of analytical, objective, or strictly rational vocabulary and the latter with abstract vocabulary and decidedly rational, logical, and objective ways of thinking—was criticized for committing the fallacies of hasty generalization and false cause. In brief, it was argued that the 1931 studies by neuropsychologist Alexander Luria that Ong cited may have discovered the same linguistic and conceptual distinctions that separate Homer from Plato; but this similarity alone is not enough to make broad cross-cultural claims about orality and literacy as such. Moreover, while literacy may have been a contributing factor to the linguistic and intellectual transformations that took place between the eighth and fourth centuries BCE, to claim that literacy or the "literate revolution" was the primary or only cause of these changes is to overlook the more important factor of institutional power that determines how literacy circulates and the ends toward which it is employed.[4] While these criticisms are not without merit, they should not tempt us to throw the baby out with the bathwater, as it were.

In contrast to the relative absence of orality and literacy theory in Plato scholarship of recent years, its influence has fared comparatively better in the history of rhetoric. Precisely because rhetoric was the first discipline devoted to the self-conscious study and theorizing about discourse and language, the idea that the rise of literacy in Greece was crucial and essential to its development (by enabling the assimilation of the very taxonomies that would later become the corpus of rhetorical theory), has been comparatively less controversial. Because rhetoric as a discipline is the architectonic discourse on language, its very existence requires the ability to analyze language *as* language. This could only be done once language was externalized via writing.

This, in essence, is one of the prime motivations for Thomas Cole's important study *The Origins of Rhetoric in Ancient Greece* (1991) and for Edward Schiappa's *The Beginnings of Rhetorical Theory in Classical Greece* (1999). Cole insists that the earliest developments in rhetorical theory were first and foremost a result of Plato's groundbreaking work, for which there is no comparable model in any earlier text:

> For the rhetorician's preoccupation with controlling the medium of transmission to come into play, two developments had to take place, neither of which would have occurred when it did without the contribution of Plato and Aristotle. First, audiences and composers had to acquire the habit of abstracting essential messages from verbal contexts: the informative core of any piece of communication from its non- or extra-informative—that is, rhetorical—residue. . . . Second, a "written" eloquence had to come into being—that is, a body of prose texts which might be read or delivered verbatim and still suggest the excitement, atmosphere, and commitment of a spontaneous oral performance or debate. Plato—along with, to a lesser degree, the other Socratics and the orator Isocrates—was the first to compose such texts. Without such texts there would have been no satisfactory data base on which to conduct the detailed precise analysis of the verbal medium that is characteristic of rhetoric. (1991, x)

For Cole, the "absolute separability of a speaker's message from the message used to transmit it" (1991, 12) appears for the first time in ancient literature in the *Phaedrus* dialogue (1991, 35), where Plato deliberately displays, on the one hand, a written speech, and on the other hand, a theoretical vocabulary based on its analysis. Prior to this, Cole argues, there is a glaring "absence of detailed analysis . . . everywhere in protorhetoric" (1991, 111). This leads to the conclusion "that the metalanguage that would have made analysis possible simply did not exist at the time to any significant degree" (1991, 111). I would extend Cole's claim to include many more of Plato's dialogues, wherein the interlocutors examine discourse that has been detached from its spoken performance, and on the basis of that examination, produce a theoretical vocabulary about discourse—what Cole refers to as "metalanguage." Plato displays again and again the same process that Cole identifies in the *Phaedrus*: through Socrates's discussions of texts that were available in writing both to him and to his readers, he engages in a critical evaluation of their language *as* language, which results in a metalinguistic vocabulary. This in essence is the development of rhetorical theory, and it illuminates through explicit demonstration how it is that reading and literacy enable self-conscious distance from and evaluation of language, which results in abstract theorizations and rhetorical terminology, or *language about language*. As Andrea Nightingale contends, the fourth-century Greeks' "spectator theory of knowledge," or *theoria*, was reliant on the themes of surveying or seeing from a distance. "Rhetorical theory" refers to precisely this kind of operation with a written text; by surveying it from a distance and, as it were, "having a look at it," one is able not only to use discourse but to theorize about it.

In agreement with Cole's groundbreaking study, Schiappa (1990) proposes the term *rhêtorikê* is Plato's intellectual property, and "rhetorics" that emerge outside the Platonic lineage are not rhetorical in the formal sense, so the term *rhetorical theory* ought to be confined "to texts containing explicit discussion of rules and principles of rhetoric which may or may not influence the compositional practices of others" (1999, 109). As Robert Wardy (1996) has similarly observed, the loose, generic uses of the term *rhetoric* indicate an impoverished awareness of the rich, complex, labyrinthine history of its development in Plato and Aristotle, and particularly of the theoretical metalanguage that filled the very content of the future discipline. "Once *named*," Schiappa writes, "intellectual practices can become what we can loosely call a discipline" (1999, 186).

The argument I pursue here is at heart a logical extension of Cole's and Schiappa's examination of the beginning of rhetoric and rhetorical theory:

because Plato's dialogues are the first and most important extant texts from the ancient world to demonstrate this process of creating, on the basis of an analysis of written eloquence, a theoretical metalanguage, I investigate how those texts function as contributions to fourth-century-BCE rhetorical theory. In this way, I not only restrict the term *rhetorical theory* to texts that contain this explicitly theoretical content in the way that Schiappa recommends, I likewise strictly identify that theoretical content first and foremost as rhetorical theory wherever it appears, even if it is in a genre not typically identified as rhetorical, as is the case with Plato's dialogues. I use the term *rhetorical theory* specifically to denote what Plato, in coining the term *rhêtorikê*, was attempting to define. By externalizing and stabilizing language, what was once visceral, ephemeral, and aural became stable, fixed, and examinable. This had the effect of creating a self-consciousness about language and verbal skill and an ability to survey and evaluate it from a distance. In the oral world, one was subjected to the power and force of language. Once that language could be inscribed, its powerful force could be questioned, studied, and repeated. Rhetoric was the metadiscursive technique that made possible repeatable and replicable linguistic power. In Plato's coining of the term, we find not just oratory, but self-consciousness about oratory: how it is produced, its essential components, and its identifiable and predictable effects.

Martin Heidegger and the Critique of Metaphysics in the West

The second revolution in the last century that I bring to bear on the understanding of rhetoric in Plato is the critique of the development of metaphysics in the West initiated by Martin Heidegger, and in particular, the role of Plato's treatment of the sophists in that development. This too is not an uncontroversial source to call on in interpreting Plato, given both the fact that Heidegger's prioritization of the Greeks is difficult to dissociate from his Nazism and the skepticism with which his interpretations of the ancients is held. Heidegger's explicit epitomizing of the Greek language and Greek thought is highly suspect, both politically and philosophically, precisely because he viewed the German language and German philosophy as its sole true heir.[5] The seeming inextricability of his ethnocentrism, Nazism, and epitomizing of the Greeks, therefore, makes it highly problematic to rely on him as a commentator on Greek thought and Greek language. Moreover, the critique of his "whimsical," "feeble," or "imaginative" etymological investigations has long alienated Heidegger from any serious classics scholarship.[6] While the importance of Greek thinkers from the pre-Socratics to Aristotle in Heidegger's phenomenology is a well-explored area of scholarly inquiry, his reliability as a scholar and a commentator on that tradition is at best highly contested.[7] The residue of this, of course, was memorably defined in the preface to the English edition of Marcel Detienne's monumental *The Masters of Truth in Archaic Greece* (1996). On the one hand, Detienne claims, "Heideggerians and 'deconstructionists' have built a veritable wall to separate themselves from the explorations of Greek scholars," while on the other hand Greek scholars hastily dismiss Heidegger, despite the fact that "the only real innovator in Greek thought is Heidegger" (1996, 26).

And yet it is possible, I believe, to lean on Heidegger as a reader of Greek philosophy while still avoiding these two pitfalls. Neither Heidegger's epitomization of Greek *Dasein* nor his dubious etymologies is essential to his account of the development of Platonist metaphysics in the history of philosophy, and it is this account, painted in broad strokes, that I believe may safely and incisively reorient our understanding of the development of rhetorical theory in Plato's texts.[8]

Of particular importance for this study is the apogee of Heidegger's 1935 lecture course, *Einführung in die Metaphysik*, published in English as *Introduction to Metaphysics* in 1953. The course was the first of Heidegger's works to be published in English, and despite the fact that Heidegger himself referred to it as a further elucidation of the question of being developed in his masterwork *Sein und Zeit* (*Being and Time*), originally published in 1927, it is not the elucidation of Greek *Dasein* that is the true value of the work. Rather, the section that traces a series of four chronological steps in the history of philosophy—or "The Restriction of Being"—that Heidegger claims constituted development of metaphysics in the West, helps, I believe, to define more precisely the crucial role that rhetoric played in the development of Platonist metaphysics. In other words, it is Heidegger's analysis of how Platonist metaphysics developed though the differentiation of being from its "other" in Greek philosophy that exposes the role of rhetorical theory in Plato's thought. These four steps were the differentiation of being from becoming, from seeming, from thinking, and from the ought. The first two distinctions—being and becoming, being and seeming—appear repeatedly in early Greek texts, a point that is obvious even to the casual reader. Heidegger's contribution to what is already obvious is his observation that, as these distinctions developed chronologically, they formed over the course of several centuries the basic building blocks of a transcendent metaphysics. The widespread familiarity of the second distinction in particular, "Being as opposed to seeming . . . what is actual as distinguished from and opposed to what is not actual—the genuine versus the ungenuine" (Heidegger 2000, 103; original pagination 75), is perhaps the most pronounced. It is indeed difficult to speak of how something seems or appears without necessarily implying that it *only* seems or appears to be in some way or another, but in fact *is not*: "The distinction between Being and seeming is familiar to us, just one of the many worn coins that we exchange unexamined from hand to hand in an everyday gone flat. If it comes up, we use the distinction as a moral directive and rule of life, to avoid seeming and instead to strive for Being: 'to be rather than to seem'" (Heidegger 2000, 104; original pagination 75). According to Heidegger, it is precisely this commonplace familiarity that obscures from view how the distinction developed initially or how it laid the architecture for Western metaphysics, and, I might add, how rhetorical theory made the distinction possible in the first place.

Although the initial distinction can be traced, Heidegger claims, to the earliest Greek philosophy and poetry, it is never firm nor taken for granted in the period of Greek thought that is of the greatest interest to him. Far from familiar and flat, "again and again, they [the Greeks] had first to tear Being away from seeming and preserve it against seeming. . . . Only by undergoing the struggle between Being and seeming did they wrest Being forth from beings, did they bring beings into constancy and unconcealment" (Heidegger 2000, 111; original pagination 80). Here, Heidegger's view of early Greek philosophy suggests that, in its repeated attempts to gain understanding of *what is*—a manifest concern from Parmenides and Heraclitus to Plato and Aristotle—the distinction between seeming and being or appearance and reality was glancing and momentary, but in no way given or familiar in the way it is for us now. It would take the full-fledged development of Platonist metaphysics for the distinction to be so ingrained in thought that it could hardly be unthought. In the beginning, by contrast, and even with Plato, it was rough and incomplete. And, as I examine in the final two chapters, these repeated efforts "to tear Being away from seeming" occur precisely in and through Plato's rhetorical theory.

The crucial break that would set the course for this development may be found, according to Heidegger, in Plato's clash with the sophists: "Only with the sophists and Plato was seeming explained as, and thus reduced to, mere seeming" (Heidegger 2000, 111; original pagination 80). Heidegger's proof in support of this claim is characteristically scant; and yet, in the dialogues analyzed in the following chapters, his claim is borne out with profound clarity. As I attempt to demonstrate, Plato's dramatic overturning of the sophists is accomplished precisely through his development of the rhetorical theories of *mimêsis*, *onoma,* and *rhêma,* which he uses both to define their *logos* as false imitations and to distance their speech from the visceral power and poetic force that is its natural property.

It is through these schisms, which took place sequentially in the history of philosophy, that metaphysics was born, and

> Being as *idea* was elevated to a supersensory realm. The chasm, *khôrismos,* was torn open between the merely apparent beings here below and the real Being somewhere up there. Christian doctrine then established itself in this chasm, while at the same time reinterpreting the Below as the created and the Above as the Creator and with weapons thus reforged, it set itself against antiquity [as paganism][9] and distorted it. And so Nietzsche is right to say that Christianity is Platonism for the people. (Heidegger 2000, 111; original pagination 80)

Before this development, however, there were sophists and Socrates, poets and Plato. Plato did not denounce the sophists' speech as false or the poets' words as dangerous on the grounds that they dealt in seeming as opposed to being; rather, as I show, it was through his dramatic portrayal of Socrates's clash with the sophists and their manipulations of the poetic tradition that the very distinction between seeming and being was forged, thus opening the chasm for the development of metaphysics in the West. And it is Plato's development and deployment of rhetorical theory that makes this distinction possible in the first place.

This, in effect, is a subtle but nevertheless crucial difference in how Heidegger may be depended on as an interpreter Plato. It is not Heidegger's precision or authority as a reader of the Greek thinkers or their language, but his genius as a reader and critic of the history of philosophy that is useful for understanding the place of Plato in Plato's own philosophical tradition. It is not inaccurate to claim that Heidegger's analysis of the development of a metaphysics-of-transcendence and truth-as-correspondence in the history of philosophy (particularly Plato's philosophy)—an interest that spans the early, middle, and late periods of his thought—has gained widespread traction in philosophy.[10] The restriction of being from its "other," particularly seeming, receives its clearest articulation in the 1935 lecture course, but this articulation is merely a reiteration of the same understanding of how metaphysics developed in the West that recurs from the beginning to the end of Heidegger's long career.[11] Although Heidegger's weakness may have been to read too much of his own social world into the Greeks (and vice versa), this should not rule out his definitive strength, which was to discern in Plato the very seeds that would eventually flower into the full-fledged metaphysical system of Western thought. By drawing our attention to how this flowering occurred as a historical process, Heidegger serves as a guidepost that leads us to question rhetoric's place within that process.

Literary-Dramatic Interpretations of Plato

The third and final revolution in Plato scholarship is the literary or dramatic readings of the dialogues that have come to the fore in recent decades. Malcolm Schofield describes the rise of this method in the following way:

> In the bad old days questions about the literary properties of the Platonic dialogues were not much canvassed by philosophical readers—unless they happened to be Straussians or (in even older days) Neo-Platonists. . . . [Today] the relation of form to content has become a prime subject of philosophical interest, sometimes handled gushingly or flat-footedly, but at best with tact and sophistication. (1992, 122)

The literary-dramatic position Schofield refers to is offered in opposition to the longstanding tendency, inherited from Neoplatonist interpretations, to discover in the dialogues dogmatic or doctrinal positions of Plato's for whom Socrates was presumed to be the mouthpiece. This dogmatic assumption has persisted in spite of numerous interventions in modern scholarship, all of which have aimed to grapple with the fact that Plato's dialogues, if read as doctrinal treatises, endorse highly contradictory views. These interventions at times challenge the doctrinal presumptions, but more often than not reinforce them. For example, despite Friedrich Schleiermacher's influential recognition in the early phase of modern scholarship that for Plato, "form and subject are inseparable, and no proposition is to be rightly understood except in its own place and with the combinations and limitations which Plato has assigned to it" (1836, 14), the dialogues nevertheless contained the whole system of Plato's thought for Schleiermacher. They comprised a static doctrinal unity that was only presented in different ways in different dialogues. So while form was important for deciphering that doctrine, there was still presumed a doctrinal totality to Plato's thought, and "the dialogues [were] a gradual and pedagogically ordered exposition of Plato's system" (Gonzalez 1995, 5).

This so-called "unitarian" view was not unilaterally monolithic; it was tempered by the "developmentalist" and "esotericist" perspectives. According to the former, Plato's views changed and developed over time, such that seeming contradictions are a product of his gradual maturation as a philosopher.[12] According to the latter, Plato's views were never communicated in the dialogues themselves, only verbally in the Academy.[13] In all three of these perspectives there remains a tacit belief that Plato was in the business of building doctrine—either synchronically, diachronically, or tacitly. Despite their differences, all three perspectives "assume that Plato's philosophy is a system of philosophical doctrines and then pursue different ways of reconciling this assumption with the unsystematic, nondoctrinal form of the dialogues, namely, by seeing the dialogues either as a *gradual exposition* of the system ('unitarianism'), or as records of the system's *evolution* ('developmentalism'), or as *propaedeutic* to a system they do not contain ('esotericism')" (Gonzalez 1995, 8).

The literary-dramatic interpretation of the dialogues is at heart an attempt to gain escape velocity from these doctrinal readings of Plato, all of which are presumptively and procedurally problematic. They are presumptively problematic inasmuch as they are committed to finding doctrine within a literary form—dialogue—whose most fundamental asset is its ability to refract and camouflage authorial voice, perspective, and opinion.[14] They are procedurally problematic inasmuch as they rely on a clairvoyance to accurately date the authorship of Plato's compositions or to discover in nonextant material the truth of Plato's convictions—two manifest impossibilities.[15] By contrast, Plato scholars such as Drew Hyland, Stanley Rosen, Gerald Press, and others have contributed to a broad movement in Plato scholarship that attempts to prioritize dramatic details over doctrine, philosophical questioning over dogmatic answering, and the posing of problems over solving them.[16] The end goal of reading Plato, by this view, is not to develop a system of thought but a way of thinking. This is not to say that Plato did not hold certain views, or even that he may have embedded those views in the text, but that deciphering those views is a matter of indirect reading and not a matter of taking the views directly expressed by Socrates as Plato's. As John Sallis describes it, "To read a dialogue thoughtfully and carefully does not mean to ferret out the opinions of which the dialogue would be the expression but rather to make explicit what the dialogue makes manifest regarding the matters which it puts at issue" (1986, 3). The question concerning rhetoric, then, becomes not, What is Plato's doctrine of rhetoric? but, How are rhetoric and rhetorical theory handled, portrayed, problematized, and most important, *created* and *used* in Plato's dialogues? With very few exceptions, this is a virtually unexplored question in the scholarship on Plato's rhetoric.[17]

Sophists and Sophistry in Plato

Any consideration of Plato's rhetorical theory necessarily provokes questions about Plato's sophists. Not only does he refer explicitly to rhetoric as the art that sophists teach, he goes to great lengths to carve a distinction between rhetoric and sophistry. In this way, one can only be defined through comparison and contrast with the other. Given the difficulties exhibited by both Socrates in the *Gorgias* and the Eleatic Stranger in the *Sophist* in their attempts at coming up with a fixed definition, it is only fitting that the concepts of "sophist" and "sophistry" should present some challenge to define. Sophists and sophistry are recurring themes throughout Plato's dialogues, and the manifestly negative portrayals of sophists and sophistic activity has, with very few exceptions, led to the dominant understanding that Plato's own view of sophists and their rhetoric—the skill the sophists taught—must have been universally negative, with the sole exception of the tempered view of rhetoric he presents in the *Phaedrus* dialogue.[18] The problem of attributing to Plato the views he puts in Socrates's mouth is discussed above, but it remains to be determined: Who are the sophists and to what, precisely, do the terms for the *sophistês* and *sophistikê* refer in Plato's texts?

At the time of Plato's writing, the term *sophist* (like the term *philosopher*) had not yet developed a technical or restricted meaning. It could mean a wise, learned, or sophisticated person generally, but it could also be used as a backhanded compliment, not unlike the word *elite* today. Even as early as the second century CE, the breadth of the term was noted by Aristides, who observed that it was applied to people as diverse as Solon, Pythagoras, Plato, Socrates, and Aeschines, and that it was Plato "who most of all rebelled against the term" (Aristides, *Orations* 46; O'Neill 1972a, 1). Nevertheless, tradition has handed down to us a slightly more formalized understanding of the term, inherited in no small part from Plato's own efforts to distinguish sophists from philosophers and to subordinate the former to the latter.

According to tradition, fragmentary works by ten figures and two additional texts of unknown authorship comprise the corpus of the so-called older sophists. These are Protagoras, Xeniades, Gorgias, Lycophron, Prodicus, Thrasymachus, Hippias, Antiphon, Critias, and Euthydemus, and the texts *Anonymus Iamblichi* and *Dissoi logoi*. Such a list necessarily implies a certain formalization of a "sophistic movement"; but as the extant texts themselves attest, there is very little cohesion or uniformity in what survives of their ideas. The texts that are supposed to comprise the sophistic corpus range from cosmological investigations to speculations about being, to display speeches both satirical and sincere, to practical guidelines for rhetoric, and more.[19]

My use of the terms *rhetoric* and *rhetorical theory* is intentionally narrow, in order to reflect the specific practice of developing a theoretical taxonomy on the basis of written eloquence that was contemporaneous with and reflected in Plato's writing. My use of the terms *sophists* and *sophistry* is, by contrast, intentionally broad and general. This breadth aims to adequately reproduce the same breadth with which the term was applied in Plato's dialogues. Throughout this analysis, the definitions of *sophist* and *sophistry* are guided by Plato's own use of the terms.

Of the "older sophists" whom we know by name, only two are not mentioned in the Platonic opera: Xeniades and Lycophron. References to these figures in the extant literature as a whole are scarce, and surviving works are scant—perhaps indicating that they were obscure and relatively unimportant characters in their own time. Neither is said to have visited Athens, and the thoughts of both are attributed to others, diminishing the importance and originality of their intellectual contributions (O'Neill 1972b, 1972c). Of the other sophists who appear in Plato's dialogues, only two, Critias and Antiphon, are not treated to a direct Socratic attack. Rather, they are minor figures, benignly drifting in the background at Callias's house or at Socrates's trial.[20] It just so happens that these two—the sophists to be treated in a friendly or neutral manner—also are the only two sophists who were also Athenian citizens. The remaining six, who are the subject of direct interrogation, attack, or ridicule, are non-Athenians: Protagoras, Gorgias, Prodicus,

Thrasymachus, Hippias, and Euthydemus all come from afar, and while ancient testimony other than Plato's treats them as being on a par with the two Athenians Antiphon and Critias, Plato singles out the foreigners for particular critique. In addition, Plato uses the term *sophist* to refer to Euthydemus's brother Dionysodorus, as well as to Evenus and Miccus.

These and other references in the dialogues indicate that Plato used the term to cast a wide net, and that it was, for him, almost exclusively pejorative. The preponderance of examples indicate that Plato used *sophist* to refer to actual historical figures who, in the dramatic action of the dialogue, were wealthy, itinerant, non-Athenians, and who indirectly wielded great power in the polis through their access to and influence over Athens's most powerful citizens. They engendered among Athenian elites an enthusiastic following thanks to their dazzling powers of speech, which they would pass on in return for exorbitant fees. In most cases, they are displayed as Socrates's rivals. This working definition is culled from the following references to the people Plato referred to by that term:

Protagoras: *Cra.* 391c; *Hp. mai.* 282d; *Soph.* 232d; *Meno* 91d; *Prt.* 309dff., 328b, 335a, 361d; 319; 349a; *Rep.* 10.600c.

Gorgias: *Grg.* 449a–60e; *Hp. mai.* 282b; *Ap.* 19e–20c; *Symp.* 198c; *Meno* 96d.

Prodicus: *Euthyd.* 277e, 305c; *Hp. mai.* 282c; *Symp.* 177b; *Lach.* 197d; *Ap.* 19d–20a; *Prt.* 315e, 341a–b, 357e; *Cra.* 384b; *Tht.* 151e.

Thrasymachus: *Rep.* 1.337d–348b; *Phdr.* 261b–71a.

Hippias: *Hp. mai.* 281d-e; *Prt.* 314c–19e, 357e ff.; *Ap.* 19e

Euthydemus and Dionysodorus (brothers): *Euthyd.* 271c–277e, 288b; *Symp.* 222b.

Evenus: *Ap.* 20b–c; *Phdr.* 267a: *Phd.* 60d–e.

Miccus: *Lysis* 204a

More important than who or what these terms referred to is the role rhetoric and rhetorical theory play in the dialogues' dramatic portrayals to define and defame the sophists. In light of a literary-dramatic interpretation, the sophists in Plato's dialogue seem to supply the author with a stock of antagonists: opponents with whom Socrates is perpetually locked in combat and who nevertheless repeatedly evade or attempt to evade categorical definition. Again, at issue for defining Plato's rhetorical theory is not, What is Plato's view of rhetoric and the sophists? but, What role does rhetorical theory play in the dramatic action with the sophists, and how does he differentiate between the two?

Plan of the Book

This book consists of six main chapters, each analyzing a dialogue or set of dialogues that were crucial for rhetoric's development: the *Gorgias*; the *Phaedrus*; the *Cratylus*, the *Euthydemus*, and the *Theaetetus*; the *Protagoras*; the *Republic*; and the *Sophist*.

The first chapter, on the *Gorgias*, addresses Socrates's analogy between sophistry and "cosmetics," which is undisputedly the most famous moment in Platonic thought for associating sophistry and rhetoric with "seeming" as opposed to "being." This standard view is ubiquitous, but perhaps most clearly articulated in E. R. Dodds's influential commentary, which maintains that "the most important element in the [analogy] is the distinction of principle which Plato draws between 'scientific' and 'unscientific' procedures (see 465a 2–5). *It is one form of that distinction between being and seeming, inner reality and outward appearance, which runs through the whole of the dialogue from this point*" (1959, 227; emphasis mine). Dodds's description accurately summarizes more than a century of scholarship on the analogy.

The standard view that sophistry and rhetoric are forms of seeming, and therefore alienated from being, depends on an erroneous translation of *kommôtikê* as "cosmetics." When translated thusly, the analogy necessarily implies that sophistry and rhetoric deal in appearances and seeming, and conversely are opposed to being and reality. But these translations overlook the fact that there is no record of the term prior to Plato's use in the *Gorgias*, nor for nearly five hundred years after. Most likely, this term is Plato's neologism, making its meaning in the *Gorgias* far from obvious. I want to suggest that Plato coined the term in Greek by improvising on the Egyptian word *kommi*, which he was using in order to evoke and criticize Athens's consumption of expensive foreign goods and luxuries such as Egyptian perfume. This change of interpretation localizes the criticisms of the *Gorgias*—he was targeting specific practices of particular sophists who whetted Athens's appetite for acquisitive luxuries and in so doing lured them into a disastrous campaign for regional domination.

My rereading of the *Gorgias* dialogue—the dialogue most frequently cited as evidence of Plato's negative views on rhetoric, and of rhetoric's affiliation with appearance as opposed to being—indicates that the critique displayed there is not predicated (as it often is believed to be) on a firm metaphysical distinction between seeming and being. The purpose of the analysis, then, is not to suggest that in fact Plato was not as critical of rhetoric as he appears to be in the dialogue, but to call into question the assumption that a firm distinction between seeming and being, grounded in a fully formed metaphysics, was the basis of his critique. This clears the way for a more capacious consideration in later chapters of how rhetoric is implicated in the very structuring of that metaphysics.

The second chapter concerns the *Phaedrus* dialogue, usually cited as the place where Plato offers a more tempered view of rhetoric, since the second half of the dialogue contains a number of recommendations for how rhetoric should be practiced. These recommendations are that it should be able to divide a topic where its "natural joints" are, to be able to group diverse things under a single category, and so on (264c, 265d–266b); and they are usually read as straightforward prescriptions whereby rhetoric is a counterpart art to the art of dialectic, defined more exhaustively in Aristotle's rhetorical theory. This view is problematic because it requires that the recommendations regarding rhetoric in the second half of the *Phaedrus* be read in isolation from the speeches delivered at the beginning of the dialogue, which both confound and are confounded by the recommendations Socrates gives. In those speeches, Plato was contrasting the new "scientific" discourse of rhetoric teachers like Protagoras and Isocrates (illustrated in Lysias's written speech at the beginning of the dialogue) and the older, muse-influenced, divinely possessed discourse of poets like Homer and Hesiod (illustrated in Socrates's inspired palinode). Understood in this light, the speeches at the beginning of the dialogue highlight how similar the visceral effects of the new sophistry are to those of old poetry—both rouse their hearer to a frenzy of enthusiasm and create what Eric Havelock has called "whole, bodily sympathetic engagement" ([1963] 1998, 152) between the speaker and the hearer. There is nevertheless a crucial difference between the two performances: unlike the *Protagoras*, where Socrates has meager means to trammel the sophists' power, in the *Phaedrus* he is able to critique and analyze Lysias's speech because he has it in writing (234e–235a; 262d–e; 264a–b). At the same time, he cannot critique the inspired speech precisely because it is no longer physically there—once he has finished speaking, the speech ceases to be (264d–e). All that is left is the trace the speech leaves on its hearers: their excitement, arousal, and persuasion. Socrates's recommendations about rhetoric (it should divide, classify, etc.) describe not what the speech or rhetorician accomplishes or should accomplish, but what Socrates and Phaedrus, as rhetorical critics, are able to identify through a dramatic analysis of only the written speech. It is a literate rhetorical theory, in this case, that breaks the sophistic oral spell. It is here that we begin to see the emergence of a more technical theory of rhetoric, consistent with the full-fledged rhetorical theory as defined by Cole (1991) and Schiappa (1999).

This method of critical resistance may be contrasted to Socrates's engagements with Protagoras and his doctrines, which are the subject of the third and fourth chapters. In chapter 3, I examine how Plato treats Protagoras's thought as a linguistic and epistemic theory that is concomitant with pre-Socratic ontology. He interprets Protagoras's main doctrines—the "man-measure" doctrine, the "*dissoi logoi*" doctrine, and the "impossibility of contradiction" doctrine—as manifestations of Heraclitean ontology of flux. In Plato's portrayals throughout the *Theaetetus*, the *Cratylus*, and the *Euthydemus*, Protagoras's doctrines are both a consequence and an embodiment of the incessant flux of the material universe; they carry out the epistemic consequences of a physical world that is perpetually generating and deteriorating. In such a state, knowledge of what is true or false is utterly unattainable. Given the agnosticism that is an inevitable consequence of Protagorean epistemology, Plato implies that the only alternative to epistemic crisis is sophistic victory. In chapter 4, I examine the *Protagoras* dialogue, which offers a view of sophistry and dialectic without rhetoric. In the *Protagoras*, we witness the sophist's verbal power firsthand—the same power compared to a *pharmakon* in the *Gorgias* and to erotic pleasure in the *Phaedrus*. Protagoras's power, by which he hypnotizes hearers "with his voice like Orpheus, while they follow where his voice sounds, enchanted" (315a–b) also ensnares Socrates. He responds in a thoroughly sophistic fashion, attempting to counter Protagoras and beat him at his own game by offering an absurd, erroneous, sophistic interpretation of Simonides's poem. Although this portion of the text is traditionally ignored as a "satire of sophistic methods," the interpretation matters precisely because it indicates how dialectic cannot stand up against or be distinguished from sophistry in the absence of rhetorical theory. Although the dialogue portrays an examination of the poem of Simonides (which would have existed in writing but is only quoted from memory in the dialogue), the examination does not result in a theoretical taxonomy. Rather, it is merely fodder for sophistic and eristic contest. Consequently, Socrates's only defense against Protagoras's superior eloquence is duplicity and doublespeak. This dispute between Socrates and Protagoras, portrayed humorously in the *Protagoras* dialogue, gains more significance and weight when considered in light of the epistemic crisis that Protagoras's man-measure doctrine and its implicit Heracliteanism causes for Socrates. I examine Socrates's intense but fruitless struggles with Protagoras in all these dialogues to show how Socrates's transformation into a sophist is his only prophylactic against the verbal powers of Protagoras. Obviously, this is unsatisfactory, and its inelegance must be remedied in the *Republic* and *Sophist* dialogues, where Plato's rhetorical theory receives its fullest development.

In chapter 5, I address how in the *Republic* Socrates demonstrates a more systematic model of critical resistance to verbal power by analyzing in great detail a written text of Homer—an obvious contrast to the loose interpretation of Simonides, a poem Socrates recalls from memory. Plato's so-called attack on the poets is possible only through an analysis of writing similar to what is modeled in the *Phaedrus*. Through his analysis of Homer's written eloquence, Socrates develops a theoretical definition of *mimêsis* by finding it in Homer's language and by comparing it to visual arts, both of which were highly irregular uses of the term *mimêsis*. The meaning of *mimêsis* in book 10 is made possible by Plato's initial innovation of the term in books 2 and 3, where he expands the word from its general meaning of imitating, emulating, or following and example to the actual words and language that the poet uses to perform his imitations. Once Plato has linked *mimêsis* and poetry in this way, he is able to link it to all other forms of manufacturing and *poiêsis* (including visual arts), and ultimately to cast doubt and suspicion on them. By this reading, rhetorical theory (the analysis of a written text to produce a theoretical vocabulary) capacitates the suspicion of imitation that will be crucial for casting doubt on the sophists, who he wants to claim are the ultimate imitators.

In chapter 6, the dubiousness of imitation developed in the *Republic* is explicitly linked to the imitative work of the sophists, who not only used imitation as a central method in their educational programs, but also used language to imitate people with knowledge. The theory-building that emerges in textual analysis reaches its pinnacle in the *Cratylus* and *Sophist* dialogues through a theory of language that detaches language or *logos* from Heraclitean *phusis* such that language can, for the first time in the history of philosophy, be defined as either true or false. In the *Cratylus* and the *Sophist*, Plato's theorizes for the first time "the assertion," through original distinctions between *onoma* and *rhêma*, or word and phrase. The result of these theories is that the sophist can no longer "make and do everything" (233d–234a). By distinguishing between these two terms, which he uses interchangeably elsewhere, Plato has his interlocutors transfer the representational and signifying function of names (*onomata*) to phrases (*rhêmata*) and speech as such (*logos*). This signifying speech is fundamentally a form of *mimêsis.* Inasmuch as *logos* is merely representational and imitative, the sophist is no longer the maker of worlds, mover of bodies, or hypnotist of the masses. Rather, because his words are no longer in *phusis* but about *phusis*, he is merely a "statement maker," an assertion-giver, and his words are not only demystified and emptied of their power, they can be definitively identified as either a true or false imitation. When discourse is transformed from something inspiring fear, respect, and terror, to something that is formalized, theorized, and pointed to, it is effectively muted. In this way, the profound changes wrought by Plato in how discourse is understood—which ultimately forged a philosophical distinction between seeming and being—could not have been accomplished without Plato's rhetorical theory. And it is this rhetorical theory that silences sophistry.

« 1 »

The "Cosmetics" of Sophistry

Seeming and Being in the *Gorgias*

The *Gorgias* dialogue is widely recognized as Plato's harshest condemnation of both rhetoric and sophistry. It is where he ultimately concludes that neither is "a *technê* but a knack, because it can give no rational explanation of the thing it is catering for, nor of the nature of the things it is providing, and so it can't tell you the cause of each. And I don't give the name *technê* to something which is unreasoning" (465a; T. Griffith 2010, 30; translation modified).[1]

Perhaps less widely recognized than the harshness of the criticism, however, is the fact that the dialogue also marks the moment in the Platonic corpus where rhetoric and sophistry most explicitly are associated with seeming and appearance, and therefore distanced from being and reality. This association with seeming (and alienation from being) arises from "the most famous passage in the dialogue" (Kennedy 1994, 37): the analogy at 464b–466a in which Socrates distinguishes between two kinds of *technai* (a word that means "arts," "sciences," or perhaps more accurately, "strategic and ordered ways of doing and making things"). These are *technai* that concern political life (*psychê politikên*), and those that concern bodily life (*sômati*).[2] He further divides these into two branches: one dealing with the healthful maintenance of the polis and the body—legislation and gymnastic—and the other dealing with curing ills in the polis and the body—justice and medicine.[3] He then matches each of these four *technai* with a false counterpart, which deals not in true maintenance or healing, but simulates maintenance and healing by means of "flattery." These false counterparts may seem to be the thing they simulate, but in fact are not. We might imagine this analogy as a grid:

	Maintenance (being | seeming)	Cure (being | seeming)
Polis	legislation | sophistry	justice | rhetoric
Body	gymnastic | *kommôtikê*	medicine | cookery

Sophistry is the false counterpart of legislation, rhetoric of justice, cookery of medicine, and "cosmetics, "self-adornment," or *kommôtikê* of gymnastic.

Upon initial investigation, the "falseness" of sophistry, rhetoric, cookery, and cosmetics seems to be a species of the familiar Platonic distinction between appearance and reality. As E. R. Dodds explains, "The most important element in the present passage is the distinction of principle which Plato draws between 'scientific' and 'unscientific' procedures (see 465a2–5). *It is one form of that distinction between being and seeming, inner reality and outward appearance, which runs through the whole of the dialogue from this point*" (1959, 227; emphasis mine).[4] Here, Dodds effectively summarizes more than a century of scholarship on the dialogue: rhetoric is relegated to an inferior status, and that status is determined by rhetoric's relationship to seeming or appearance and consequential divorce from being and reality. Brian Vickers makes the same point: "Binary oppositions were extremely common in Greek thought, of course, but their function in Plato's hands is to relegate rhetoric to the inferior, the lowest possible category" (1988, 113). In other words, gymnastic *is* healthful maintenance of the body, or so the story goes, while cosmetics *seem like* healthful maintenance. Legislation *is* healthful maintenance of the polis, while sophistry only *seems like* healthful maintenance, and so forth. The false practices deal in "images or reflections" (Kennedy 1999, 62), appearances, opinion, or what seems to be, and not in reality, knowledge, or truth.

As modern readers, when we encounter the *Gorgias* dialogue (and in particular the analogy regarding rhetoric and sophistry), this distinction seems natural to us. That is, we presume a natural demarcation of that which seems to be from that which is, and moreover, we presume that that which only seems to be *is not* that which is. But as I explain in the introduction, for the Greeks by contrast, including for Plato and Gorgias, this demarcation was far from obvious. Rather, it is in these very texts that the distinction was forged in the first place.[5]

The larger aim of this book is to reevaluate the history of rhetoric-as-appearance, and to trace both its sophistic roots and the process by which it was reduced to something privative and derivative (*mere* appearance, in opposition to truth, reality, and being); the smaller aim of this chapter is to dismantle the anachronistic concept of appearance that reduces appearance to mere seeming or semblance, particularly where this reduction concerns rhetoric, and particularly at the crucial point in the *Gorgias* dialogue where this association has been most influential and severe: in the analogy between sophistry and rhetoric, cosmetics and cookery. The guidance offered by Heidegger on this point requires that we adjust the question we pose to the *Gorgias*: we are no longer concerned with where to slot rhetoric, as an enterprise either for truth and reality or falsity and unreality. Rather, we are concerned with how rhetoric functions in the original delimitation of true and false, the real and the unreal. Moreover, we are interested in how rhetoric as such makes possible the original delimitation.

The focus of this chapter isolates a single term within the analogy that I believe has determined the fate of the analogy as such, and by association, the dialogue as a whole. I will begin by explaining the difficulty as well as the importance of the term *kommôtikê*, commonly translated as "cosmetics" or "self-adornment." I will outline the reasons why this translation is inadequate, if not misleading—a point of particular concern since the general interpretation not only of this analogy but of the dialogue as a whole is inflected with an implicit opposition between seeming and being on the basis of this single term. None of the other seven terms carries a connotation of appearance or seeming. Through "cosmetics" alone, rhetoric and sophistry anachronistically are handed over to seeming and appearance, and therefore dissociated from being and truth. The importance of this term is manifest through its collateral damage—all the terms are presumed to derive their falseness through an association with seeming and appearance and their consequential dissociation from being and reality.

However, I suggest that Plato constructed this term not, as is commonly believed, from Greek terms referring to hair care and self-adornment (*komaô*) but from an Egyptian term referring to gums and unguents (*kommi*).[6] This seemingly minor translation adjustment creates ripple effects throughout the dialogue, since it pulls us away from a presumed Platonic distinction between seeming and being, and toward a historical economic problem of profligate consumption that imperiled Athens, making Socrates's analogy concerning rhetoric and sophistry more in line with the larger themes of political justice and temperance that are the focus of the rest of the dialogue. Ultimately, by challenging the translation of *kommôtikê*, I suggest that the analogy is transformed from a distinction between seeming and being into a distinction between foreign profligacy and domestic austerity. This transformation discharges the vulgarization of appearance as *mere* appearance and *mere* seeming that have long infected and hampered our understanding both of Platonic thought and of early rhetoric.

In what follows, I summarize the place of the analogy within the dramatic structure of the dialogue as a whole. I then discuss the interpretive problem that arises from the traditional interpretation of *kommôtikê* as "cosmetics," "hair care," and "outward adornment": the common interpretations that attribute *kommôtikê* to *komaô* (the presumed root for the neologism) fail to account for Plato's bizarre insertion of a double *mu* (or μμ). I then propose an alternate interpretation, which links *kommôtikê* not to *komaô*, but to the Egyptian term for "gum," *kommi*, used in the production of perfume, a costly and exotic but also much-demanded good in fifth-century Athens, emblematic of Athens's thirst for foreign and expensive luxury items. Finally, I explain how this adjusted interpretation is supported by the dramatic context of the Peloponnesian War, explicitly referenced throughout the dialogue. I develop the latter two points through reading the *Gorgias* alongside two contemporaneous texts: Xenophon's *Symposium* and Thucydides's *History of the Peloponnesian War*. The result, a seemingly minor translation adjustment of a single term, enables a more unified reading of the dialogue as a whole, where the critiques of rhetoric and the critiques of Athenian greed can be knitted into a single critique of the acquisitiveness that led Athens into a war of imperial domination. The effect is that the *Gorgias* can no longer be read as a text about rhetoric and sophistry as such. Rather, it is a critique of the specific practice of rhetoric in fifth-century Athens, which exploited Athenian greed in order to provoke imperial reach.

The *Gorgias* Dialogue and the Role of the Analogy

At the opening of his 1959 commentary, E. R. Dodds poses the question that hums as an undercurrent to any investigation of this dialogue: How is rhetoric rendered in the *Gorgias*? The centrality of this question is inescapable, given the fact that, since antiquity, the *Gorgias* has carried the second title *Peri rhêtorikês*, or "Concerning rhetoric." Indeed, if R. G. Hoeder's (1957) hypothesis is correct, that the second title originated with Plato himself,[7] then we are correct to seek to understand how it is that rhetoric unites the diverse and sometimes meandering themes of the dialogue that are seemingly irrelevant to rhetoric as such, including war, justice and injustice, freedom and slavery, wealth, power, desires (both satiable and insatiable), moderation, and the ultimate "ends" of life.

An initial reading of the *Gorgias* might lend the impression that it is one of the less puzzling Socratic dialogues, and certainly one that presents less immediate resistance than the other dialogues considered in this study. Unlike the *Protagoras*, where we struggle to account for Socrates's manifestly unvirtuous and duplicitous behavior toward his interlocutor, here he is direct and sincere even as he is harsh. Unlike the *Phaedrus*, where the myth ruptures the conversation and the textual unity, the myth in the *Gorgias* is woven subtly into the texture of the discussion and provides an important moment of illumination. Unlike the *Republic*, where the conversation protracts, meanders, and maintains a bland docility, often dulling and blunting the intrigue, the conversation in the *Gorgias* remains compact, contentious, and lively throughout, keeping the reader alert amid the fray, and never stalling out in lengthy and digressions. And unlike the *Sophist*, which moves through a series of distinctions and divisions that grow increasingly abstract and paradoxical, the numerous Socratic distinctions and discriminations in the *Gorgias* remain sensible and concrete, never branching into abstraction or metacategorization.

Moreover, the thematic development of the dialogue is mirrored by dramatic shifts, so that the dramatic structure supports the content structure. These developments and shifts are marked by three turns in the conversation, from Gorgias to Polus to Callicles. Beginning with Gorgias, the interlocutors set out to define *rhetoric*—this ineffable thing at which Gorgias excels, prompting Socrates to wonder: "Faced with phenomena like this, it comes across as something supernatural, a divine power" (456a; Waterfield 1994, 19; translation modified). Once Socrates leads Gorgias to the contradictory view that the rhetorician both can and cannot use this supernatural power for immoral purposes, Gorgias's student Polus steps in and changes the direction of the discussion (461a–b). Polus accuses Socrates of using sophisms with Gorgias, and the focus shifts from Gorgias's definition of rhetoric to Socrates's. It is at this point that Socrates offers the crucial analogy, defining rhetoric and sophistry by comparing them to cookery and *kommôtikê* (464e–465b), and then moves to his discourse on the uses and misuses of this power, leading to his famous claim that suffering wrong is superior to doing wrong (469c). In the final turn of the conversation (481b), Callicles steps in to challenge as stridently as he can Socrates's moral vision, bringing Socrates ultimately to link the exercise of power with the aims of self-satisfaction and acquisitive pleasure, and the moral life to the practice of self-discipline and restraint. Ultimately, this calls into question the ultimate aims of life, which cannot be defined as the mere prolongation of life (511b–c) since the ultimate end of life is death. The close of the *Gorgias* reverberates with the sound of the *Phaedo*, where Socrates claims that philosophy is ultimately a preparation for death.

The crisp structure of the dialogue can't entirely overcome the difficulties caused by these radical shifts in topic. After all, the final meditation on death as the end of life (in both senses: where life ends, but also the ultimate *telos* of the living) is thematically quite far removed from the question concerning rhetoric introduced at the beginning of the dialogue. As James Doyle has pointed out, this poses a problem for contemporary scholarship on the *Gorgias*, since there is virtually no unifying account of the "important connections" (2006, 93) between rhetoric and the other themes in the dialogue. More often, studies tend to focus on one topic in the dialogue rather than on how the disparate topics ought to be woven together. This leads translators to conclude that the dialogue doesn't even seem really to be about its professed topic (rhetoric) but is about something different entirely, aimed not at a local audience but a universal one.[8] And *Gorgias* scholarship tends to puzzle over not the relation between Socrates's view of rhetoric and the other themes of the dialogue, but the fact that the view of rhetoric in the *Gorgias* runs so contrary to the view in the *Phaedrus*—a seeming contradiction that some commentators attribute to the dating of the dialogues, indicating that Socrates's or Plato's view of rhetoric softened over time.[9] The tentative relationship of these other topics to rhetoric itself poses a problem in any approach to the rendering of rhetoric, since it works to seemingly pull the discussion away from the theme identified both in the second title and in the initial analogy. Where connections have been discussed, the readings are relatively straightforward, implicitly suggesting that the dialogue is exceptionally and uncharacteristically nonparadoxical—a reading that any seasoned reader of Plato should view with suspicion.[10]

Despite the disunities in our readings of the dialogue, it is no surprise, given the prominence of place of the analogy, that it has had enormous impact in the history of ideas and the disparagement of rhetoric. As Robert Wardy suggests, "The *Gorgias* falls little short of the *Republic* in the continuous influence it has exerted on Western intellectual and political history" (1996, 56). The impact for rhetoric is well known: Kennedy writes that the *Gorgias* is "the earliest example of the identification of rhetoric with flattery and deceit, a view that has recurred throughout western history" (1999, 66). Consequently, we are driven alongside Gorgias himself "to the humiliating admission that the master of oratory lords it only over those who do not know: ever since, philosophers have approached the wiles of rhetoric with circumspection, while its self-professed champions have indignantly denounced Plato's defamation as a piece of shoddy rhetoric" (Wardy 1996, 57). The analogy alone, once and for all, defines rhetoric as having the appearance of truth but not knowledge or truth as such, and this in spite of our incomplete understanding of how the analogy coordinates with the other themes under discussion.

Given both its pride of place and its hefty impact on the history of ideas, this analogy is worth careful attention, as well as extensive quotation. As I summarize briefly above, Plato's initial division is between those *technai* that concern political life (*psychê politikên*), and those that concern bodily life (*sômati*):

> For these two things I say there are two *technai*: the one which looks after the life of the *polis* I call politics; as for the one which looks after the life of the body, I can't give you a single name for it, just like that. And though the care of the body is a single science, I say it has two subdivisions—gymnastic and medicine, while the counterpart to medicine is justice. . . . Now, there [are] these four sciences, two taking care of the body and two of the *psychê*, and always with a view to what is best. (464b–c; T. Griffith 2010, 30; translation modified)

These *technai* that aim for the best are not left inviolate. Rather, each is corrupted by "sycophancy"[11], which

> divides itself into four, attaching itself to each of the subdivisions, and *is the very thing it attaches itself to* [ὑπδῦσα ὑπὸ ἕκαστον τῶν μορίον, προσποιεῖται εἶναι τοῦτο ὅπερ ὑπέδυ]. It has no concern with what is best,

> but uses the pleasure of the moment to ensnare and deceive folly, masquerading as something of the greatest value. . . . The mask of medicine, as I say, is worn by the sycophancy which is cookery; that of gymnastic, in just the same way by *kommôtikê*, since it is pernicious, illusory, demeaning, and slavish, deceiving with shapes and colours smooth skin and clothes. *It makes people import an alien beauty and neglect that beauty of their own which comes from gymnastic.* . . . As *kommôtikê* is to gymnastic, so cookery is to medicine. And moreover, as fashion is to training, so the skill of the sophist is to the science of the legislator; and as cookery is to medicine, so rhetoric is to justice. (464c–465c; T. Griffith 2010, 30; translation modified, emphases mine)[12]

As noted above, the term *kommôtikê* is the only truly puzzling term in this section. Other terms in the analogy have received serious scholarly attention given the likelihood that, as Edward Schiappa (1990) has argued, this marks the spot where Plato probably coined the term *rhêtorikê*. But this coinage is not so very unusual, since the root *rhêtôr* is so prevalent in the literature prior to the *Gorgias* dialogue.[13] Rather, the more unusual terminology is the rhyming tail to the newly minted *rhêtorikê*'s head: *kommôtikê*.[14]

Aristotle, writing only a generation after Plato, refers implicitly to the Platonic and Gorgianic analogy in his definition of rhetoric found in the first book of the *Rhetoric*; however, in the Aristotelian definition, the term *kommôtikê* is eliminated. He writes:

> Let rhetoric be [defined as] an ability, in each [particular] case, to see the available means of persuasion. This is the function of no other art; for each of the others is instructive and persuasive about its own subject: for example, medicine about health and disease . . . and similarly in the case of the other arts and sciences. But rhetoric seems to be able to observe the persuasive about "the given," so to speak. That, too, is why we say it does not include technical knowledge of any particular, defined genus [of subjects]. (1.2.1; Kennedy 2007, 37–38)

Even though Aristotle, following Gorgias and Plato, retains the indirect comparison to medicine in his definition of rhetoric, he does so by eliminating the other terms of Plato's more elaborate version, including *kommôtikê*, and by upgrading rhetoric to the status of a *technê*. Indeed, his elision leads one of the modern commentators to suggest that the term *kommôtikê* should be likewise struck from the *Gorgias* dialogue,[15] a view that was influential for a time but ultimately short lived.[16]

There is a reasonable explanation for why both Aristotle and modern commentators might be inclined to strike *kommôtikê* from the text. There is no record of the term's use prior to its appearance in the *Gorgias* dialogue, making it difficult to know either what Plato would have meant by the term or how his readers would have interpreted it. The newness of the term is not itself strange—it was not unusual for Plato to innovate with language, after all. What makes the term puzzling, rather, is the fact that, unlike other terms Plato coined (such as *rhêtorikê*), *kommôtikê* did not begin circulating as currency. It never appears again in the Platonic corpus, and the next instances of its use do not show up until the first and second centuries CE with preparers of Neoplatoism, such as Plutarch.[17] Although the term does see widespread use in the Platonist tradition from late antiquity through the Middle Ages, by authors who were self-consciously taking up Plato's vocabulary, there is no record of the term's use before the *Gorgias* dialogue, nor for nearly five hundred years following it. This absence indicates that, in addition to the terminological puzzle confronting modern commentators and translators, the term's meaning was equally confounding to Plato's own readers and followers.

Since the term was unlikely to have had an obvious meaning at the time Plato used it in the fourth century, we must consider what neighboring Greek terms Plato would have been drawing on to construct this strange word *kommôtikê*—roots that would have been familiar to his audience and therefore capable of inflecting the neologism with a similar familiarity. In other words, which familiar source terms would have helped his audience glean the meaning of the neologism? Most modern scholarship concurs that, despite the term's "uncertain lineage" (Thompson [1871] 1973, 147), Plato probably constructed it out of the homophonously rooted words referring to care and tendance (the verb *komeô* and the noun *komidê*), hair (*komê*) and ostentatious grooming or letting the hair grow long (*komaô*). The similarity between Plato's neologism and the terms for self-care, hair, and hairstyling moved Olympiodorus in the sixth century CE to suggest that the term refers to when one "adorn[s] the hair with an artificial elegance and colour" (14.2.131). Most modern translators and commentators follow Olympiodorus's lead. Gonzalez Lodge, for example, in his 1890 commentary, suggests that the term refers "not only to finery in dress, but also hair—curling, ointments, cosmetics, etc." (1890, 81). While typical English translations for this term are "cosmetics" or "self-adornment," these translations grew out of an early preference to interpret the term as a linguistic descendent of *komaô* and therefore as an implicit reference to a form of self-adornment that involved hairstyling.[18] But if this is in fact the source for Plato's neologism, then there are logical problems that ensue, which I discuss in the following section.

The Problem of the Double *Mu*

If contemporary etymological accounts of *kommôtikê* are correct, (that the term is derived from the homophonously rooted *komaô* or *komeô* and therefore is intended to refer to a controversial manner of self-adornment or cosmetic enhancement) then a curiosity arises. Namely, the root term *komaô* is sufficient in itself for evoking the concept of excessive self-adornment—to a shameful and socially controversial degree—without the full extent of etymological adjustment that Plato offers. *Komaô* referred not only to letting one's hair grow long, but also to arrogance and putting on airs, since long hair was a mark of aristocracy. Cosmetic enhancement centered on haircare and elaborate self-adornment would be more readily apparent if the *komaô* were more transparently linked to Plato's neologism (as, for example, the neologism *rhêtorikê* is derivative of *rhêtôr*).

The broader cultural significance of the practices associated with the terminological parent *komaô* is discussed in a recent article by Mark Griffith (2006), who shows that the hairstyling denoted by these terms was a common practice among upper-class Athenians, and it was regarded with particular suspicion in the fifth century BCE. According to Griffith, the terms were used to refer to the dressage and adornment of hair, both for aristocratic humans and their prized horses. In both cases, ostentatious display was key. The hair was "braided, clipped into patterns, arranged in pom-poms, or decorated with bows, bells, or ribbons, oiled, and even perfumed" (M. Griffith 2006, 308). Griffith's analysis suggests that the same terms were applied in these different scenarios (indeed, "no other animal hair except lions' manes seems to be so designated," 2006, 309) not merely because of a visual similarity between human hair and horses' manes, but primarily because the practices carried similar cultural and socioeconomic significance. Namely, both were expensive and ostentatious displays symbolic of wealth and cosmopolitanism. Excesses of this sort were deemed particularly controversial during the fifth century (the dramatic setting of the *Gorgias* dialogue) because of the threat they posed both to economic parsimony and to cultural purity. Griffith writes: "*Hippotrophia* itself and other ostentatious displays of elegance might be resented in contexts of increasing conflict over the distribution of wealth and the proper indices of civic worth. Hellenic (or 'democratic') simplicity and manliness came increasingly to be contrasted with 'Asiatic' (or aristocratic) luxury and effeminacy as the fifth century progressed" (M. Griffith 2006, 310).

We can see this identification of hairstyling with both Asianism and excess in Plato's contemporary Thucydides, for example—who, reflecting back on the recent history of his own time during and following the Peloponnesian War, suggests that the Athenian culture of simplicity was the reason for their historic stability and wealth. He describes how the Athenian upper classes were among the first of the Greek aristocracies to give up wearing expensive linens and costly adornments, preferring instead a more moderate fashion. He points specifically to the moderation and simplicity in their hairstyling, when they no longer wore their hair in ostentatious buns or attached gold cricket barrettes to it (1.6).[19] Thucydides offers evidence to support the probability that elaborate hairstyling and adornment, the activity associated with *komaô*, was an upper-class preference during the dramatic setting of the *Gorgias* dialogue. Furthermore, Thucydides's testimony indicates that in the period following the dramatic setting—in other words, at the time the dialogue was written—such an activity was subject to the critique of posterity, both for its excess and its foreignness.

If it is the case that this terminological parent referred to practices that were, as the commentaries suggest, not only common during the dramatic date of the dialogue but also relevant to its themes and retrospectively controversial at the date of composition, then Plato might have made this critique much sharper had he simply written his neologism as *komatikê* rather than obscuring this meaning with strange spelling and gemination.

In order to determine what possible meaning Plato may have been introducing by coining this term, it is most important to attend precisely to what is *new* about the neologism. While the commentators may be correct that Plato expected his reader to inflect the meaning of his neologism with some meaning borrowed from *komaô*, his basic innovation includes the bizarre addition of a double *mu* (μμ). Gemination in itself is not necessarily strange—adding or removing letters was not an unusual practice, particularly in poetic compositions. In a given piece of text, letters could be added or removed at the discretion of the writer to lengthen or shorten the sound of words in the service of greater parity and harmony. This convention makes it particularly strange, then, that Plato uses a double *mu* in his term *kommôtikê,* since the addition of the *mu* makes the term less, not more, similar to the terms he uses in conjunction with it, having the overall effect of creating greater dissonance both visually and aurally, since gemination caused prolonged pronunciation.

The possible significance of this dissimilarity is even more striking when we consider what lengths Plato took to create terminological similarity in this analogy. All eight terms are given the rhyming suffix *-ikê*; six terms have four syllables, and two have five syllables. In sequence, he introduces first the four legitimate *technai*: *gymnastikê, iatrikê, nomothetikê, dikastikê,* followed by their counterparts *kommôtikê, opsopoîkê, sophistikê,* and *rhêtorikê.* The close proximity of these terms emphasizes their assonance, homophoneity, and rhythmic regularity. It is all the more strange, then, that Plato uses a double *mu* here, given that it sets the term apart as the only term of the eight to contain a geminated consonant.

There is a term that, with only one exception, has been overlooked by both ancient and modern commentators on the *Gorgias*, and which I believe is the hidden terminological root of the neologism. I suggest that a fuller appreciation of the sources of Plato's neologism severs the word from an association with seeming and appearance by binding it to foreignness and profligacy. It is a brilliant innovation—its fuller understanding has the effect not only of expanding the meaning of *kommôtikê* such that the reader can understand why Plato would have felt a new term was necessary, but also of uniting rhetoric and sophistry with the other, seemingly disparate themes of the dialogue: justice, pleasure, and death, the ultimate *telos* of life.

The *Kommi* in *Kommôtikê*: Athenians and Luxury

I wish to explore an etymological source for *kommôtikê* that to my knowledge has been proposed only once before, in Platonic scholia. William Thompson notes this attribution but then immediately dismisses it: "The word κομμοῦν is of somewhat uncertain lineage. A scholiast derives it from κόμμι, *gummi,* which can hardly be true" ([1871] 1973, 147).[20] In this section I offer reasons in support of this proposal, given the probable way in which this term and its material referent entered Athenian culture and the Greek tongue.[21] The dubiousness with which scholiast etymologies are now viewed is not groundless. Nevertheless, as Benjamin Jowett once rightly cautioned, we should not be tempted to dismiss scholiast interpretations out of hand. "The value of each Scholiast," Jowett writes, "like that of each [manuscript], must of course be judged alone, remembering, as is obvious in the Scholiasts on Homer, that he may often repeat or preserve the opinions of older or wiser writers than himself." While it may be true that many scholiasts were "deficient in grammatical knowledge and falling according to our standard into remarkable grammatical blunders," they nevertheless had "a curious dialectical insight into the meaning of passages." Jowett sagely cautions against the hubris of presuming their philological irrelevance: "That with all Greek literature lying open before them, themselves the students of an art which, commencing with the Sophists and Alexandrian grammarians, lived and flourished for above 1500 years, they should have added so little to our knowledge either of the classics or of language generally, is a valuable warning of the tendency of such studies when pursued in a false and narrow spirit" ([1894] 1973, xx–xxi).

The term *kommi*, meaning "gum," "paste," or "unguent" (and the precursor to the English word "gummy"), first entered the Greek tongue through commerce with Egypt. The term still would have been relatively young in the Greek language at the time Plato wrote the *Gorgias* in the early fourth century BCE, and it would have carried natural associations not only of foreignness, but also of luxuriousness—particularly the luxury of perfumed unguents that came to Greece through trade with Egypt and Phoenicia (Forbes 1955, 35; Pliny 7.59; Herodotus 3.107–112) and which had close associations to cosmetic and medicinal self-care and luxurious, costly self-adornment. In this way, both the word and its matter are of a foreign extraction for the Greeks.

The earliest appearance of the term in Greek literature occurs with Herodotus, who recounts how it is used in the embalming practices of the Egyptians—an emulsion rubbed on the linen bandages in only the costliest funerals. In this context, *kommi* is connected to mortuary trim levels available only for the wealthy. Herodotus recounts how in the most expensive procedure, "the body is washed, and wrapped round, from head to foot, with bandages of fine linen cloth, smeared over with *kommi*, which is generally used by the Egyptians in place of a *kolla*. . . . Such is the most costly way of embalming the dead" (2.86–96; Rawlinson 1928, 108–09). The use of gums and aromatics, by Herodotus's account, is an additional luxury in the embalming practice, superfluous to the more essential purposes of preserving the body against decay.

We might infer from Herodotus's marginal explanation of the term he uses for "gum" (that it is a similar substitute for the flour paste—*kolla*—used by Greeks as a glue) that the term, along with its material referent, was either unfamiliar or had been only partially imported from the Egyptian to the Greek vocabulary at the time of his writing in the fifth century, and that Herodotus was transliterating the term for the sake of his audience. This introduces the possibility that the term may still have been relatively new, bearing the trace of its foreign origin, when it was used by Plato in the early fourth century.

While Herodotus may mark the entrance of Egyptian *kommi* into the Greek language, it's unlikely that the term gained wide circulation through association with the Egyptian funerary uses he documented. More likely is for *kommi* to have gained wide circulation through association with the perfume trade, given the fact that the term bore an essential connection to the manufacture of perfume, an Egyptian good that came to be traded with and highly valuable to Athenian society. This relation would have been established through the material process by which perfumes were made. Archaeologist Jean-Pierre Brun has recounted how gums and unguents were integral to the ancient Egyptian perfume-making process, dating to the second millennium BCE. In this process, fats were heated in order to be made astringent, and then they were mixed with aromatic plants and "fragrant woods, gums [*kommi*], and musk" (Brun 2000, 277). The perfumes themselves, in their finished form, were solid gums or emulsions, suggesting that the term itself could have functioned metonymically for perfume. In this way, the term is materially related to perfumes, which were highly prized in Athenian society and introduced initially through trade with Egypt.

Ultimately, it is through the perfume trade with Egypt and the consequent widespread use of perfume in Athens that, I believe, this term develops in its significance as a component of Plato's neologism *kommôtikê*. Once trade (both etymological and material) of Egyptian *kommi* began with Greece, perfume use in Greece eventually became more widespread. Brun recounts how, in the earliest days of the trade, only the wealthiest Greeks could afford it. But in the seventh and sixth centuries BCE, it became more widely available as the trade center moved from Alexandria to Corinth. Brun also notes how the nature of the trade changed during this time—from importing perfumes themselves that had been manufactured abroad and packaged in small alabaster vials, to importing the raw materials from abroad (including *kommi*) and manufacturing and packaging the perfumes domestically. It is likely that this material shift is what led to the assimilation of the Egyptian term into the Greek language.

While the domestication of production had the effect of making perfumes more widely available, they retained their association with luxuriousness and aristocratic profligacy, such that "what soon distinguished the aristocracy from the common people was not the use of perfumes but the quality and relative rarity of perfumes used" (Brun 2000, 277). In other words, it was a status symbol that, through wide market demand, demonstrated a widespread Athenian status consciousness.

There is a significant amount of ancient testimony that provides insight into the symbolic social status and significance of perfumes and perfumeries in Athens from the classical to the Hellenic period. While this may seem to be a detour of sorts, my sense is that the material and economic association of the Egyptian term *kommi* with perfume is essential for understanding the social controversies that inflect Plato's neologism. Athenaeus cites texts from the fourth through the second century BCE, all of which attest to the exorbitant cost of perfumes—sums that were relatively equal to more than five hundred days of citizen dues (15.691). But its costliness did not stem its use in Athens. Athenaeus recounts: "When the price of perfumes was exorbitant . . . they did not abstain from their use any more than we do nowadays" (15.691; Gulick 1941, 205). Athenaeus also refers to the accounts of Demosthenes and Lysias, who record that the perfumers' shops near the agora were popular meeting places. Athenaeus describes a speech by Lysias that provides insight into the social status and prosperity of the perfumers near the end of the fifth and beginning of the fourth century. According to Athenaeus, Lysias derides Aeschines for going into debt so that he could acquire a perfume shop—Lysias accuses him of corrupt morality and wrongful accounting in his endeavor to promote "himself from the condition of peddler to that of perfume-seller" (Athenaeus 13.612e; Brun 2000, 282).[22] This testimony demonstrates the class and status consciousness that would have been associated with the use of perfumes.[23]

Finally, the potential relevance of Egyptian *kommi*, essential in the production of Egyptian perfumes traded with Athens, for Plato's neologism is made more plausible through what seems at first to be a passing remark about perfumes made by Socrates in Xenophon's *Symposium*. The text, which dates to the same time as Plato's *Gorgias*—380 BCE—recounts a feast hosted by Callias, a great patron of the sophists whose home we will visit again in chapter 4, and attended by (among others) Antisthenes, who was a follower not only of Socrates but also of Gorgias. In this text, both perfume and sophistry are topics of conversation, and they are treated, albeit obliquely, as similar practices by Socrates.

At the outset of the dialogue, Socrates responds to Callias's invitation by drawing attention to the host's patronage of the sophists: he has "paid a good deal of money for wisdom to Protagoras, Gorgias, Prodicus, and many others" (1.5; Todd 2006, 537), Socrates says in a show of false admiration. This prompts Callias to respond that if Socrates comes to the feast, Callias will indeed demonstrate that he is "a person of some consequence" (1.6; Todd 2006, 537).

It is in an effort to prove his consequence and wealth that Callias offers to share perfumes with his guests. After a performance by a male and a female dancer, Socrates praises his host, both for the excellent food and the excellent entertainment. Callias responds by suggesting that they feast not only on food and dance, but on aromas as well. He will bring in his perfumes, he says. Socrates stops him:

> No indeed! . . . For just as one kind of dress looks well on a woman and another kind on a man, so the odours appropriate to men and to women are diverse. . . . The odour of the olive oil, on the other hand, that is used in the gymnasium is more delightful when you have it on your flesh than perfume is to women, and when you lack it, the want of it is more keenly felt. (2.3–4; Todd 2006, 542–45)

Twice Socrates condemns the perfumers in this dialogue, blaming them even (through a quote from Theogenes) for the corruption of society: "Good men teach good; society with bad will but corrupt the good mind that you had" (2.4; Todd 2006, 545). He recommends against the use of feminine perfume in favor the more appropriate and truly Athenian, male, gymnastic practice of using olive oil. Here we see an explicit indication that Socrates saw the use of perfume as, on the one hand, an opponent to gymnastic (the same opposition we find in the *Gorgias* between *kommôtikê* and gymnastic), and on the other hand, a source of corruption in the polis.[24]

It is clear from the ancient testimony and from Socrates's statements that perfume occupied a controversial place in Athenian society; it was viewed as a sort of cultural corruption in itself. Moreover, the archaeological record confirms that it was widely desired and used in practices of self-adornment that had become popular among both men and women. Socrates laments these practices because they corrupt cultural purity and austerity with profligate self-indulgence, and he contrasts them to Athenian gymnastic arts and the purer use of olive oil. Aligned with this is his further critique of foreign sophistry, which is hidden in his analogical and ironic praise of pimps, who dress and coif their personnel to greatest advantage (4.57–62). It is not self-adornment alone that is problematic; rather, it's the use of expensive, foreign goods—including foreign sophistry—in the act of self-adornment that is problematic.

Taking this economic and social context into consideration, we find that the meaning inflected in *kommôtikê* by *kommi* carries a much more complex connotation than is captured in "cosmetics" or "self-adornment." The *kommôtikê* that comes from *kommi* is not suspect because it alters the appearance or causes a person to seem different from how he or she is; rather, it corrupts through foreign influence, which comes at great cost—foreignness makes it expensive, and expensiveness both makes it undemocratic and necessitates imperial reach.

In fact, Plato provides something like a clue that his neologism is drawing on a foreign term. The hint is supplied in the passing definition he offers soon after using the term *kommôtikê*. He emphasizes that the term he has just used indicates something that "*makes people import an alien beauty and neglect that beauty of their own which comes from gymnastic*" (465b).[25] In my view, this explicit reference to importing or "dragging in" [*ephelkomenous*] "foreign" [*allotrion*] goods binds the term *kommôtikê* to the foreign-sounding word *kommi,* adding to the concept of *komaô* the consumption of expensive, luxurious, foreign goods in the practices of self-adornment—the imported, perfumed gums of the wealthy as opposed to the native olive oil of the gymnast.

It is altogether possible that Egyptian *kommi* is also the source of other inflections of the stem *komm*–. Other terms similarly demonstrate that this stem is consistently associated with profligate pampering, suggesting therefore that the derivation from the foreign and expensive *kommi* is not entirely unlikely. For example, the term *kommôtria,* meaning "ladies' maid," "dresser," or "tire woman," appears in the *Republic* during a discussion of the bloated, enlarged city, filled with a multitude of unnecessary comforts (373b), which is also the source for the scholiast etymology discussed above. To supply the city with these items necessarily requires manufacturers of excess, especially those having to do with feminine adornment (373c): cooks, nurses, maids, *kommôtria*, and many other pampering servants. The term also appears in Aristophanes's *Ecclesiazusae* in a similar context. Here a character is arranging an imaginary stock of luxurious belongings and indulgent attendants: a sunshade carrier, a water carrier, a flute girl, a perfume carrier, and a *kommôtria* (734–44). In both of these examples, which satirize and ironize fifth-century profligacy and self-indulgence, the term relates to a constellation of activities defined primarily by their wasteful extravagance and not to appearance and seeming.[26] All these inflections confirm that the stem *komm*- was young in the fifth century and that, despite the uncertainty regarding its origins (which has baffled numerous philologists), it was routinely used to refer to the self-indulgent excesses of fifth-century Athenian society. These excesses may well be linguistically and materially explained by the surge of imported goods during the fifth century, including Egyptian perfume and Egyptian *kommi.*

War: The Historic Context and the Thematic Unity of the *Gorgias*

As noted above, there is far too little discussion of how the disparate themes in the dialogue are of a piece with one another. Instead, there tend to be two views: the *Gorgias* dialogue is about Socrates's condemnation of rhetoric, and therefore contrary to the views expressed in the *Phaedrus* dialogue; or the dialogue is really about political and personal justice, and therefore thematically more in line with the *Republic*.[27] To conclude this chapter, I will propose how the altered definition of *kommôtikê* might ultimately unify these two views by suggesting that the *Gorgias* is not a polemic against rhetoric, but a subtle portrayal of the cultural shift in Athens that was in the process of taking place during the dramatic dating of the dialogue, and which would come to threaten the very existence of the Athenian polis as such. (In chapter 2, I follow one implication of this unified reading by suggesting that, understood in this way, the *Gorgias* dialogue is not as distinct from the account of rhetoric offered in the *Phaedrus* dialogue as it is commonly believed to be.)

From the beginning of the dialogue, two ideas are introduced that, in my opinion, run through the entire dialogue. An altered understanding of the analogy, informed by a new interpretation of *kommôtikê*, stitches together the various manifestations of these two ideas. In the very first lines of the dialogue, Callicles says, "You're in nice time, Socrates. For a war or a battle, as the saying goes"; Socrates responds, "Does that mean we're too late? Have we missed the feast, as they say?" (447a; T. Griffith 2010, 7)). I propose that these two themes—warring and feasting—cut through every discussion: from Gorgias's claim that, through the *polemos* of rhetoric, he can make a feast of his opponent, to Socrates's inquiry toward the end of the dialogue of whether it is better instead to "rule the pleasures and desires within [oneself]" (491d; T. Griffith 2010, 67) rather than to see the ultimate purpose of life as the pursuit of pleasure and the prolonging of life. This essential contrast reflects some basic conditions of existence for a fifth-century Athenian and fourth-century survivor of the Peloponnesian War. Is it better to feast without limitation, and therefore go to war to fill Athens's walls with consumable goods? Or is it better to limit one's appetite, and therefore nullify both the appetite and the need for war? The answer to this question may seem implicit in the asking, particularly when Plato is read in light of Platonism, but it raises a further question: Is it better to fortify the distinction between inside and outside, between domestic and foreign, rather than to efface that distinction? The latter implies a longer empirical reach, a greater regional domination, a larger military presence abroad, a more formidable naval fleet—necessary for the inflow of foreign goods, available within the walls of Athens at a high price. The former, by contrast, implies careful austerity, consuming only what can be produced through local labor, fortified through both the disciplined abjuration of excess and the cultural distrust of exterior influences that would tempt Athens to ingest the luxuries of cosmopolitanism.

This same tension between "acquisitiveness and injustice" (Balot 2001, 179) is found later in Aristotle's *Politics* but, as Ryan Balot discusses, has its roots in the sixth century in Solon's laws and poems.[28] Solon saw justice as tethered inversely to acquisitiveness: acquisitiveness is suspect precisely because it compromises justice (it is perhaps not incidental that one of Solon's laws banned the selling of perfume in Athens). Balot shows how these Athenian values reached a peak of concern between Solon and Aristotle, as it were, in the late fifth century, when "a unified discourse on greed arose in response to the changing social, economic, and military conditions in Athens. . . . In the intellectual controversies of the time, as well as in the two oligarchic revolutions at the end of the century, Athenians played out conflicts between rich and poor and between individual self-interest and collective responsibility" (2001, 179). Aristotle in the fourth century, with Solon in the sixth century, was "urging the rich to observe self-restraint for the sake of Athens as a whole" (Balot 2001, 58).

This tension between greed and collective responsibility or justice may be seen clearly in Thucydides's account of the Peloponnesian War, a dramatic setting that should not be overlooked, given the copious references to the war in the *Gorgias* dialogue.[29] Indeed, all the historical references contained in the dialogue refer to events that occurred during the war; Plato poetically suspends the conversational account of an event during Gorgias's one and only visit to Athens (427 BCE) across the historic span of the war—Pericles has "recently died" (503c), which took place in the plague at the beginning of the war (429 BCE), and the trial of the generals that dates to the end of the war in 405 happened just "last year" (473e). In a way, Gorgias's visit to Athens reinforces this temporal suspension, since Athens received two Sicilian ambassadorial delegations—one in 427 BCE (four years after the start of the war) and another in or around 415 BCE (eleven years before the end of the war). These deliberately impossible temporal references emphasize the importance of the war as a backdrop for the dialogue.

And it is in the war that the tension between greed and justice is thrown into relief. Plato's contemporary Thucydides, writing what he hoped would be the true and accurate history of the same events that serve as dramatic setting for the *Gorgias* dialogue, shows how the general response in Athens to the second ambassadorial campaign demonstrated precisely this problematic clash of values, most evident in the Athenian general Nicias's arguments against the proposal that Athens send a fleet to Sicily. In his speech to the Athenian assembly, he questioned the motivation of those who favored the Sicilian campaign. The implicit target of his critique is Alcibiades, the treacherous oligarch, who "advises you to set sail, when he is only looking out for his own interests . . . and really hopes to benefit from the prerequisites of his office while being admired for his fine stable of horses" (Thuc. 6.12; Blanco 1998, 238). Against this self-interested acquisitiveness, Nicias advises caution: "Don't put it in the power of such a man to endanger the city just so that he can show off. Bear in mind that such men violate the public trust and squander their private fortunes" (Thuc. 6.12; Blanco 1998, 238). In response, Nicias too invokes the common medicinal remedy: "The city's mind is not right, and you must be its physician" (Thuc. 6.14; Blanco 1998, 238). By contrast, Thucydides recounts Alcibiades's defense for the greed of the wealthy elite, given that his extravagances are ultimately good for the polis. He gloats: "All things that make me notorious are really an honor to my ancestors and to me, as well as an advantage to the state. . . . When I distinguish myself here in Athens with a dramatic production or some other such thing, it's only natural for my fellow citizens to envy me; but to foreigners they are a sign of strength" (Thuc. 6.16; Blanco 1998, 239).

The sophist is fitted into the barrier between the two sides of this dichotomy that unite the beginning and end of the *Gorgias* dialogue. The sophist in this case is, historically and situationally, Gorgias, and not sophistry as such. In other words, this is not "a universally valid critique of rhetoric" (Vickers 1988, 88), but a situationally contingent critique of Gorgias, the wealthy and profligate foreigner who enchanted Athens with his verbal sorcery, and as a result lured them into a longer imperial reach—a thirst for war, whetted by the promise of filling the Athenians' purses and bellies. Gorgias, by this interpretation, is not metonymic for rhetoric or sophistry, but for the lure of foreign riches, the answer to Athenian acquisitiveness and greed, and the counterweight to a more appropriate Athenian austerity, parsimony, and domesticity. He stands between Callicles's two citizens: the one who remains under the edict of democracy, who believes that "equality is admirable and right" (484a; Waterfield 1994, 66), and the Nietzschean antecedent who lays claim to his will to power. The latter will "shake off all these limitations, shatter them to pieces, and win his freedom; he'll trample all our regulations, charms, spells, and unnatural laws into the dust; this slave will rise up and reveal himself as our master, and then natural right will blaze forth" (484a; Waterfield 1994, 66). It is not rhetoric and sophistry as such, in other words, but the wealthy Gorgias's sophistry in particular that aimed to exploit Athens's desire for a power capable of maximizing pleasure and self-indulgence. Gorgias promises to deliver this pleasure by teaching Athens his arts of rhetoric, such that they will be able to squeeze whatever they want from whomever they want: "As for the businessman, it will become clear that he is not in business for his own benefit, but for someone else's—yours, since you are the one who has the ability to speak and persuade large groups of people" (452d–e; T. Griffith 2010, 14–15).

Gorgias serves as the perfect symbol for the dangerous fulfillment of this promise not only because of the temporal plot arch of the Sicilian delegations, but also because of the greedy responses the delegations prompted. Of the first delegation, we know from Thucydides's account that it succeeded in persuading Athens to send ships by tapping into their desire for "prestige and profit" (Thuc. 2.65; Blanco 1998, 83): "The Athenians did send ships, allegedly because of their long-standing relationship, but really . . . to feel out whether it would be possible to take control of things in Sicily" (Thuc.

3.86; Blanco 1998, 132). The first Sicilian campaign became typological in the war itself, prefiguring the very thing Thucydides calls Athens's "biggest mistake": the second campaign in 415, when Athens would lose its navy and ultimately destroy itself (Thuc. 2.65; Blanco 1998, 83). In the second campaign, the admonitions of the likes of Nicias (which mirror those of Socrates) failed. Instead, Athens was persuaded by the lure of riches promised by the likes of Gorgias and Alcibiades (and his mirror Callicles).

By Thucydides's account, it is precisely the self-serving greed of Athenians like Alcibiades and those he persuaded that led to Athens's greatest defeat:

> They sent the second delegation to Sicily in order to maintain the appearance of helping their kinsmen and their newly acquired allies, but what they really wanted was to rule over the whole island. They were especially egged on by some ambassadors from Egesta who were in Athens and who were very eager for the Athenians to come and help them. . . . The Egestans reminded the Athenians of the alliance they had made with Leontini during Laches' previous campaign and begged Athens to send a fleet to their defense. . . . And so the Athenian delegation was sent to Sicily. (Thuc. 6.6; Blanco 1998, 235)

And he writes feelingly of the scene at Piraeus when Athens dispatched the ships to Sicily, the moment that would seal their fate in the war:

> Almost the whole population of Athens, citizen and alien alike, went down to the sea with them. The citizens came to send off their own—friends, relatives, sons—with hope and sadness, hope of conquering Sicily and sadness because they thought of how far the ships were sailing and wondered whether they would ever see their loved ones again. At that moment, just as they were about to leave each other, they were filled with dread, as they had not been when they voted for the expedition, yet they took heart from the sheer might and plenitude of what they saw. . . . For this first armada was the greatest, the most magnificent, and of course the most expensive ever launched by a single Greek city up to that time. . . . A vast sum of money indeed was sailing away from Athens. . . . It was the greatest, longest voyage ever attempted from Athens, and it offered the hope of a huge addition to their empire. (Thuc. 6.30–31; Blanco 1998, 244)

The sense of foreboding and dread is most likely a literary embellishment on the part of the author. Nevertheless, as we know, the Sicilian campaign failed miserably, ultimately determining the outcome of the war. It would be impossible for any fourth-century reader of the dialogue (which refers to the first of the two Sicilian diplomatic envoys that bookend the war) not to think—cringing—of this as a backdrop of the dialogue. A devastating defeat at Sicily, Alcibiades's treachery, the fall of Athenian democracy, and the installation of the tyrants in Athens would necessarily be evoked by any reference to Sicily, the very thing that is foregrounded in the *Gorgias* dialogue.

Socrates's critique of sophistry and rhetoric cannot be detached from the disasters that are necessarily invoked by this explicit reference to the Sicilian ambassadorial visit. To define precisely Socrates's criticism, we must acknowledge the role Plato's sophists played in exploiting Athens's acquisitive greed that would ultimately lead to its downfall. The term *kommôtikê* serves as a subtle reference to that greed, indicating that the "universally valid critique" (Vickers 1988, 88) has more to do with gluttony and excess than with sophistry and rhetoric as such.

Conclusion

If there is a timeless critique encased in this dialogue, it is a critique that aims to expose how an empire's domination abroad can be ensured only if it is necessary, and it will only be necessary if there is profligate consumption at home. It is through the constant desire for more, and the consequential ever-widening reach of military, industry, and voracity that the empire can require and therefore attain its domination and power as an empire. The observation that bottomless desire at home is a necessary prior condition for domination abroad has a long political history, reaching at least as far back as Plato and his contemporary Thucydides.

For these two, the greed that promotes imperial domination is the same greed lurking beneath the demand for foreign luxury goods, including the use of foreign perfumes. Thucydides explicitly blames Athenian acquisitiveness for the destruction brought about through the war; Plato explicitly makes the war the dramatic backdrop and then explicitly critiques Athenian acquisitiveness for making Athens pursue pleasure rather than justice. In the end, the definition of rhetoric and sophistry offered in the analogy coheres with this larger critique of Athenian appetites and imperial policies precisely inasmuch as the term *kommôtikê* is capable of reflecting these wedded critiques: the consumption of goods and foreign entanglements. A *kommôtikê* derived from Egyptian *kommi* is capable of managing the connotation of both imperial domination and profligate consumption; *kommôtikê* derived from Greek *komaô* is not.

Although translations regularly impose the distinction between seeming and being in a way that is consistent with E. R. Dodd's reading, which suggests that the analogy introduces an opposition of seeming to being that is recurrent and upheld throughout the rest of the dialogue, the analysis here suggests the distinction is absent from the dialogue. It is found neither in the analogy nor in other places where it is commonly presumed to be. As I discuss above, translators commonly describe the false *technê* as *impersonating* or *seeming to be* the real thing, whereas Plato describes the false *technê* not as impersonating or seeming but as "attaching itself to each of the subdivisions, and *being the very thing it attaches itself to*" (464c; T. Griffith 2010, 30; translation modified, emphasis mine). Similarly, translators typically identify a distinction between seeming good and being good at the end of the dialogue. However, the language there actually draws a distinction between a false *expectation* of goodness and actual goodness (527b). Once the anachronistic distinction is removed from the analogy, its greater absence may be felt throughout the dialogue.

When Plato finally introduces the myth of the afterlife at the end of the *Gorgias*, it's to add valuative force to the contrast he's developed between a life that pursues pleasure and a life that aims instead at self-discipline and the avoidance of wrongdoing. Up to that point, both seem as though they may be viable accounts of what is good. But the myth reminds us that both end in death; in death, both are stripped of their clothing and every other luxury—"attractive bodies, noble birth, and wealth" (523c) are shed. What remains are the products of the *psychê*: "the scars which every dishonest and unjust action imprinted on it, utterly crippled by lies and arrogance and warped by a truth-free diet" (525a; Waterfield 131). As Gilles Deleuze explains (in a point that will be explored more thoroughly in the final chapters of this book), Plato's myths function to subordinate one idea to another in the absence of truly representational thinking—in other words, in the absence of a metaphysics that separates seeming from being, appearance from truth, the myth intervenes to deliver a judgment about the lines of distinction that have been drawn and to give one "probative force" (1995, 61) while subordinating the other. In the *Gorgias*, the myth functions in precisely this way.

The dialogue has set up no contrast between truth and its appearance, but between two equally alluring models of goodness: the Calliclean (later the Nietzschean) lion who takes what he wants, and the Socratic citizen who disciplines what he wants. It's the myth of the afterlife that allows the reader to subordinate the former to the latter. This is one indication that the apparent critique of rhetoric in the *Gorgias* is not predicated on a metaphysical distinction between seeming and being, but is also not a critique of rhetoric as such. Rather it is a critique that passes *through* the rhetoric of the sophist Gorgias and arrives ultimately at its true object: the use of power for acquisitive gain. In other words, rhetoric and sophistry serve as a medium for the critique; they are not the target of the critique.

Plato's critique of rhetoric in the *Gorgias* cannot be taken at face value, but neither should his apparent embrace of rhetoric in the *Phaedrus* be viewed as straightforward. In the following chapter, I examine how the view of rhetoric in the *Phaedrus* functions as a dramatic portrayal of the erotic, irrational effects of the poetic tradition, inherited by the sophistic arts of rhetoric. Plato does not make literal recommendations about rhetoric in the *Phaedrus*; rather, he engages in a display that demonstrates how the rhetoric of the sophists replicates the visceral effects of poetic expression, while at the same time rhetoric offers a prophylactic against those effects. In this way, it is both the drug that induces irrational, poetic ecstasy, and the *pharmakon* that protects against such inducement.

« 2 »

The Oral Poet and the Literate Sophist

Divine Madness and Rhetorical Inoculation in the *Phaedrus*

Upon initial reading, Plato's *Phaedrus* seems as though it were "divided into two parts" (Kennedy 1994, 39). In part 1, Phaedrus and Socrates deliver speeches on the topic of love. In part 2, they discuss rhetoric and writing. The speeches, which culminate in Socrates's famous palinode, seem to present "several basic Platonic doctrines" (Kennedy 1994, 39), whereas the discussion that follows the speeches offers practical observations and recommendations not unlike what might be found in a classical rhetorical handbook. As Charles Griswold describes it, "The first half of the *Phaedrus* is normally thought of as being mythic and playful in tone, whereas the second half seems considerably more technical and sober. Indeed, it is this fact that has helped make the unity of the *Phaedrus* so problematic and the significance of the first half of the dialogue so difficult to gauge" (1986, 138). Moreover, the apparent division in the text accordingly bifurcates most scholarship on the dialogue. Investigations of rhetoric in the *Phaedrus* gravitate toward the recommendations at the end and ignore the speeches at the beginning, which seem at best irrelevant to and at worst incongruous with those recommendations, while investigations of Plato's concept of *eros* do the reverse, gravitating instead toward the speeches on love.

The break between the two parts is emphasized by the stylistic caesura of the dialogue's centerpiece—Socrates's famous, "best" speech: the palinode. There Socrates presents an elaborate theogonic account of the *psychê*, represented as a winged chariot, pulled by an unruly dark horse and a docile white horse. The chariot driver ascends to the heavens, where he encounters the procession of the gods who, from that height, have a "view of things as they really are" (248b; Waterfield 2002, 31). Because the mythical content of this speech and the practical remarks that follow it are so alien to each other in terms of both form and content, the dialogue reads as though there were a deep rift, which, as I discuss more fully below, develops a profound interpretive disunity, problematizing scholarly efforts to define the interrelevance of the palinode and the practical theory of rhetoric.

Despite this puzzle of apparent disunity (indeed, *because* of it), I suggest that the palinode is essential for discerning and understanding the discussion of rhetoric that follows it, and that viewing the recommendations with this context in mind, they no longer seem to be a straightforward set of prescriptions. Rather, they are a demonstration of the critical analysis that's possible when and only when one has a discourse in writing. One side effect of this reading, however, is that it problematizes the general understanding that the palinode should be viewed as a serious presentation of Platonic doctrines. Rather, I believe, along with Aristotle (*Rhet.* 3.7.11), that the enthusiasm Socrates displays and comments on in his delivery of the speech is an imitation full of irony and cheek—a display of the plastic powers of *logos* made possible by Plato's own writing technology.[1] Plato's greatest feat in this case is his ability to replicate—in writing—not only the verbal tricks of the sophists in his imitative version of Lysias's oratory (who was famous for having written his speeches), but also the inspired, muse-made poetry that prior to Plato could only be explained by divine power.[2] Plato uses writing to pull back the curtain, as it were: the sophists and poets alike may fill their hearer's breast with lust, pity, fear, and terror, but if the rhetorician is able to criticize their abilities through an analysis of their written eloquence, then the sophists' power is no longer supernatural, nor the poet's skill divine. Socrates's seeming condemnation (in the myth of Theuth) of writing and his apparent recommendations regarding rhetoric are refracted through this ironic display. In this way, he only seems to condemn the very thing (writing) that has made it possible for him to mimic both the sophistry of Lysias and the poetry of Homer and Hesiod. Writing, in other words, heralds the death of the poetic tradition, captured as a death mask in Socrates's palinode. Rhetoric, then, is meant to inoculate hearers against a sham divine power: the sophist, who is able to produce effects identical to those of the divinely inspired poet. This inoculation works by raising critical awareness of the sophist's verbal skill. In so doing, Plato breaks the aural spell. I suggest the dialogue be read not as a "tempered view of rhetoric" or a "philosophy of *eros*" but as a demonstration of how the theoretical apparatus of rhetoric identifies, catalogs, and exposes the sophists' simulation of the same effects of the divine, erotic *logos* of the poet. In this way rhetoric separates the sophists' more "scientific," apodeictic *technê* of speech making from their ability to produce profound visceral effects.

In this chapter I propose that the speeches—which evoke in both Phaedrus and Socrates a palpable, erotic bodily frenzy, characteristic of religious and cultic revelry—indicate a coherence between the old tradition of epic poetry (illustrated in Socrates's palinode) and the new "scientific" mode of apodeictic discourse (illustrated in Lysias's speech). In this way, the radical innovations in *logôn technê* that so impress Phaedrus are of a piece with the oldest poetic habits. Despite drastic differences in the mode of presentation, the overall effects of the speeches are the same: both excite their hearer to a height of frenzied, erotic, irrational ecstasy. Nevertheless, the particular benefit of the new mode of discourse is that the same technique that enables the profound innovation also enables rhetorical critique, as Socrates's discussion of rhetoric demonstrates. A speech that once irresistibly provoked strong emotion—even to the point of erotic arousal—may now, upon reconsideration, be dissected, criticized, and belittled.[3] The sophists' writing may replace the living memory of the poet and drug its hearers, but it also may be used to inoculate those hearers against these visceral effects by exposing the rhetorical means by which they are achieved.

In what follows, I offer a brief summary of the recommendations on rhetoric from the second half of the dialogue. I then turn to an analysis of the speeches (particularly the palinode), which appear at the beginning of the dialogue and which have been for the most part ignored by scholarship on Plato's view and critique of rhetoric. Finally, I examine how Plato's writing enables Socrates to break the powerful link between epic and sophistry through the use of rhetorical criticism.

Rhetorical Disunity in the *Phaedrus*

As is well known, in the second half of the dialogue, Socrates makes several recommendations on rhetorical expertise, and in so doing enlists rhetoric as a tool in service of dialectic. In contrast to the *Gorgias*, where, as discussed in the previous chapter, rhetoric receives Plato's harshest condemnation and Socrates renders it as a "civic depravity" (Crick and Poulakos 2008, 2), in the *Phaedrus*, Socrates seems to suggest that rhetoric might be a legitimate *technê* so long as it meets certain requirements. These requirements are summarized as follows.

Rhetoric should not be reduced to the basic skills of arrangement, as they'd been set down in the popular handbooks of the time. These include the basic structure of the speech (proem, exposition, proofs, etc.; 266d–e), particular figures of speech (reduplication, maxims, imagery, etc.; 267b–c), correctness of diction (267c), and the use of emotion (267c–d). These techniques are not enough on their own because using them does not necessarily indicate genuine and proper understanding. The techniques found in the handbooks are merely the "preliminaries" of a technique (269c). Similarly, natural ability can bring one only so far, even when that natural ability is honed by knowledge and practice (269d). True expertise must surpass both the codified "rules" and the natural "knack": it must "enumerate all its aspects and . . . see with which of these aspects it is naturally equipped to act and to what effect, or with which of these aspects it is naturally equipped to be acted upon, by what, and to what effect" (270d; Waterfield 2002, 62). And since all rhetoric is directed at the movement of the human *psychê* (270e), it naturally follows that the proper rhetorician must be able to classify the *psychê* "with absolute precision" (271a; Waterfield 2002, 63), to know how it is likely to be affected by different types of speech, and to determine "all the causes, fitting each type of speech to each type of *psychê* and explaining what it is about the nature of particular kinds of soul which makes them inevitably either persuaded or unpersuaded by speeches of a particular kind" (271b; Waterfield 2002, 63). Socrates's summary of the requirements indicates a vast scope for any legitimate rhetorical *technê*:

> When he can not only say what kind of person is persuaded by what kind of speech, but also spot that kind of person before him and tell himself that here, in real life and before his eyes, is the kind of person and the kind of character which was the subject of those earlier discussions, and to which such-and-such a kind of speech should be applied in such-and-such a way to persuade him of such-and-such—once he is capable of doing *all* this, and moreover has understood the proper moments for speaking and for keeping quiet, and can also recognize the appropriate and inappropriate occasions for concision, arousing pity, shocking the audience, and all the various

modes of speech he has learnt, *then and only then* will his expertise have been perfected and completed. (271c–272a; Waterfield 2002, 64; emphases mine)

Obviously, rhetorical *technê* so defined is nothing less than enormous. The scope and breadth of these requirements not only render rhetoric a high art, obtainable only through "a great deal of effort" (273e; Waterfield 2002, 67), but they also imply that Socrates is arguing for an omniscient rhetorician. One who would speak on issues concerning statecraft, legislation, or adjudication would need to meet the prerequisite that he or she know everything about everything and everyone. Elsewhere I have called this "Cinderella Rhetorica" (Reames 2012, 138)—she can go to the ball, but only after she has done so many chores that would naturally preclude her from doing so.

By such an interpretation, there is not necessarily any conflict between the views on rhetoric presented here and those presented in the *Gorgias*. In both cases, we might conclude that Plato's opinion (articulated in the voice of Socrates) was intractable. In the *Gorgias* he demeans it as a civic canker, and in the *Phaedrus* he presents an unrealizable cure.[4] According to such a reading, his apparent acceptance of rhetoric is merely a display of Socratic irony. Nevertheless, the tempered tone and the apparent affability and friendliness of the exchange between Phaedrus and Socrates—an obvious contrast to the bitterness and acrimony of the *Gorgias*—lead many to suggest that Plato indeed had a change of heart, and that the apparent conflict between the view of rhetoric here and the one offered in the *Gorgias* is resolved by the likelihood that *Gorgias* was an early dialogue and *Phaedrus* a late one, so Plato's opinion (via Socrates) must have softened over time.[5] By the latter view, Aristotle's *Rhetoric* is read as an earnest attempt to fulfill the rigorous requirements set forth in the *Phaedrus* dialogue.[6] And by at least one proponent of the former view, Aristotle's *Rhetoric* may have been the implicit target of the critique hidden within the *Phaedrus* dialogue.[7]

I am critical of both of these readings. Interpretations that would slot Plato as "for" or "against" rhetoric seek definite conclusions within a compositional form—dialogue—whose particular merit is the possibility of refracting and misdirecting meaning and deferring conclusions. Seeking such a fixed end for interpretation threatens to counteract a crucial aspect of the dialogue form: the possibility of indirect reasoning and hidden understanding.[8] As Drew Hyland has famously argued, any doctrine Plato may have had is necessarily obscured by the dialogue form in which he wrote (1968, 40). Moreover, the for/against readings tend to isolate the recommendations regarding rhetoric from the rest of the dialogue, and particularly to alienate them from the third speech in which Socrates poeticizes at length. In other words, as I hope to make clear in this chapter, in order to read the *Phaedrus* as a definition of rhetoric that contrasts with the one Plato offers in the *Gorgias*, one must neglect what otherwise seems to be "the main thrust of the dialogue" (Curran 1986, 71): the Socratic palinode. The tendency to separate Socrates's recommendations on rhetoric from the rest of the dialogue contributes to an additional problem that has plagued interpretations since antiquity; namely, the apparent and profound "disunity of the *Phaedrus*."[9] Finally, both of these interpretive tendencies wherein one reads the dialogues in search of a propositional or doctrinal "point," and each point must be reconciled and unified with the other doctrinal positions in Plato's corpus as a whole, arise from the Neoplatonist readings of Plato. Given the manifest anachronism of Neoplatonist interpretation—not to mention the dubious Neoplatonist assumption that "Plato simply cannot be wrong" (van den Berg 1997, 149)—we are right to be suspicious of these tendencies.

The interpretive line we must walk is seeing apparent disunity as a guise for some hidden unity, not due to thick assumptions about Plato's status as a doctrinal author, but due to the merits of the compositional form of dialogue for hiding meaning, the "philosophic importance" of the dramatic structure of the dialogue (Hyland 1968, 38), and the clues planted for us within that dramatic structure. These clues are not subtle, and should not be overlooked. It is no accident that Socrates praises the act of "bringing things which are scattered all over the place into a single class by gaining a comprehensive view of them" (265d; Waterfield 2002, 55) in a dialogue that is itself very scattered. Along with Richard Rutherford, I believe this is an explicit indication that the author is self-consciously aware of the importance of a unified discourse even as he is crafting a discourse that is, at least on the surface, highly disunified. According to Rutherford, this simply cannot be incidental or accidental: "That Plato praises unity in a work which seems to most readers bafflingly diverse and varied in matter and tone is neither coincidence nor incompetence, but deliberate" (Rutherford 1995, 266). This observation is not original to Rutherford: it follows Jacques Derrida's recognition in 1968 that the discourse of the *Phaedrus* is unified in a way that is neither crude nor obvious; rather, its unity is accomplished "with suppleness, irony, and discretion" (1981a, 67).

I suggest that our attention should be drawn to the very place of the dialogue where the unity seems most fraught: between the practical recommendations regarding rhetoric in relation to dialectic, and the palinode's mythical story of the charioteer. It is these two moments in the dialogue that mutually ensure the irrelevance of the other and fracture the work. This occurs precisely because the palinode, which Socrates regards as the "greatest" of the three speeches, violates every guideline for the production of a great speech outlined in his own practical recommendations.[10] For one thing, it is "both too magnificent and too long; the balance of the dialogue is upset and the structural plan at least partially obscured" (Hackforth 1952, 136). Since Plato offers, immediately following the speech, a set of guidelines that allow us to make this determination, Socrates's violation of his own rules should not escape our notice. At the beginning of the palinode he seems as though he will remain tethered to some sophistic conventions—he claims he will offer proofs (245b–c), he enumerates types of madness (244c–d; 245a), and he recapitulates earlier points (245b). But this opening is in stark contrast with the palinode's myth once it gathers momentum. As Gerrit de Vries notes, "The whole of the speech until 256e3 is meant as an ἀπόδειξις" (1969, 120), indicating that the beginning of the speech still bears the trace of the earlier sophistic displays, which structure the content as an offering of proofs. But the discourse resembles proof less and less as it progresses. Instead, Socrates admits, "It would take too long—and beyond the slightest shadow of a doubt require a god—to explain [the *psychê*'s] character" (246a; Waterfield 2002, 28), thus explicitly signaling that he will not fulfill the requirements that he demands. In addition to these failures, once he has finished the speech, Socrates cannot give any account for why the speech was persuasive, either to Phaedrus or to himself, or what in particular was so effective or moving about it. Although he praises the speech at length, his praise is merely a recapitulation of its overwhelming effect and not an identification of the mechanics provoking that effect. It is Plato's reader and not Socrates himself who is able to offer these explanations. As Hackforth describes the speech, its "magnificence of expression . . . imaginative power . . . [and] richness and grandeur of its portraiture" (1952, 136) may account for its effect on Socrates and Phaedrus, but we do not gain this view from any self-conscious awareness on Socrates's part, despite the fact that it is that very self-conscious awareness of how and why speeches create their effects that determines rhetorical greatness, in Socrates's view (271b–272a).

Given Plato's explicit signal that his readers should attend to the overall unity of a work, the key conflict between the myth of the third speech (presented as a grandiose theogony) and the recommendations regarding rhetoric that follow (presented as a set of straightforward and practical recommendations) grows in importance. In other words, by highlighting unity, Plato subtly draws our attention precisely to the relationship between these two profoundly disunified parts of the dialogue. Despite their apparent disunity—indeed, *because of* their apparent disunity—a fuller consideration of the mutual illumination between the speech and the recommendations on rhetoric is in order. In the following section, I show how the recommendations regarding rhetoric are presented as a method by which Socrates and Phaedrus can rupture the psychic power of sophistry by dissociating it from the tradition of epic poetry, a tradition that I show is richly and elaborately represented in the palinode.

The Speeches in Contrast

The palinode that precedes the discussion of rhetoric takes place as a culmination of the speeches that Socrates and Phaedrus deliver to each other. At the beginning of the dialogue, they have wandered outside Athens's walls discussing a speech on love that Phaedrus has just heard the speechwriter Lysias deliver. Phaedrus is dazzled by Lysias's ability to subvert conventional wisdom and reverse common expectations. He gushes: "Lysias' work is designed for the attempted seduction of a good-looking boy—but (and this is the exquisite aspect of it) by someone who *isn't* in love with the boy! He claims, you see, that you should gratify someone who is *not* in love with you rather than someone who *is*" (227c; Waterfield 2002, 3; emphases mine). The speech is impressive to Phaedrus, in other words, because it has convinced him of something that should be unbelievable: that the one most worthy of love is the one who does not love.

When Phaedrus reveals that he has purchased a copy of the speech, the two agree to turn off the road and find a shady spot so Phaedrus might deliver the speech himself and demonstrate to Socrates the reason for his great admiration of Lysias's verbal accomplishments. They settle in an auspicious spot—it might just have been the place where, sometime in the deep past, Boreas, the god of the north wind, absconded with Oreithuia to ravish her and keep her as his wife, or so the oral tradition recounts. Phaedrus recites Lysias's speech for Socrates, and in so doing reveals how he came to be so convinced of Lysias's unlikely prothesis: the speech is characterized by a systematic presentation of proofs, characteristic of the "scientific" apodeictic mode of fifth-century sophistry. This is particularly evident in the fact that the speech begins with a proem that forecasts the proofs to be offered, and in the vocabulary of Lysias's speech, which contains the regular repetition of apodeictic terms like "moreover"/ἔτι δὲ (231a–b, 232a, 233d) "furthermore"/καίτοι (231c), and "therefore"/τοίνυν (231e).[11] This vocabulary, along with the language Socrates uses to describe Lysias's speech, is characteristic of the "scientific" style of discourse that came into widespread use during the dramatic period of the dialogue—terminology that sharply demarcates and self-consciously indicates the steps of the argument.[12]

After Phaedrus delivers Lysias's speech, Socrates attempts to improve upon it by offering a speech of his own. He alters little of the content, but in place of a demonstrative proem, Socrates begins with the "fiction" (de Vries 1969, 82) of epic inspiration: "Come, then, clear-voiced Muses . . . grant me your support" (237a; Waterfield 2002, 16), and then continues, "Once upon a time there was a boy, or rather a young man, who was very beautiful, and he had a great many lovers. One of these lovers was a cunning man. . . . And this is what he said" (237b; Waterfield 2002, 16). This beginning contrasts strongly with the beginning of Phaedrus's speech, which is a direct appeal, in the speaker's own voice, to a beautiful young boy: "You are aware of my situation and you have heard me explain how, in my opinion, it would be to our advantage if this were to happen" (230e; Waterfield 2002, 8).[13] And instead of a straightforward and systematic presentation of proofs of the sort Phaedrus offers, signaled by the regular repetition of apodeictic vocabulary, Socrates claims to use the affected and florid dithyrambic style of fifth-century poetry, and indicates that he is in danger of possession by nymphs or perhaps inspired by a god (238c–d).[14] This change in form between Phaedrus's and Socrates's speeches indicates a chronological step backward since, according to de Vries, "in Plato's time the dithyramb was in full decay; the fifth century already mocked at it" (1969, 88).[15] The "improvement" that Socrates attempts is marked by a more embellished style, by a shift from demonstration to storytelling, and by a chronological step away from new sophistic oratory and toward old poetry.

This temporal and stylistic shift is reemphasized when Socrates interrupts his own speech to give his palinode. When he pauses, he notes that he has "stopped chanting dithyrambs and [is] now coming up with epic verse" (241e; Waterfield 2002, 22).[16] In other words, he's receded even further into the past, from dithyramb to epic. He explains the reason for his breaking off: he says that he was just about to cross the river when he heard a divine voice, compelling him to purify himself for an offense he had committed against the gods (242b–c). Following his explanation that the previous two speeches were irreligious, for they spoke of love as though love were not a god (the son of Aphrodite) Socrates claims he will offer a palinode to purify the blasphemy. In this speech, Socrates departs even further from the apodeictic style of the initial speech and offers instead a mythological and allegorical account that follows in the epic tradition, describing the *psychê* as a winged charioteer pulled by two horses, a black one and a white one.

It is necessary to pause here briefly and to note the importance this speech has had in Plato scholarship since late antiquity, beginning with Proclus and continuing even today. As indicated above, the final speech on the transcendence of the *psychê* found in Plato's *Phaedrus* is ubiquitously regarded as the "best" of the three speeches offered by Phaedrus and Socrates in the first half of the dialogue. The speech is prioritized for various reasons:

- Because it corrects the previous views by presenting Plato's own view of *eros* and philosophy (Rowe 2009, 144)
- Because, through inspiration of the muses, it stylistically overcomes (Slaveva-Griffin 2003, 239) the limitations of Lysias's "highly rational, unemotive style, in the tone of a reasonable man, pointing out advantages, disadvantages, options to be chosen and dangers to be avoided" (Rutherford 1995, 252) by "wax[ing] poetic without reservation, and entranc[ing] Phaedrus with a prose-poem which far surpasses Lysianic performance" (Rutherford 1995, 256; see also Cook 1985, 430)
- Because it is one of the most important places where Plato works out
    - his theory of the Forms (Lebeck 1972, 272; Dyson 1982, 309; Stoeber 1992, 276)
    - the tripartite structure of the soul (Clegg 1976, 57)
    - and the immortality of the soul (Stewart 1965; Griswold 1986, 145–47)
- And, above all, because Socrates and Phaedrus explicitly praise the speech in the dialogue, unlike Lysias's speech, which they critique; this assumption works implicitly in the preponderance of the scholarship cited above

In other words, the "greatness" of the third speech is designated as such because Socrates's praise and the content of the speech are taken as a straightforward representation of Plato's own views, because its style is marked by divine inspiration, and because it contains Plato's essential metaphysical doctrines. Daniel Werner calls this the "Dogmatic View of Platonic myth."

"On this view," he writes, "we should regard the palinode . . . as a serious attempt by Plato to make substantive philosophical claims—claims that, moreover, he would himself be willing to defend. Platonic myth, in this view, is little more than a vehicle to express philosophical truth, and hence myth is 'dogmatic'" (Werner 2012, 11).

The trend of ranking Socrates's palinode as the best of the three speeches, full of dogmatic content, stems originally from the Neoplatonist commitment to syncretizing Plato's thought as a systematic metaphysics. Indeed, the very question of how the Platonic myths as a whole should be read in relation to Platonic philosophy, a perennial question in Plato scholarship (Frutiger [1930] 1976, 1–8; Clegg 1976, 52; Griswold 1986, 142–56; Deleuze 1995, 61; P. Murray 1999, 251; Rowe 2009, 134–35), appeared as an outgrowth of the Neoplatonist insistence that Plato's thought must be internally consistent. As R. M. van den Berg puts it, "All Neoplatonists . . . are in agreement that Plato simply cannot be wrong and that a philosopher's task is to clarify Plato's real meaning" (1997, 149–50). Proclus in particular, to whom we are indebted for the original attribution of dogmatic content to the myth of the charioteer, carried this tendency to an extreme; for where other Neoplatonists prioritize the philosophical content and deeper meaning of the text, Proclus further emphasizes the dogmatic consistency of every aspect of Platonic thought. Simply put, his objective was "to place Homer and the so-called Theologians alongside Plato as comprehensive and mutually consistent expressions of a seamless metaphysical world-view" (Smith 2007, 234). We see this in the proem of Proclus's book, for example, where he writes:

> [Plato], who, after the gods, has been our leader to every thing beautiful and good, receiving in an undefiled manner the most genuine and pure light of truth in the bosom of his soul, made us a partaker of all the rest of Plato's philosophy, communicated to us that arcane information which he had received from those more ancient than himself, and caused us, in conjunction with him, to be divinely agitated about the mystic truth of divine concerns. (1.1; T. Taylor 1985, 2)[17]

Buckley (2006) notes that Proclus's view that Plato had been initiated into divine mysteries and that certain trustees (including himself) were his rightful heirs and fellow initiates, was unequivocally influenced by the myth of the charioteer in the palinode. The very language Proclus uses to describe the appearance of Plato's first philosophy, which came into being through

Plato's "divine agitation" and through the revelation of the higher truths by divine beings, explicitly recalls the terminology Plato uses to describe the train of the gods and their followers from the myth: "[Proclus's] proem leans more heavily on the *Phaedrus* than any other dialogue—and on the myth in which these images appear above all" (Buckley 2006, 126).[18]

Proclus's intent to syncretize and canonize Plato's thought helps to explain how the myth of Socrates's palinode came to be interpreted as a vessel of philosophical and theological content—a capsule, as it were, of themes and ideas deeply resonant with and influential on the later development of Christian metaphysics. These themes are summarized as the soul-body relation, the immortality of the soul, the afterlife and transmigration of the soul, the soul's ability to recollect the Forms, the divine beauty of the Forms that transcend sensible reality, and "the truly real world to which the human soul naturally belongs and to which it always longs to return" (Rutherford 1995, 258). The third speech is believed to contain all this prototheology, and as such it is without question the "best" of the speeches and the apex of the dialogue. Every major study of Plato's psychology (in the sense of his *logos* about the *psychê*) points to the myth of the charioteer for evidence of the eternal, self-moving, and unoriginated nature of the soul, and this fact alone demonstrates how thoroughly influential the Neoplatonist readings of Plato—and particularly of Socrates's palinode—continue to be.

In addition to the manifest unreliability of the Neoplatonist prioritization and "doctrination" of the myth, the context of the dialogue itself gives us further reason to resist the interpretive tendencies we have inherited from this tradition. In the dialogue itself, Socrates's second speech is not explained as an exposition of theological or philosophical truths. Rather, it is offered as a correction for the first two speeches, which themselves constitute reversals of received or common wisdom—the common wisdom that would have been scrupulously preserved in the very oral epic tradition that the palinode mimics. In earlier Greek culture, prior to the rise of literacy and the craft of the sophists, it was the epic tradition that preserved the conventional wisdom—its history, customs, ethics, and social codes. In the epic, not only the poet but the culture as a whole was invested in "saying over and over again what has been learned arduously over ages" (Ong 1982, 41). And once it had been learned, the traditional sayings "must not be dismantled" since "it has been hard work getting them together over the generations. . . . Once a formulary expression has crystallized, it had best be kept intact" (Ong 1982, 39). Indeed, the very style and formulaicity of the epic verse is itself a mnemonic device for linguistic and cultural preservation, as Albert Lord hypothesized. Plato's pastiche of a Lysianic speech demonstrates an inversion of this wisdom and a fearlessness about what Ong calls the "high-risk procedure" of "breaking up thought" (1982, 39). In place of the epic formula, which "inhibits intellectual experimentation" (Ong 1982, 41), the speechwriters, according to Socrates, "used the power of speech to make trivia appear important and important things trivial, they got novelties to sound old and old things fresh and new" (267a–b; Waterfield 2002, 57). The important no longer need be described as important, nor the old described as old. Achilles can now be cowardly, Odysseus feckless, Helen virtuous, and the nonlover the best kind of lover. Writing—and particularly, written speeches—means that knowledge is no longer "hard to come by and precious" (Ong 1982, 41), so there is no longer any need scrupulously to conserve it. The sophist, who has acquired writing technology and is willing to exploit it, sees very little at stake in linguistic innovation and inversion.[19] Since the knowledge is inscribed in writing, it is not lost. Thus sophistic subversion is nothing more than an amusement, diversion, and ironic display.[20]

Socrates's change of speech is prompted by a concern over his own complicity with this sophistic subversion that offends the old ways: "I was rather worried, as Ibycus says, 'lest the cost of winning honor among men is that I sin in the eyes of the gods.' But now I see where I went wrong. It was an awful speech, Phaedrus, just awful—the one you brought with you, and the one you forced me to make. . . . It was stupid and almost irreligious, and speeches don't come more awful than that" (242b–d; Waterfield 2002, 23). So it is to correct this wrongdoing that Socrates famously begins the palinode, quoting the early sixth-century lyric poet Stesichorus, who, Socrates claims, corrects a fault of his predecessor Homer by being conscious of having told a falsehood: "'False was the tale' that you should gratify a non-lover rather than a lover" (244a; Waterfield 2002, 25).

Socrates's self-conscious identification with the poets and poetic inspiration is a deliberate reference to the chronological development of different language arts, or *logôn technê*, from the epic to sophistic oratory.[21] G. R. F. Ferrari similarly has observed the counterchronological progression of at least one aspect of the dialogue. In his reading of the preamble to Socrates's palinode, Ferrari notes its "historical presentation":

> Whereas in his critique of rhetoric, as befits a theoretical account which aims to legislate current rhetorical practice, he invokes the most modern

> strain of medicine (the Hippocratic [270b-c]) and contemporary poets (Sophocles and Euripides [269a]), in his mythic hymn he adduces rather those ancient rites of healing which Hippocratic physicians in his day were casting in the unfavourable light of superstition; and he names no contemporary poets, but rather emphasizes how true poetry adorns the achievements of the ancients. (1987, 114)

Ferrari groups much under this mantle of ancient rites that work as a counterweight to contemporary "science": prophecy, the Delphic oracle, the Pythia and Sibyl, all of which "invoke a rich tradition of involvement in the grand events of Greek history" (1987, 114). The significance of how Socrates begins the palinode is, according to Ferrari, a hymn of praise for the archaic world (1987, 115), and, he explains, this is a deliberate contrast with the contemporary Lysianic speech and the recommendations on rhetoric. In Socrates's world, archaisms had been overtaken by sophists and their rhetoric: "Key speakers in political assemblies could now be regarded as having the kind of power over social planning for the future that was once a prerogative of oracles (cf. 260c6–d1)—and which Plato dreamed of committing to the hands of philosophers" (Ferrari 1987, 115). This observation is crucial: if the palinode is designed to evoke the sounds and images of archaic Greek thought, and rhetoric itself is what separates his world from that thought, then there is an indispensible link between the recommendations regarding rhetoric and the seemingly bizarre content of Socrates's elaborate myth of the charioteer.

These archaisms are evident in numerous elements of the palinode—in Plato's Homeric turns of phrase, to which Plato's Socrates explicitly draws the reader's attention; in the themes of the chariot and the divine procession that cohere unambiguously with Homeric and Hesiodic epic themes; and in the religious and mythological symbolism of horses and Bacchic and Corybantic religious initiation rites. All of these should be understood as a deliberate contrast to the modes of presentation and forms of thought made accessible through rhetorical theory, represented in Phaedrus's speech.

The Palinode as Epic: Themes, Formulae, Symbols

In this section, I explain how the palinode works as an elaborate and deliberate portrayal of archaic poetry, which, I believe, makes it less compatible with the doctrinal, dogmatic interpretation described above. As I discuss in the final section, this shift of interpretation impacts how we receive the recommendations on rhetoric that follow the palinode.

The explicit markers that indicate a discursive shift from contemporary apodeixis of the first speech to archaic poetry of the palinode are apparent both in the themes and the diction of the latter, and reinforced by its imagistic and symbolic content. As the voice of the divine overtakes Socrates's own voice, the speech reverberates more and more with the traditions of the epic past.

To begin, the very setting for the theogony—with the gods in the heavens, emphasizing as it does the association of the divine with ascent and height (247a)—is a theme that is "as old as humanity" (de Vries 1969, 130). The *psychê* has wings, and wings naturally want to carry things upward (246d), and gods also dwell in upward places. For the gods, the natural tendency is to ascend skyward on their chariots, in ordered procession to the heavenly banquet. But for we mortals, the way is more difficult. The human *psychê* must steer the direction of two horses, "only one of which is thoroughly noble and good, while the other is thoroughly the opposite [which] inevitably makes driving, in our case, difficult and disagreeable" (246b; Waterfield 2002, 28).[22] Nevertheless, the purpose of the *psychê*'s journey is ultimately "a recollection of the things which our *psychê* once saw during its journey as a companion to a god, when it saw beyond the things we now say 'exist' and poked its head up into true reality" (249c; Waterfield 2002, 32; translation modified).

These thematic references to the epic tradition are extensive, specific, and deliberate. Svetla Slaveva-Griffin has noted the striking similarity between the myth of the charioteer, the proem of Parmenides's book, and a panoply of references that saturate the ancient tradition. The references to the charioteer, Zeus, and the procession of the gods link the myth, she argues, to Parmenides's proem, which in itself is a direct bridge to Homer. For example, when Socrates refers to Zeus as 'the great leader' (246e, *ho megas hêgamôn*), he forges a deliberate link "to Parmenides' portrayal of the gods (especially the Heliades, who also 'lead,' ἡγεμόνευον, the way in B1.5) and his adaptation of the Homeric theme of divine chariot rides (especially the one of Zeus in B1)" (Slaveva-Griffin 2003, 247). By including the literary allusion to Zeus and his chariot, Plato is summoning in the voice of Socrates one of the most central themes of the epic tradition. And not only

Zeus's chariot (*Il.* 8.41–52), but heaven's gates, Hera's chariot (*Il.* 5.748–52), and Telemachus's journey from Pylos to Sparta (book 3 of the *Odyssey*), are all enfolded in Socrates's reference to the charioteer's skyward journey (Slaveva-Griffin 2003, 232n22).

By drawing on Parmenides's proem for the myth of the charioteer, Plato is drawing likewise on the more than two hundred allusions to Homer and Hesiod contained therein. The similarities are obvious when the Socrates's palinode is compared directly with Homer and Hesiod:

A third kind of possession and madness comes from the Muses. It takes hold of a delicate, virgin soul and stirs it into a frenzy for composing lyric and other kinds of poetry. (245a; Waterfield 2002, 27)	[22] It was they who taught Hesiod beautiful song as he tended his sheep at the foothills of god-haunted Helikon. Here are the words the daughters of aegis-bearing Zeus, the Muses of Olympos, first spoke to me. (Hesiod, *Theogony*; Athanassakis 1983, 13)
The supreme leader in the heavens is Zeus. He goes at the head, in a winged chariot, arranging and managing everything, and behind him comes the host of gods and spirits in an orderly array of eleven squadrons. (246e; Waterfield 2002, 29)	[47] Then they sing of Zeus, the father of gods and men— they begin and end their song with him and tell of how he surpasses the other gods in rank and might. (Hesiod, *Theogony*; Athanassakis 1983, 14) I will sing of Zeus, chiefest among the gods and greatest, all-seeing, the lord of all, the fulfiller. (Homer, *Hymn to Zeus*; Evelyn-White 1914, 449)
For Hestia stays alone in the gods' house. (247a; Waterfield 2002, 29)	Hestia, you who tend the holy house of the lord Apollo, the Far-shooter at goodly Pytho, with soft oil dripping ever from your locks. (Homer, *Hymn to Hestia*; Evelyn-White 1914, 449)

When the souls we call "immortal" reach the rim, they make their way to the outside and stand on the outer edge of heaven, and as they stand there the revolution carries them around, while they gaze outward from heaven. The region beyond heaven has never yet been adequately described in any of our earthly poets' compositions, nor will it ever be. But since one has to make a courageous attempt to speak the truth, especially when it is truth that one is speaking about, here is a description. This region is filled with true being. (247b–c; Waterfield 2002, 30)

[105–11] Sing the glories of the holy gods to whom death never comes,
the gods born of Gaia and starry Ouranos,
and of those whom dark Night bore, or briny Pontos fostered.
Speak first of how the gods and the earth came into being and of how the rivers, the boundless sea with its raging swell,
the glittering stars, and the wide sky above were created.
Tell of the gods born of them, the givers of blessings, how they divided wealth, and each was given his realm, and how they first gained possession of many-folded Olympos. Tell me, O Muses who dwell on Olympos, and observe proper order for each thing as it first came into being. (Hesiod, *Theogony*; Athanassakis 1983, 15–16)

Once back home, the soul's charioteer reins in his horses by their manger, throws them ambrosia to eat, and gives them nectar to wash the ambrosia down. (247e; Waterfield 2002, 30)

[639–42] But when Zeus gave the three gods what strengthens the body,
the very nectar and ambrosia of the gods,
and they drank nectar and ate exquisite ambrosia, then the spirit rose bold in the hearts of all. (Hesiod, *Theogony*; Athanassakis 1983, 29).[23]

Throughout the palinode, epic archaisms, too copious to exhaustively treat here, abound.

These descriptions explicitly evoke not only the themes but also the formulaic language of the epic tradition. For example, the description of the gods' drivers and horses as "good and of good descent" (*agathos kai ex agathôn*) is an epic turn of phrase, a construction repeated elsewhere in the dialogue (249d, 274a). As de Vries (1969) notes, the precedent of this description is set, among other places, in Homer's *Iliad*, when Aias describes fallen Archilochus as "no mean man . . . nor of mean descent" (14.472, *ou . . . kakos . . . oude kakôn hex*). The formulaicity of such phrases, de Vries argues, should be understood as a deliberate reference to epic formulae: "In the fifth and fourth century Greek this and comparable phrases had long since become stereotyped. . . . A stereotyped phrase can occasionally be revivified, and in some of the passages referred to this may be the case. If this is so in the present passage, *this should be regarded as a conscious play*" (246a; de Vries 1969, 126–27; emphasis mine).

This description of the charioteer draws richly on the epic tradition not only in terms of themes and formulaic phrasing, but also in terms of imagery. In particular, the horse occupies potent symbolic role in preliterary cultural practices, evocative of both sexual power and archaic religious rites and initiation. The dark horse—the one who holds back and does not readily give in—weighs us down and tethers us to the earth (247a–b) in a way that, Elizabeth Belfiore (2006) notes, evokes a tradition of using horses as erotic symbols.[24] For example, in both Theogenes 1249–52 and Anacreon fragment 360, the beloved is compared to a horse. The comparison often turns on a kind of taming—in the same way that wild horses must be broken, the wildness of the beloved must be tamed through sexual domination (Belfiore 2006, 194n25). The nature of this eroticism in the literary tradition is particularly wild and untrammeled, "characterized by *hybris* and lack of restraint, especially in sex, and failing to achieve its sexual goals" (Belfiore 2006, 195). This wild eroticism is merged through the image of the black horse with early ecstatic mystery and religious initiation rites that long predate the Greek literary tradition. In particular, Belfiore cites the Corybantic rites, in which as Plato recounts in his *Laws*, "internal, mad movement (μανικὴν κίνησιν, 791a3) is calmed by the application of ordered movement" (2006, 208).

The Corybantic and Bacchic rites are referenced not only in the palinode through the image of the black horse, but also, it just so happens, in Socrates's and Phaedrus's excited responses to Lysias's speech. Plato refers explicitly to these rites when he has Socrates say that Phaedrus was in a "frenzy" after hearing Lysias's speech. When Phaedrus, who must have pored over it until he learned it by heart, encounters Socrates, "who is sick with passion for hearing speeches," he has found "someone with whom he [can] share his *frenzy* [*sygkorubantiônta*]" (228b; Waterfield 2002, 4; emphasis mine). The term here refers specifically to someone who shares in the frenzy of the Corybantic revels, reflected also in the taming of the wild horse (Belfiore 2006, 208).[25] Similarly, once Phaedrus has delivered the speech, Socrates is also infected with the Corybantic frenzy: "It's out of this world, my friend. I was amazed. And you were the reason I felt this way, Phaedrus, because I was looking at you while you were reading, and it seemed to me that the speech made you glow with pleasure. . . . I followed your lead, and so came to share in the ecstasy of your enthusiasm [*synebaccheusa*]" (234d; Waterfield 2002, 12). And later, producing a speech of his own, he continues the erotic theme: "Do not be surprised if I become possessed by the Nymphs as my speech progresses" (238d; Waterfield 2002, 18).

The obviously erotic overtones and the language that evokes the frenzied and frantic celebration of the Bacchic mysteries and "nymphaphilia," as it were, indicate an important connection between these two parts of the dialogue. This deserves emphasis—Plato's language to describe Socrates's and Phaedrus's excitement is descriptive also of the frenzy, wildness, and *madness* of ancient divine rites. This same concept is repeated again in the divinely inspired speech: the black horse leaps and neighs in a disorderly way that mimics the wild lust of erotic conquest and the bodily frenzy of the archaic Corybantic rites. By couching this imagery within Socrates's speech, and at the same time drawing on ancient religious rites and the oral traditions of epic themes and vocabulary, Plato is subtly linking the verbal performances in the *Phaedrus* dialogue. The titillating language of sexual arousal and satisfaction creates a prismlike relationship between Phaedrus's and Socrates's sympathetic responses to hearing the speeches, the frantic arousal of ancient cultic rites, and the archaic poetic experience as such. When the lover sees a beautiful object of desire, he swells with passion just as Socrates and Phaedrus do: "His wings begin to grow and he wants to take to the air on his new plumage. . . . The quills of the feathers swell and begin to grow from the roots upwards. . . . His whole *psychê* seethes and pounds" (249d–251c; Waterfield 2002, 33–35).[26] The aroused lover "seethes and pounds," just as the words "gush forth" and "flow" from the poet's mouth (Hesiod 84, 97; Havelock [1963] 1998, 154). This visceral, bodily frenzy, sensory, *irrational* arousal, characteristic of religious revelry, is present in *both* speeches, despite their numerous formal differences. The madness of divine inspiration (the source of the palinode), the wildness of the dark horse (the content of the myth of the charioteer), and the frenzy of both Socrates's and Phaedrus's responses to Lysias's speech are of a piece with one another, and more important, indicate how the new, scientific mode of apodeictic discourse, such as Lysias's speech, is not so very different from the deepest, oldest poetic habits. Despite its new "logical" mode of presentation and "scientific" method of demonstration, the effects are the same. Phaedrus and Socrates are worked into an irrational frenzy by the speech, demonstrating a confluence between the old poetry and the new rhetoric.[27]

If Eric Havelock is correct that Plato's account in the *Republic* was "the first and indeed the only Greek attempt to articulate consciously and with clarity the central fact of poetry's control over Greek culture", and moreover, that Hesiod represents a stopping-off place of sorts between the oral tradition of Homer and the critical tradition of Plato, representing "the first to attempt a statement of how the minstrel viewed himself and what his profession meant," then this similarity (in addition to the other similarities discussed above) between Homer, Hesiod, and Plato are in all likelihood not incidental but intentional ([1963] 1998, 97).[28] Just as "Homer simply invoked the Muse who is figuratively responsible for anything he says [and] Hesiod in effect asks, Who is the Muse? What precisely does she do, and how does she do it?" (Havelock [1963] 1998, 99), Plato synthesizes both of these gestures in his palinode in order to ask, ultimately, what is at stake for these different types of *logôn technê*? And how, moreover, might this manic frenzy be wrangled and brought under control?

In the end, the poetic palinode, an offering from the madness of divine inspiration to praise the madness of love, praises neither madness nor love. Rather, it is restraint and control that are praised, in the same way that the nonlovers of the first two speeches are praised for their restraint. The white horse, restrained by a sense of shame, is obedient to the charioteer's commands. The dark horse, by contrast, is truculent and, compelled by lust and desire, barrels toward the beloved, dragging the charioteer and white horse with him (254a–b). This speech, in which Socrates has promised to show definitive proof that in love, like in prophecy and poetry, madness is to be praised over sanity, ends by offering yet another encomium to restraint and sanity. The good horse, like the nonlover, is marked by its restraint and good sense of shame and decorum (254a, c), and it is only this control that leads the charioteer ultimately to subdue the untrammeled will of the bad horse, "pinning its legs and haunches to the ground, and causing it pain. Once the same thing has happened to it over and over again, the bad horse calms down, and now that it has been humbled it lets itself be guided by the charioteer's intentions. . . . At last the lover's *psychê* follows his beloved in reverence and awe" (254e; Waterfield 2002, 39).[29]

Ultimately, at the close of the palinode, we find the familiar Socratic preference for restraint over ecstasy and sanity over madness. It is this orderly behavior that he defines as "a wonderful, harmonious life here on earth, a life of self-control and restraint, since they have enslaved the part which allowed evil into the soul and freed the part which allowed goodness in . . . [and] which brings greater benefits than either human sanity or divine madness can supply" (256a–b; Waterfield 2002, 41). We are left at the end of the palinode to wonder what can bridle and tame the unruly discourse of poetic frenzy—what can trammel, dominate, and subdue the power of visceral, erotic drives, which are only symbolically represented in the content of the palinode, but literally present in the effects of the *logôn technê*? By what mechanism or means is such discursive restraint possible?

It is this need for restraint over the physical frenzy and psychical hypnosis of verbal performance that, I believe, offers a necessary context for understanding both the remarks on rhetoric and the discussion of writing that follow the presentation of the speeches in the second half of the dialogue.

Writing and Rhetoric

Despite promises to the contrary, the third speech subordinates the madness of love to the sanity of restraint. It promises to offer proofs that will exculpate madness but veers instead into a proofless theogonic account of love and erotic desire—an account that in both imagery and phrasing drinks deeply from the epic tradition. As readers, we expect either Socrates or his interlocutor to take note of this failure to fulfill the promise. However, this is not what happens at all. The palinode is invulnerable to criticism because once it is finished, it is—at least for Phaedrus and Socrates in the dramatic action of the dialogue—no longer physically extant. The critical remarks about Lysias's speech, by contrast, are a performative demonstration that rhetorical criticism is possible only with the written text. In other words, critical resistance to the verbal spell of the sophists and the poets is possible only because writing stabilizes speech long enough for it to be critically considered—pinning it to the ground and subduing it, forcing it to submit to the speaker's will (254e).

Lysias's speech, in contrast to the palinode, is vulnerable to criticism precisely because, after the frenzy of the delivery has died away, it is still there in front of them in written form. As Socrates and Phaedrus indicate, Lysias did not deliver his speeches extemporaneously but, like many of the sophists, wrote them out ahead of time.[30] When Socrates asks Phaedrus to recount the speech, Phaedrus responds, "Do you think an amateur like me could remember and do justice to a composition it took Lysias, the cleverest speech-writer of today, ages to write in his free time?" (228a; Waterfield 2002, 4). Socrates is doubtful that the speech would need to be remembered at all, guessing that Phaedrus would have "nagged [Lysias] to read it again and again. . . . And I doubt that even this was enough for Phaedrus. Eventually he borrowed the scroll himself and pored over those parts of the speech he particularly wanted to look at" (228a–b; Waterfield 2002, 4). It is this suspicion that inspires Socrates to urge Phaedrus, with flirtatious doubleness of meaning, to disclose his secret: "Show me what you've got in your left hand under your clothing. I suspect you've got the actual speech. . . . Come on, then, show me what you've got" (228d; Waterfield 2002, 5). When Phaedrus commences with his delivery of the speech, we are given no room to doubt that the speech is being read directly from the scroll (230e). Through all these explicit indicators, Plato simply makes it impossible for us to ignore the written-ness of the first speech. And unlike the unwritten, inspired speech, the written-ness of the read speech opens it up to self-conscious evaluation and assessment by its auditors. It is only the first speech, the written one, that may be critiqued, and it is this criticism of the written speech that enables his discussion of rhetoric.

Once Phaedrus has delivered the speech, it is clear that, despite its visceral effect, Socrates is able after the fact to gather his critical faculties in an evaluation of it:

> Are we also required to praise a speech because its writer has included the necessary content, and not just because he has written a clear and compact speech, and has finely honed his vocabulary? . . . I was paying attention only to the form of the speech, and I got the impression that even Lysias himself was dissatisfied with the content. In fact, Phaedrus, unless you correct me, I thought he repeated himself two or three times, as if he had some difficulty finding a lot to say on the subject, or perhaps because he wasn't interested in such matters. And so I thought that in an immature fashion he was showing off his ability to say the same thing in two different ways and to find both times an excellent way of expressing himself. (234e–235a; Waterfield 2002, 13)

It is only with the written speech that Socrates is able to practice the proper *technê* of identifying the best type of speech to use with different sorts of people. The necessity of reading and rereading a written speech to facilitate this kind of evaluation is indicated even more clearly later in the dialogue, when Socrates asks Lysias to go back and reread the beginning of Lysias's speech (262d). When Lysias does so, he repeats verbatim the same lines he had recited earlier in the dialogue (262e). Socrates interrupts him to critique the speech: "Stop. So we have to point out his mistakes and where his composition lacks expertise, do we?" (262e; Waterfield 2002, 51). The exercise is repeated when, a few lines later, Socrates asks Phaedrus to read the same portion again. After the second reading, Socrates's response to the speech changes dramatically from what it had been at the beginning of the dialogue. Now he no longer shares in Phaedrus's enthusiasm (234d), but takes critical aim at the speech. Whereas earlier Phaedrus and Socrates had marveled together at how "extraordinary," "amazing," and "out of this world" the speech was, causing them both to "glow with pleasure" and experience a shared "ecstasy" (234c–d; Waterfield 2002, 12), upon rereading, the speech's powers shrink before their very eyes: "He certainly seems to be nowhere near doing what we wanted him to be doing. He doesn't begin at the beginning at all, but tries to swim through his speech on his back and the wrong way round, starting at the end. . . . What about the rest of his speech? Don't you think it's thrown together indiscriminately?" (264a–b; Waterfield 2002, 53). This speech, which in its actual performance, had made both Socrates and Phaedrus alike swell with a sympathetic ecstasy (234d), is now, upon consideration as a written text, dissected and critiqued. What was sublime in its performance is disorganized, indiscriminate, and messy in its reading.

When Socrates attempts to engage in a similar analysis of his own extemporaneous speech, the conversation cannot get of the ground—there's no longer anything *there* for them to analyze, and their attention turns back to the written text in front of them (264d–e). According to Thomas Cole (1991), it is only with the written speech that this separation of form and content, and the self-conscious critical reflection to discern the separation, becomes possible—not only in the case of Lysias's speech, but in the Greek culture at large. Cole even proposes that the concept of rhetorical *topoi* emerged out of precisely the kind of activity Phaedrus and Socrates model together at this place in the dialogue. Through pointing to a particular *place* (*topos*) on a written scroll, one might identify, discern, and separate the different kinds of content in a speech. It's only given this context that Socrates is able to point to Lysias's speech and make his larger recommendations concerning rhetoric: it should systematically divide its subject matter (263b), it must be able to generalize by categories (263c), and so on. Ultimately, these recommendations merely recapitulate what he has been able to identify in Lysias's speech once he has a text of the speech in front of him. He can point to places where Lysias makes divisions or defines categories and determine whether he has done so well or badly.

Much has been made of these recommendations, whether they are offered sincerely or satirically, or whether they are the template of a full-fledged rhetorical theory that Aristotle's *Rhetoric* aims to follow. However, the actual content of the recommendations matters less than their subtly constructed context, which shows how critical reflection of the seemingly divine power of speech is possible only when that speech is stabilized long enough that it might be studied. In this way, the idea of rhetoric Plato offers us in the *Phaedrus* is less important as a set of literal recommendations than it is as a demonstration of the rhetoric that writing makes possible. Through the analysis of a written speech, rhetoric exposes its hidden deficiencies and tricks, and in so doing demystifies the force that, in its performance, was capable of exciting palpable frenzy. This separation of form and content, and the self-conscious critical eye that discerns the separation, is made possible by writing because Socrates and Phaedrus "could as it were take a look at it" (Havelock [1963] 1998, 208). Even though the verbal performance of the written speech is capable of creating bodily effects that are reminiscent of both of frenzied religious rites and the untrammeled force of the black horse (234d), the measured reflection, the self-conscious evaluation of that effect, and rhetorical theorizing are reminiscent of the restraint and self-control of the charioteer and the white horse.

And of course, the subtle joke is that unlike Socrates and Phaedrus, we do have the palinode in writing, since it is inscribed in the *Phaedrus* dialogue itself. I do not think Plato means for his reader to ignore this fact when, following the speeches, Socrates admits, "It's perfectly clear, then, that speech-writing is not shameful in itself. . . . What's really shameful, though, is getting it wrong—speaking and writing shamefully badly. . . . So how does one write well or badly?" (258d; Waterfield 2002, 44). We are meant to conduct an analysis similar to the one performed by Socrates and Phaedrus on Lysias's speech, and thus we cannot fail to recognize that it promises to exonerate madness but praises restraint, and that it intends to offer proofs but never does. Like Socrates and Phaedrus do with Lysias's speech, we too are invited to see the deficiencies and tricks of Socrates's written palinode. Just as Socrates and Phaedrus expose the flaws of the writer who is hiding beneath the words written on the page, we the readers are meant to expose Socrates hiding beneath the hood of divine inspiration.[31]

In answer to the above question, we learn that merely identifying and repeating the features that work like a *pharmakon* on the audience is not a suitable strategy. In an explicit reference to the rhetorical theories circulated by the sophists of Socrates's day (including Gorgias), Phaedrus says, "What I've heard about this, my dear Socrates, is that it isn't essential for a would-be orator to learn what is *really* right, but only what the masses who are going to assess what he says might *take* to be right. Likewise, he doesn't need to learn what is really good or fine, but only what they think is good or fine, because that, not the truth, is the basis for persuasion" (260a; Waterfield 2002, 46). The assessment of the masses, we might imagine, is borne on their very bodies—in the excitement, the beating of their hearts, the arousal of their desire that marks their visceral response to hearing a speech. Based on this bodily, sympathetic response, Socrates and Phaedrus, along with the masses, might take the palinode to be true and right. But this visceral response can be misleading; thus there must be a critical mechanism that can check those responses so that the speech may be judged by some category other than its ability to evoke strong reactions in the hearers.

In his series of well-known essays on "Plato's Pharmacy" Derrida famously refocused this dialogue, claiming that the myth about writing and not the palinode about the *psychê* lay at the heart of the dialogue—"it is called for from one end of the *Phaedrus* to the other" (1981a, 67). Derrida rightly noted that Plato's ultimate target was the sophists, who may have been able to imitate living memory, but whom Socrates could also imitate, since writing makes both these imitations possible. Consequently, writing is not the remedy but a poison. But just as "there is no such thing as a harmless remedy" (1981a, 99), there is likewise no such thing as an entirely nonremedial harm. In order for writing to truly be "ambiguous" (1981a, 103) as Derrida claimed it was for Plato, it must be capable of both harm (killing the live memory of poetic speech) and benefit (protecting us against the noetic powers of poetic speech). Because Derrida too quickly conflated sophists and rhetoric (1981a, 115), he did not fully appreciate the depth of the very Platonic ambiguity he was after—a *pharmakon* that is truly "at once good and bad" (1981a, 115). Between what Derrida described as Plato's poisonous writing and Theuth's curative writing, I would insert, via rhetoric, inoculating writing. Only with a written speech can rhetorical analysis occur, and it is this analysis that inoculates against the druglike powers of *logos*. Writing may indeed kill the living *logos*, but this living *logos* is no less deadly, as the myth of the cicadas reminds us. Those who had it first were "ecstatic with pleasure and were so busy singing that they didn't bother with food and drink, so that before they knew it they were dead. They were the origin of the race of cicadas, whom the Muses granted the gift of never needing any food once they were born; all they do is sing, from the moment of their births until their deaths, without eating or drinking" (259b; Waterfield 2002, 45). The cicadas were vulnerable to the power of song in the same way that Oreithuia was vulnerable to Boreas's ravishment, to the violent force of his sexual desires, which, in a powerful gust of *pneuma*, swept her away, and "as he spoke, he shook his dreadful wings . . . embraced the maid, and wrapt in dusky clouds, far off conveyed" (Ovid 1961, 6, 198). The prophylactic of writing kills this wind, distances us from the song, subdues its frenzy, and returns us to our senses. It is writing qua rhetoric that, as Socrates's analysis models, makes this return to earth possible.

Conclusion

In the progress from the first speech to the palinode, we bear witness to a gradual recession into the past in both form and content. As Sean Kirkland rightly observes, *Phaedrus* gives us a glimpse into a period in which "the mythical understanding of the world and the place of the human in it were first explicitly subjected to the demands of reason" (2004, 313–14). The speeches of the *Phaedrus* supply ample evidence for this replacement. From the outset of the dialogue, when Phaedrus asks Socrates whether he believes the Boreas and Oreithuia myth is "true," "Socrates's response (229c–230a) is illuminating. He states that he could perhaps reject such myths, as do the 'wise men [σοφοῖ, "sophists"].' If he wished to be one who 'argues cleverly and subtly [σοφιζόμενος]' he could explain that the girl simply came too near the edge and was blown over the rocks by the wind. He does not see fit, however, to spend his time debunking myths" (Kirkland 2004, 315). Here Kirkland suggests Socrates is setting up physical, scientific knowledge against its counterpart, myth, which deals in monsters and fabulae. Although Kirkland aligns this scientific knowledge (via Francis Cornford) with pre-Socratic natural science of the seventh through the fifth century, it is more accurate to align this scientism with the proofs of the sophists and writers of speeches. They could marshal proofs to make what was only plausible seem to be a scientific fact. According to their method, Aristotle would later note, the power of rhetorical proof invented by the rhetorician mirrors exactly the material proofs that are not invented because they simply exist in the world as such (*Rhet.* 1.2.2; 1355b). The evidence for this scientific form of reasoning is supplied both in the apodeictic vocabulary of the first speech and in the rhetorical analysis Socrates offers of the structure of the three speeches. Socrates further indicates his awareness that this speech conforms to other standards of the new scientific discursive forms when he claims that it is "clear and compact, and has a finely honed vocabulary" (234e; Waterfield 2002, 13).

Ultimately, the important connection between the speeches, which seem so alien from one another in terms of form—the first speech being an example of sophistic, modern, "scientific," apodeictic discourse and the last speech being an example of poetic, ancient, "irrational," epic discourse—is forged by the fact that they are able to elicit identical responses from their audience. Both speeches bring their hearers to a point of ecstasy, although the poetic speech seems to do so more effectively simply because it is never subjected to critical analysis. And both are able to use language to create plausibility. Regardless of whether the myth is "true" or the nonlover is the most worthy lover, the poet's unlikely story seems truly real, in the same way that the sophist's unlikely premise seems truly proven. The sophistic reversals use "the power of speech to make trivia appear important and important things trivial . . . novelties to sound old and old things fresh and new" in the same way that the poet makes the inaccessible and unimaginable—the gods, the heavens, the deep past, etc.—manifest before our eyes. The true danger, however, is that both convince the masses. The bodily *ekstasis* is dangerous precisely because these effects operate independently of the truth, since "it isn't essential for a would-be orator to learn what is *really* right, but only what the masses who are going to assess what he says might *take* to be right" (260a; Waterfield 2002, 46).

The images and terms that refer to religious, sexual, and aural frenzy offer implicit and explicit ways of emphasizing the bodily ecstasy that underlines the experiences provoked by both the sophists and the poets. By placing the speeches on a par with one another in this way, we are introduced to the possibility that Plato's main consideration is not the composition of the soul or the theory of the Forms, but a consideration of the different noetic effects of the range of verbal modes in Greek linguistic culture. One may be inclined to object that these two purposes of the palinode are not necessarily exclusive to one another. However, the interpretations that assign dogmatic or doctrinal content to Socrates's speech are not only implicitly reliant on dubious Neoplatonist receptions of the myth, they also naively take Socrates's and Phaedrus's reluctance to criticize the palinode as an indication that it is above criticism. In the dialogue, Socrates and Phaedrus are able to offer reflections and critiques only of Lysias's speech because it, and it alone, exists in written form, and its written form makes possible not only Socrates's discussion of rhetorical theory but rhetorical theory as such. Critique, self-conscious awareness, and ultimately the restraint that trammels poetic frenzy are possible in and as writing and rhetoric. Such criticism should not be interpreted as a literal endorsement of the palinode, a literal condemnation of writing, or literal recommendations about rhetoric. Rather, rhetoric should be viewed as a mechanism of restraint against poetic madness that is made possible through writing. If writing inoculates us against the dangers of poetic verse and the raw material word, then it becomes more difficult to understand that raw material word as Plato's doctrinal vessel, which it has long been believed to be.

Are the myths "true"? Does the epic vocabulary and thematic tradition give us access to things as they are? As the example of Boreas and Oreithuia at the beginning of the dialogue indicates, the answer is probably no. In most cases, a scientific explanation of the "raw data" that supplies myth with its content is far simpler and more reliable than the myths would have us believe. One is more likely to have been pushed from rocks by a strong wind than to have been abducted by a god, after all (229c). Though the bodily tide of the poetic experience is strong, that potency does not make the myths true. Rather, their potency inures us to proper skepticism regarding their truth. But does that mean we can place blind faith in a more scientific mode of discourse that favors apodeictic demonstration over storytelling and mythmaking? Again, no. In the latter case as in the former, it is the function of speech to create things that are not. Indeed, their presentation as apodeictic makes them seem truer than myth, even though we have just been persuaded to define one thing (love) in terms of its opposite (nonlove). And moreover, the scientific mode of speech is similarly capable of greasing the wheels of belief with the bodily ecstasy, as both Phaedrus's and Socrates's physical response to the first speech indicates.

The aim of the three speeches at the beginning of the dialogue, then, is to demonstrate how the rhetoric of the sophists belongs to a different lineage than the one it claims: it is not the scientific discourse of demonstration and proof, but the poetic discourse that enchants the hearer. By demonstrating this natural connection, Socrates means to break it. Once broken, rhetoric might be brought to union with the *logôn technê* of dialectic. The question, then, is not how sympathetic Plato might have been to rhetoric, or even how rhetoric might be the proper counterpart of dialectic in the *Phaedrus*. The real question is, To what extent might the *antilogikê* of rhetoric, which subverts received wisdom and traditional understandings, be emptied of its poetic, linguistic power? This is the fundamental question that is raised implicitly by the three speeches at the beginning of the dialogue, without which we have no real context for the recommendations regarding rhetoric. Plato, through the rhetorical theories he develops across several dialogues, attempts to do precisely this: limit the power the sophists can wield through their arts of rhetoric by proposing an alternative set of linguistic theories.

« 3 »

Heraclitean Opposition and Parmenidean Contradiction

Pre-Socratic Ontology and Protagorean Sophistry in the *Cratylus*, the *Theaetetus*, and the *Euthydemus*

Before Gorgias, there was Protagoras, the oldest of the "older sophists" (O'Brien 1972, 3). He is credited with being the first to observe that for every issue there are two opposing arguments (*dissoi logoi*, or "two sides to every story," as we now say); the first to charge a fee for his instruction and in so doing break with the traditional methods of transmitting knowledge; and the first to develop a method of arguing through question-asking (DK 80a1, a2; Diogenes Laertius 9.50; Philostratus, *Lives* 1.10.1). Although the dispute between Socrates, Gorgias, and his followers in the *Gorgias* dialogue is widely regarded as Plato's most acrimonious treatment of sophists and sophistry, Protagoras was without a doubt a more serious and formidable thinker for Plato (Zilioli 2007), and his "voice like Orpheus" (*Prt.* 315a) reverberates across Plato's entire body of work.[1] It is not inaccurate to suggest that, in numerous portrayals of Protagoras and his thought, Plato treats Protagoras as a more profound and capacious thinker even than Socrates.

The previous two chapters examine how the two dialogues most commonly cited for "Plato's view of rhetoric"—the *Gorgias* and the *Phaedrus*—might more fruitfully be understood as Plato's dramatic portrayal of the rhetorical consequences of sophistic activity. The sophists of these dialogues (Gorgias and pseudo-Lysias) reinscribe the linguistic sorcery and power of the archaic poets; when they apply those verbal powers to legal and political ends as opposed to mere display or diversion, disastrous consequences may ensue. They direct nothing less than the rise and fall of empires. This rereading (and the crucial etymology of *kommôtikê*) unlaces the long-held belief that Plato's critique of rhetoric is predicated on a firm distinction between seeming and being, where rhetoric is suspect because it shows the appearance of truth but not truth as such. Rhetoric is not critiqued on these grounds; rather, it is critiqued because, through the verbal bewitchment of the sophists, it can be manipulated to whet the appetite of Athens and exploit imperial greed, leading to conquest, war, and destruction. Rhetoric is not inherently an art of seeming and appearance for Plato; on the contrary, the following chapters suggest, rhetorical theory is a crucial tool for Plato's forging the distinction between seeming and being in the first place.

Making this distinction is an overriding aim spanning numerous dialogues—particularly the dialogues where Socrates struggles with Protagoras and his thought. In the *Theaetetus*, the *Cratylus*, the *Euthydemus*, and the *Protagoras*, Plato's Socrates doggedly attempts to resist the paradoxes of Protagoras's epistemology by distinguishing between truth and the appearance of truth, being and seeming. This distinction fails to emerge only because Plato's Socrates cannot (yet) develop an adequate theory of *logos*; in other words, he cannot develop a rhetorical theory.

The purpose of this and the following chapter is to illuminate how Plato portrays Socrates's struggle with the epistemic consequences of Protagorean thought, embodied in three of Protagoras's famous doctrines and the relationship between them: the man-measure doctrine, the doctrine of two-*logoi*, or "*dissoi logoi*" (and its companion doctrine, the "stronger/weaker" *logoi*),[2] and the doctrine of the impossibility of contradiction. His struggle is depicted across several dialogues as a relentless but ultimately fruitless attempt to distinguish between seeming and being, true and false, by extracting a sound dialectic method from the related practices of eristic and antilogic, all three of which are argumentative activities Plato associates with the sophists. In this chapter I examine Plato's treatment in the *Cratylus*, the *Theaetetus*, and the *Euthydemus* of the pre-Socratic ontology implicit within Protagoras's famous doctrines. These treatments combine to create an epistemic crisis for Socrates, leaving him "like a fish caught wriggling in a net" (*Euthyd.* 302b; Rouse 1961, 416), unable to distinguish between truth and falsehood, knowledge and belief, or being and seeming. In the following chapter I examine how the absence in the *Protagoras* of an external, fixed measure thwarts Socrates's attempts to overcome this epistemic crisis or to extract dialectic from eristic and antilogic. In all these cases, Socrates fails to develop an adequate theory of language that can overcome sophistic linguistics and epistemology, embodied in Protagoras's language games that both enact and entail his man-measure doctrine.

In what follows I define the three Protagorean doctrines in relation to their pre-Socratic antecedents. In spite of numerous obvious similarities and overlaps, the historical relationship between pre-Socratic thought and the sophistic movement of the fifth century BCE cannot be established definitively, since the complete works of both groups of thinkers are now lost.[3] Nevertheless, on the basis of Plato's portrayal alone, it is noncontroversial to conclude that Plato wanted his readers to associate Protagoras's thought with pre-Socratic ontology, particularly Heraclitus (van Eck 2009), and that Socrates associated many of the sophists of his day with both Heraclitean and Parmenidean ontologies.[4] What follows is an examination not of the historical influence of the pre-Socratics on the sophists, nor the contributions of the sophists to pre-Socratic philosophy, but how Protagoras's thought is portrayed in the *Cratylus*, *Theaetetus*, and *Euthydemus* as being derivative of pre-Socratic ontology—a derivation that provokes profound epistemic problems for Socrates.

Heraclitean Etymologies and Protagorean Relativism in the *Cratylus*

Protagoras was (and perhaps is) most famous for the first lines of his book *On Truth*: "Of all things the measure is man: of things that are that they are, and of things that are not that they are not" (DK 80b1: πάντων χρημάτον μέτρον ἄνθρωπος, τῶν μὲν ὄντων ὡς ἔστιν, τῶν δὲ οὐκ ὄντων ὡς οὐκ ἔστιν).[5] Schiappa has observed that of all the extant fragments from the Older Sophists the dictum is the most "difficult to interpret and understand," and that its "ambiguity has allowed it to be all things to all people," not the least of whom is Plato himself (2003, 118). In addition to Schiappa, Laszlo Versenyi (1962), Michael Gagarin (1968, 1969), and Ugo Zilioli (2007) all have noted that the ambiguity of Protagoras's man-measure doctrine is recognized in the earliest commentaries, and that it was very likely intentionally given an uncertain, paradoxical meaning.

In this section, I examine how this "man-measure" doctrine is grappled with in Socrates's interpretations in the *Cratylus* and *Theaetetus* dialogues as a troubling species of Heraclitean thought. Socrates's engagements with the doctrine betray a desire to overcome the epistemic crisis that the doctrine both reflects and provokes—a desire that leads to a nascent but incomplete attempt to distinguish between seeming and being.

In the second century CE, Sextus, the father of empiricism, offered in his *Outlines of Pyrrhonism* (1.216–219) a view of what relationship Protagorean thought may have had to Heraclitean ontology. I offer Sextus's summary as a backdrop (albeit a much later one) for how Plato treats the natural theory of names and Heraclitean ontology in the *Cratylus*. Sextus summarizes Protagoras's thought in the following way:

> Protagoras, too, will have it that of all things the measure is man, of things that are that they are and of things that are not that they are not [B 1]. . . . So he says, in effect, that man is the standard of judgment of all things, of those that are that they are, and of those that are not that they are not. And for this reason he posits only what appears to the individual, thus introducing relativity. . . .
>
> Now what he says is that matter is in a state of flux, and that as it changes there is a continuous replacement of the effluvia which it gives off; that, moreover, one's sensations undergo change and alteration in accordance with one's age and other aspects of one's bodily condition. He says too that the *logoi* of all the appearances [*phainomenôn*] are present in the matter itself [*hulê*], so that the matter is capable, as far as lies in its own power, of being everything that appears to everybody. Men, however, apprehend different things at different times according to their various dispositions. For the man whose condition is in *phusis* grasps, out of what is contained in *phusis*, what can appear to those in that condition [in *phusis*], whereas the man whose condition is not in *phusis* grasps what can appear to those not in *phusis*. . . .
>
> And so, according to him, man becomes the standard of judgment of things that are. For all things that appear to men also exist, but things which appear to no man do not exist either. *We see, therefore, that he dogmatizes not only about the flux of matter, but also about the presence in it of the* logoi *of all* phainomenôn, although these are obscure matters on which we suspend judgment. (O'Brien 1972, 10–11; translation modified, emphasis mine)

This testimony of Sextus is invaluable for explaining precisely how Protagoras's thought—in particular, his man-measure doctrine—is intricately wedded to the Heraclitean doctrine of flux, both of which are explicitly disputed in the *Cratylus* and the *Theaetetus*.[6] The most important aspect of the above passage is the observation that, according to Protagoras's interpretation of Heraclitus, *logos* is inextricable from the material universe that is perpetually in the process of coming into being (*phusis*)—"the *logoi* of all *phainomenôn* are present in matter itself, so that matter is capable . . . of being everything that appears to everybody."

The Heraclitean doctrine of flux is best summed up in the maxim of *panta rhei*: everything flows. The structure of the universe is defined by a fundamental unity of opposing forces; it is a perpetual process of change arising from the unending strife of opposites. Numerous examples from Heraclitus's fragments—the bow, the lyre, the river, fire, war—illustrate the basic Heraclitean principles that "in differing, it agrees with itself—a backward-turning connection, like that of a bow and a lyre" (DK 22b51; Barnes 1987, 102), and "that war is common, that justice is strife, that all things come about in accordance with strife and with what must be" (DK 22b80; Barnes 1987, 114). *Logos* belongs to the physical human body, which itself changes "in accordance with one's age and other aspects of one's bodily condition" (Sextus 1.217; O'Brien 1972, 11). Just as one's physical embodiment is subject to the flow of *phusis*, so the speech or account (*logos*) is inextricable from the this principle of *phusis* as such. Thus *logos* is inexorably subject to the same laws of flux and incessant change that define the material universe.[7] In Sextus's interpretation, Protagoras's dictum that "of all things the measure is man: of things that are that they are, and of things that are not that they are not" is a natural consequence of the fact that *logos*—the quintessential human practice and the very means for knowing what is—cannot be stripped of the flux and flow of *phusis*. This perspective on the role of language in Heraclitean philosophy is consistent with Plato's own description in the *Theaetetus*, where Theodorus describes the confluence between the ontology of flux and the instability of words:

> If you ask any one of them [i.e., a Heraclitean] a question, he will pull out some little enigmatic phrase from his quiver and shoot it off at you; . . . indeed they never reach any conclusion with each other, they are so very careful not to allow anything to be stable, either in an argument or in their own souls. I suppose they think that if they did it would be something that

> stands still—this being what they are totally at war with, and what they are determined to banish from the universe. (180a–b; Levett 1990, 309).

Because *phusis* is in flux, *logos* is in flux; because *logos* is in flux, human understanding, knowledge, and reason are perpetually unstable.

It is clear from the beginning of the *Cratylus,* which considers different arguments concerning the correctness of names, that there lies a deeper question: the correctness of *logos* as such. In the dialogue, Hermogenes resists Cratylus's (Heraclitean) view that names are correct according to *phusis.* In order to discover the underlying reasons for Hermogenes's resistance, Socrates asks whether it is possible to speak truth or lies (*alêthê legein kai pseudê*), whether there is such a thing as true *logos* and a lying *logos* (*logos alêthês ho de pseudês*), and whether one can speak of what is and what is not (*legein ta onta te kai mê*) (385b).[8] Here the deeper motivations for their investigation of the smaller units of language—*onomata*—is revealed to be much more than idle speculation: both Hermogenes and Socrates seek a method for defining true and false *logos* as a whole. This examination of the correctness of words is, we will see, a training ground for this attempt to define linguistic truth—*logos alêthês*—as such.

The debt Protagoras's man-measure doctrine owes to Heraclitean ontology and the instability of words is subtly indicated in the etymologies of the *Cratylus* dialogue. The influence of Heracliteanism on Protagorean linguistics may be observed throughout the interlocutors' prolonged consideration of whether the smallest unit of language—names [*onomata*]—"are correct as what they are by nature [*tôn onton phusis*]" (383a, my translation) or by "agreement," "convention," and "custom" to call things what they are called (*sunthemenoi kalein kalôsi* [383a]; *sunthêkê kai homologia* [384d]; *nomô kai ethei tôn ethisantôn te kai kalountôn* [384d]).[9] The former position, Cratylus's, which Hermogenes would like to overturn, is the outworking of the Heraclitean view that *logos* is among the things that are in *phusis.*[10] Thus the opposing view, articulated by Hermogenes, ought to constitute a departure from Heracliteanism. Nevertheless, as we will see, Socrates ultimately reduces both views to two seemingly inescapable manifestations of Protagorean (and therefore Heraclitean) thought. In this way he illustrates the frustrating inexorability of the Protagorean system of ideas—to oppose him is to agree with him.

Cratylus's view, consistent with Sextus's description of Protagoras's Heracliteanism, is not that there is an inherent rightness of names, but that language, including names (*onomata*), comes from—and perhaps is even inextricable from—*phusis*. Given Cratylus's view that *onomata* are a process and product of *phusis*, they are also necessarily an instrument of distinguishing and revealing *phusis* as such. This, in a nutshell, is the rationale for the lengthy etymologies of the *Cratylus*. Socrates explains (386d–388c) that, according to Cratylus's *phusis*-theory of language, *onomata* reveal *phusis* because they are in *phusis*: "[The *onomata*] have their own proper being; not in relation to us or caused by us, swaying one way and another according to our fancy, but they are independent and maintain their own being according to *phusis* [*pephuke*]" (386d–e; Jowett 1961, 424–25; translation modified).[11] This ultimately leads to the suggestion that an *onoma*, at heart, can be probed in order to distinguish *phusis*: "Then an *onoma* is an instrument of teaching and of distinguishing natures [*diakritikon tês ousias*]" (388c; Jowett 1961, 426; translation modified).[12] An investigation of language, by this logic, should lead to a discovery of *phusis* for itself, independent of a fluctuating, subjective measure or human estimation.

The very terms of the etymologies are, not incidentally, a demonstration of Heraclitean flux—a point that has been made by Charles Kahn, who writes:

> The central etymologies of this dialogue, the long series of words all interpreted to mean flux or motion of some sort (from 401d to 421c, prefigured at 397c–d, prolonged at 426c–427b, recalled at 436e and 439c) are introduced by an apparent quotation from Heraclitus: "Doesn't Heraclitus say 'all things move on and nothing stands still,' and comparing beings to the stream of river he says, 'you cannot step twice into the same river"' (402a). The name-givers were prehistoric Heracliteans, as the etymologies show! (1986, 254–55).

Kahn's point is borne out in nearly all the etymologies, as well as the numerous direct references to the fact that Heraclitean cosmology lay at the heart of the *phusis* theory that the etymologies are meant to investigate. I offer a few examples: *psychê* (ψυχή) "gives the power of breath and revival (ἀναψῦχον), and when this reviving power fails then the body perishes and dies" (399d–e; Jowett 1961, 437); the body (σῶμα) "is the grave (σῆμα) of the soul which may be thought to be buried in our present life" (400b–c; Jowett 1961, 437); the goddess Persephone "is wise (σοφή). For seeing that all things in the world are in motion (φερομένων), that principle which embraces and touches and is able to follow them is wisdom. . . . She touches that which is in motion (τοῦ φερομένον ἐφαπτομένη), herein showing her wisdom" (404c–d; Jowett 1961, 441); the light (σέλας) of the moon (σελήνη) "is always new (νέον) and always old (ἔνον)" (409b; Jowett 1961, 445); air (ἀήρ) is "ever flowing (ἀεὶ ῥεῖ)" and aether (αἰθήρ) "is always running in flux about the air (ἀεὶ θεῖ περὶ τὸν ἀέρα ῥέων)" (410b; Jowett 1961, 446). Not only do these examples echo the theme of Heraclitean flux, they stylistically imitate Heraclitus's own maxims: "The path up and down is one and the same" (DK 22b60; Barnes 1987, 103); "The sea is most pure and most polluted water: for fish, drinkable and life-preserving; for men, undrinkable and death-dealing" (DK 22b61, Barnes 1987, 104); "Immortals are mortals, mortals immortals: living their death, dying their life" (DK 22b62; Barnes 1987, 104).

The above examples illustrate how the etymologies of the *Cratylus* are meant to be instruments for distinguishing Heraclitean *phusis,* as Socrates himself acknowledges:

> The primeval givers of names were undoubtedly like too many of our modern philosophers, who, in their search after the nature of things, are always getting dizzy from constantly going round and round, and then they imagine that the world is going round and round and moving in all directions. And this appearance, which arises out of their own internal condition, they suppose to be a reality of nature: they think that there is nothing stable or permanent, but only flux and motion, and that the world is always full of every sort of motion and change. The consideration of names which I mentioned has led me into making this reflection. . . . Perhaps you did not observe that in the names which have just been cited the motion or flux or generation of things is most surely indicated. (411b–c; Jowett 1961, 447).[13]

Here is a true outworking of Heraclitean linguistics. If all matter is in a state of flux, and *logos* is part of that matter, then it necessarily follows that an investigation of the *onomata* that compose *logos* would uncover the material flux and unity of opposites that inhere in the material universe as such.[14] Though truth can only be sought through speech and *logos,* Cratylus's Heraclitean theory of *logos* does not provide any such access to truth and knowledge. On the contrary, the flux and flow of *phusis* is intensified by the flux and flow of *logos.* Socrates seeks the antidote: a *logos* that can be stabilized against the flux and flow of *phusis,* such that knowledge and understanding will be possible.

The instability that results from Cratylus's view that language arises from *phusis* rules out the possibility of true or false discourse. The flux of *phusis*, when applied to *logos*, results in Protagoras's "two-*logoi*," or *dissoi logoi*, doctrine: "There are two *logoi* in opposition about every 'thing' (*pantos pragmatos*)" (Schiappa 2003, 90). As Schiappa has convincingly established, this doctrine is best understood "as a logical extension of the Heraclitean . . . theory of flux and his 'unity of opposites' doctrine" (2003, 92). If the same tension of opposites and strife of opposing forces that inheres in *phusis* inheres also in *logos*, then the principle that there are two opposing *logoi* about every matter necessarily results. Furthermore, as we shall see, this entails that "whatever you assert, I can always deny, with equal correctness; but my denial can never be so correct as to rule out your assertion" (Denyer 2008, 2). This, in sum, is the logical consequence of the two-*logoi* doctrine: although contradiction is inexorable, true contradiction is nevertheless impossible. Thus a *logos* will never be definitively true or false. This helps explain what Socrates means when he says that "our modern philosophers . . . think that there is nothing stable or permanent, but only flux and motion," and that a consideration of the instability of their *onomata* led him to that reflection. The epistemic consequences of Cratylus's Heraclitean and Protagorean view, and Hermogenes's sense that there *must* be such a thing as true and false discourse, is precisely what motivates Hermogenes to reject Cratylus's *phusis* theory.[15]

By contrast, and in resistance to such radical instability and flux, Hermogenes endorses the opposing principle: that correctness in names [*orthotês onomatos*] is exclusively a matter of convention and agreement [*sunthêkê kai homologia*]. For example, he says, "we frequently change the names of our slaves, and the newly imposed name is as good as the old." This example illustrates the general principle that "there is no name produced by nature [*phusei*]; all is convention and habit of the users [*nomô kai ethei tôn ethisantôn te kai kalountôn*]" (384d; Jowett 1961, 422; translation modified).

Nevertheless, in spite of Hermogenes's contention that there must be such a thing as a true or a false *logos*, Socrates reduces his position to another version of Protagorean relativism, according to which no *logos* can ever be fully true or fully false. He does this by following the consequences of Hermogenes's view: if Hermogenes believes that words are correct according to convention and agreement (as opposed to *phusis*), then mustn't he also believe "that what is [*ta onta*] differs as the names differ? And are they relative to individuals, as Protagoras tells us? For he says that man is the measure of all things, and that things are to me as they appear to me, and that they are to you as they appear to you" (385e–86a; Jowett 1961, 424; translation modified). At this point Hermogenes confesses: "There have been times, Socrates, when I have been driven in my perplexity to take refuge with Protagoras, not that I agree with him at all" (386a; Jowett 1961, 424). In other words, Hermogenes is *avoiding* Protagorean linguistics by ascribing to the theory that *onomata* are the by-product of convention and agreement, but is nevertheless unable to escape Protagoras's Heraclitean embrace even as he retreats from *phusis* toward convention and agreement.

Both positions come to the same end: either *logos* is the product *phusis*, and therefore is always changing because *phusis* is by definition always in a process of flux, and structured by the same oppositional sensibilities that structure *phusis*; or *logos* is the product of agreement and convention, and consequently always changing according to the measure of human agreement and convention, just as *phusis* is always changing. Thus Socrates concludes that "no man of sense will like to put himself or the education of his mind in the power of *onomata*" (440c; Jowett 1961, 474; translation modified), since to do so is to have the feeling of being swept up in the Heralclitean tide: "Having fallen into a kind of whirlpool . . . they are carried round, and want to drag us in after them" (439c; Jowett 1961, 473).[16] In both cases, the Protagorean relativism inexorably results, while an ability to distinguish between true and false discourse fades into obscurity.

The "Man-Measure" Doctrine and Heraclitean Flux in the *Theaetetus*

Plato's most direct and extensive engagement with Protaogoras's man-measure doctrine occurs in the *Theaetetus*. There, he makes explicit the epistemic crisis that the doctrine reflects and provokes for Socrates and his interlocutors Theaetetus and Theodorus. The interaction constitutes Plato's most intense attempt to distinguish between seeming and being—an attempt that is ultimately incomplete and unsuccessful. As the following analysis shows, Socrates's endeavor to separate seeming from being is inextricable from his attempt to overcome the Heraclitean ontology implicit in Protagoras's doctrine, and his inability to do so is the result of his failure to develop a theory of *logos* that can unseat the one encapsulated in Protagoras's two-*logoi* and impossibility of contradiction doctrines.

The overriding theme of the *Theaetetus*—"What is knowledge?"—arises in the first place from Socrates's baffled epistemic quandary, which itself is provoked by Protagoras's doctrine. The outer frame of the dialogue is set a few years after Socrates's death. Eucleides and Terpsion, both of whom had kept Socrates company on his death day, meet in Eucleides's home in Megara and reminisce about a memorable conversation that occurred some years earlier in 399 BCE, not long before Socrates's death. Eucleides had committed the conversation to writing soon after it had taken place, and this account forms the inner frame of the dialogue. The two sit down and have the dialogue read to them by a slave, who recounts the conversation between Socrates, Theaetetus, and Theaetetus's teacher (the mathematician Theodorus) that occurred years before. The conversation opens with Socrates's complaint that he "can't get a proper grasp of what on earth knowledge really is. Could we manage to put it into words?" (145e–146a; Levett 1990, 264). Protagoras's man-measure doctrine is first introduced as a response to this complaint (151e–152a); however, as the dialogue progresses, one gets the distinct impression that Protagoras's doctrine was what provoked Socrates's epistemic query in the first place. Even where the discussion in the *Theaetetus* is not explicitly about Protagoras or his man-measure doctrine, Protagoras is never far from Socrates's mind.

The test of Protagoras's man-measure doctrine begins when Socrates equates it to Theaetetus's definition of knowledge [*epistêmê*] as "perception" [*aisthêsis*] (151e) and attributes both to Heraclitean ontology. Theaetetus's definition of knowledge as perception and Protagoras's doctrine are equivalent, Socrates suggests, because perception, appearance, and belief are more or less equivalent with what Protagoras must mean by "measure." Socrates paraphrases the doctrine, and as can be plainly observed, swaps terminology to make it compatible with Theaetetus's definition of knowledge.[17] In particular, he substitutes "measurement" [*metron*] and "what is" [*ontôn*] with "appearance" [*phainomenôn*]: "Then you know that he puts it something like this [*pôs legei*], that as each thing appears [*phainetai*] to me, so it is for me, and as it appears to you, so it is for you—you and I each being a man?" (152a; Levett 1990, 272).[18] He then attempts to further elaborate and interpret what he has just paraphrased by linking appearance to perception and belief. These terminological substitutions to the original language are executed deliberately and transparently by Socrates:

> Now doesn't it sometimes happen that when the same wind is blowing, one of us is cold and the other not? Or that one of us is rather cold and the

> other very cold? . . . Shall we listen to Protagoras and say it is cold for the one who shivers, and for the other, not cold? . . . And this is how it appears [*phainetai*] to each of us? . . . But this expression "it appears" [*phainetai*] is the same as "he perceives" [*aisthanesthai*]? . . . The appearing of things, then, is the same as perception, in the case of hot and things like that. So it results, apparently, that things are for the individual such as he perceives them. . . . I was delighted with his general statement of the theory that a thing is for any individual what he believes [*dokoun*] it to be. . . . If whatever the individual believes by his perception is true for him [*alêthes estai ho an di aisthêseôs doxazê*] . . . what he believes [*doxan*] is always true and correct. (152b–161e; Levett 1990 272–85; translation modified)[19]

Because these two theories are equivalent, investigating Theaetetus's hypothesis that knowledge is nothing more or less than perception requires a further investigation of "the veiled truth in the thought of the great man" (155e; Levett 1990, 277). It is in that endeavor that he tells Theaetetus that Protagoras's "mysteries begin from the principle . . . that everything is really in motion, and there is nothing but motion" (156a; Levett 1990, 277). The mysteries of Protagoras, which baffle Socrates, are both mysterious and baffling precisely because they are built on the ever-shifting sands of a Heraclitean foundation. Since Heraclitus's ontology dictates that all *phusis* is in a process of perpetual motion and change, "the things of which we naturally say that they 'are,' are in process of coming to be, as the result of movement and change and blending with one another. We are wrong when we say they 'are,' since nothing ever is, but everything is coming to be" (152d–e; Levett 1990, 273). If there is no being, only becoming (since "all things, of all kinds whatsoever, are coming to be through association with one another as the result of motion," [157a; Levett 1990, 279]), then there is little hope for a stable *logos* that can hold fast against the sway. According to Socrates's interpretation, Heraclitean flux is precisely what gives rise to Protagoras's man-measure doctrine: because all things are in motion, creating incessant change and countless differences, "different things both are and appear to be to different subjects"; and this leads to the inexorable conclusion that "each one of us is the measure both of what is and of what is not" (166d; Levett 1990, 292). And, we are led to understand, if nothing ever *is*, but is only perpetually becoming, then knowledge of *what is* must remain forever out of grasp.

Socrates's equation of appearance, perception, and belief is a means to a larger end. His paraphrase that "aimed at getting words to mean the same thing" (164c; Levett 1990, 289) places a heavy emphasis on appearance, perception, and belief—an emphasis that persists even when, later in the dialogue, he corrects his dubious interpretation. By equating "measure" [*metron*] with "appearance" [*phainomenon*], "perception" [*aisthêsis*], and "belief" [*doxa*], Socrates is attempting to define the epistemic object of Protagoras's measure as "seeming" as opposed to *what is* or "being." Even though he eventually retracts the terminological wordplay that equates the "measure" with "appearance," "perception," and "belief," as we shall see, he nevertheless maintains that Protagoras says "that things are for every man what they seem to him to be [*to dokoun ekastô touto kai einai phêsi pou hô dokei*]" (171a; Levett 1990, 296).

Here can be detected the hazy contours of an emergent distinction between seeming and being. The possibility of overturning Protagoras's doctrine resides precisely in the full-fledged emergence of this distinction: if he is able to dissociate the doctrine from being and *what is*, and associate it instead with what appears or what we perceive and believe—in other words, with *what seems*—then the doctrine itself would then be categorized among those things that *are not*. Instantiating a difference between seeming and being would give him the tool he needs to overturn the doctrine. Perhaps even more important is the possibility that overturning the doctrine will enable him to overturn its implicit Heracliteanism. The incessant flux and perpetual becoming of *phusis* may be understood as how the natural world *seems*, but not how it *is*. Perhaps beyond the physical world, there is a metaphysical one that is not coming into being and falling out of being, but stable, transcendent, whole. This metaphysical world is still a distant mirage on the horizon, however, and not yet a tangible reality.

Socrates attempts to overcome Protagoras's doctrine in two separate ways. One, he uses the paraphrase discussed above to reduce the doctrine to absurdity, interpreting it to mean that "all beliefs and all statements are true, from which it follows that there cannot be any falsehood" (Hestir 2000, 11). Two, following Protagoras's apology, he uses the logic of the doctrine to make it refute itself. Myles Burnyeat calls these the "superficial" and "serious" refutations (1990, 252).

In the reductio ad absurdum, he claims that the doctrine entails that when a madman believes he is a god, "or a dreamer when he imagines he has wings and is flying in his sleep" (158b; Levett 1990, 280), he really *is* a god, really *is* flying in his sleep. He likewise claims that to speak of anything actually *being* at all is necessarily an absurdity (157b, 160b). If being, *what is*, is entirely a matter of continual flux and change, then it follows that "the verb 'to be' must be totally abolished . . . nor should we allow the use of such words as 'something,' 'of something,' or 'mine,' 'this' or 'that,' or any other name that makes things stand still. We ought, rather, to speak according to *phusis* and refer to things as 'becoming,' 'being produced,' 'passing away,' 'changing'; for if you speak in such a way as to make things stand still, you will easily be refuted" (157b; Levett 1990, 279). His version of the doctrine is so extreme that it would make the very act of speaking impossible.

But Socrates confesses that this conclusion is illegitimate because it stems from a faulty interpretive method—one that is far too similar to those used by the "professional controversialists [*antilogikôs*]" (164c; Levett 1990, 289). By performing his series of terminological equations (from measure to appearance, appearance to perception, perception to belief), he has "aimed at getting words to mean the same thing; and we feel complacent now that we have defeated the theory by the use of a method of this kind. We profess to be philosophers, not champion controversialists [*agônistai*]; and we don't realise that we are doing just what those clever fellows do" (164c–d; Levett 1990, 289; translation modified). In other words, Socrates has just confessed that his interpretation was an exercise in making words equivalent that perhaps should not be, which led to too easy of a victory over Protagoras's doctrine, and which is precisely the kind of dubious method that the "controversialists" (like Protagoras) use.[20]

Socrates gives Protagoras's corpse the chance to present a hypothetical rebuttal to his first interpretation in the famous "apology of Protagoras." If Protagoras were still alive, Socrates suggests, it would not have been so easy for Socrates to get away with these dubious techniques. Rather, Socrates admits, "if the father of the other tale were alive," he would have been able to defend his doctrine against Socrates's attempted reductio ad absurdum. Only because Protagoras is dead is Socrates able to treat his formidable doctrine as though it were "an orphan we are trampling in the mud" (164e; Levett 1990, 289). He introduces the next section of the dialogue by claiming that he will play the devil's advocate and provide the strongest possible defense of Protagoras's position, and he will do so without resorting to sophistic wordplay and terminological equivocation.

In the voice of Protagoras, Socrates defends the doctrine and proposes "to make its meaning clearer" (166d; Levett 1990, 292). Socrates has Protagoras suggest that, while it is true that knowledge is perception, this doesn't entail that all perceptions are *true*. Rather, it entails that what Socrates insists on calling "knowledge" is nothing more than perception. If perceptions are a person's "own private events," Socrates reasons in the voice of Protagoras, then "the thing which appears 'becomes' or, if we may speak of being, 'is' only for the one to whom it appears" (167c; Levett 1990, 292; translation modified). What Socrates wants to call "knowledge" Protagoras limits to a local, individual experience. He gives the example of a sick person and a healthy person. To the sick person, food appears and is bitter, while it is the opposite to the healthy person. It makes no sense in this case to insist that the food *is* one way or another—"what we have to do is to make a change from the one to the other, because the other state is *better*. In education, too, what we have to do is to change a worse state into a better state; only whereas the doctor brings about the change by the use of drugs, the professional sophist does it by the use of words" (167a; Levett 1990, 292–93; translation modified).

Whereas Socrates seeks a method for drawing firm distinctions between true and false, Protagoras subordinates such a distinction to a superior one: the distinction between better and worse. "Some people," he continues in the voice of Protagoras, "who are still at a primitive stage, call [these appearances] 'true,' my position, however, is that the one kind are *better* than the others, but in no way *truer*" (167b; Levett 1990, 293; translation modified). While Socrates presumes the existence of the truth he hopes to define, Protagoras substitutes the better for the true. As Marina McCoy describes Protagoras's apology, "Plato does not present Protagoras as a fool bent on preserving a strange or inconsistent system, but rather as an intellectual who rejects a strong notion of truth but then supplants the concept of truth with alternative concepts of goodness and wisdom" (McCoy 2005, 32).

For a brief moment we get a glimpse of Protagoras's philosophy in the absence of Socrates's opposition. It is not an absurd thesis that all statements are true or that none are false, but a suggestion that there is no knowledge that cannot be reduced to some form of perception, and that any claim to know absolutely is ultimately untenable. This view is visible only temporarily; Socrates never authentically engages with it. He remains devoted throughout the rest of the dialogue to seeking the very thing—truth beyond perception—that Protagoras has reasoned does not exist.

As he continues to attempt to overturn the doctrine, he aims to show that Protagoras's doctrine is no theory of knowledge at all, still presuming that knowledge must be something other than perception, and still equating Protagoras's "truth" with something that must lie outside the scope of individual perception and experience. He claims that the doctrine implies that all opinions are equally true, and this further implies that the refutation of the dictum—the claim that the dictum is false—is as true as the dictum itself (170a–171d). As Burnyeat describes this portion of the dialogue, he reminds the reader, "We must be careful, both in this dilemmatic passage [170cff.] and in the self-refutation argument to follow, about that little qualifying phrase 'for *a*' which distinguishes the Protagorean idiom from the language of ordinary people" (1990, 29). He points out that "at a critical moment (171ab) the relativizing qualifiers are dropped and Protagoras is made to speak of truth and falsity in absolute terms" (Burnyeat 1990, 29). In this way, Socrates is refusing to interact with the ultimate conclusion of Protagoras's apology, preferring instead to presume the existence of the very thing he hopes to prove: an unqualified and a-perspectival truth.

In the second refutation of Protagoras's doctrine, Socrates reasons "that the contrary opinion about Protagoras's own opinion (namely, that it is false) must be true. . . . And in conceding the truth of the opinion of those who think him wrong, he is really admitting the falsity of his own opinion" (171a–b; Levett 1990, 298; translation modified). While those who claim that Protagoras is wrong do not admit the falsity of their own position, Protagoras would be driven by the doctrine to concede the truth of their position—a position that confirms the falsity of his own (171b). As Burnyeat rightly points out, Socrates's noticeably omits the qualifier "for *a*" at this point: "Protagoras must agree (171a) that his opponents' disbelief in his *Truth* is true (query: why omit 'for them' here?)" (1990, 29). It is this omission that enables him to conclude: "Then since it is disputed by everyone, the *Truth* of Protagoras is not true for anyone at all, not even for himself" (171c; Levett 1990, 298). Although the qualifier "even for himself" is reintroduced in Socrates's ultimate claim that the doctrine is self-refuting, whether he reaches this conclusion legitimately by previously omitting the qualifier is an open question.[21] Nevertheless, the heart of the matter is not whether Socrates's conclusion is legitimately derived. Far more important and more interesting is the fact that his refutation of Protagoras's doctrine, legitimate or not, ultimately delivers him back to the doctrine itself.

Burnyeat's commentary provides a brief excursus on the apparent paradox inherent in Protagoras's doctrine. It is Protagoras's avoidance of this paradox through his "contradiction is impossible" doctrine that, I argue in the following section, obstructs Socrates's escape from Protagoras's thought-world. Burnyeat articulates a commonplace objection to relativism, Protagorean or otherwise: "Isn't there something inherently paradoxical about someone asserting (or believing) that *all truth is relative*? That proposition sums up the message of a completely general relativism, but when asserted it is propounded as itself a truth, which would indeed be self-refuting. . . . A commitment to truth absolute is bound up with the very act of assertion" (1990, 30).[22] But the man-measure doctrine cannot and should not be read independently of his other surviving doctrines. The two-*logoi* (*kai prôtos ephê duo logous einai peri pantos pragmatos antikeimenous allêlois*, "there are two opposing *logois* in every matter") and "contradiction is impossible" (*ouk estin antilegein*) doctrines enable him to avoid such absolutist commitments and to refute his self-refutation.

These doctrines may seem at first to be in direct contradiction to each other, since one claims that contradiction is ubiquitous while the other claims it is impossible. However, they are not contradictory but logically (and paradoxically) coextensive: if there are in fact two contradictory *logoi* in every matter, then any contradiction to a *logos* is likewise contradicted by another *logos*, and so on. According to the doctrines two-*logoi* and "contradiction is impossible," there will inevitably be a contradiction to each and every *logos*, including Protagoras's. But the fact that there likewise is a contradiction of each and every contradiction means that no contradiction can ever be fully refuted, including the self-refutation of the man-measure doctrine. This principle is illuminated more fully in the conversation of *Euthydemus*. In the following section, I explain how in his conversation with the sophist brothers Euthydemus and Dionysodorus Socrates attempts to deal with the Parmenidean paradox of nonbeing implicit in Protagoras's "contradiction is impossible" maxim. I show that the net result of all these dealings is an incapacity on Socrates's part to overcome the inexorability of Protagoras's man-measure doctrine.

The "Impossibility of Contradiction" and Parmenidean Nonbeing in the *Euthydemus*

The *Euthydemus* portrays a "wordy warfare" (272a; Rouse 1961, 386) between Socrates and the two brothers and sophists Euthydemus and Dionysodorus. Socrates claims their art is "disputation" [*eristikê*] (272b; Rouse 1961, 387), and their eristic techniques illuminate the maxim that contradiction [*antilegein*] is impossible, which Socrates explicitly attributes to Protagoras (286c). For example, Euthydemus and Dionysodorus trap Ctesippus into admitting that to lie or to speak falsely [*pseudesthai*] is impossible by claiming that "things that are not, are not [*mê onta onta estin*]" (284b; Rouse 1961, 397), and that orators, when speaking, do not do nothing, they do *something* (284b). Consequently, "no one ever says the things that are not—for he would at once make them something, and you have admitted that no one can make that which is not" (285c; Rouse 1961, 398). Since one cannot speak of that which is not (*hôs ouk esti*), speaking against [*antilegein*] is impossible (see 284d–286e).

Speaking falsely and speaking against are equally impossible, according to Euthydemus and Dionysodorus, because both are equivalent to speaking *what is not*. As G. B. Kerferd explains, this follows because "anyone who speaks the truth is saying what is the case about that which is the case. A person who is speaking untruthfully is saying what is not the case about that which is not the case. But that which is not the case is simply not there. So the person who says what is not the case is not talking about anything at all" (1981, 88).

The idea of speaking *what is not* is clearly a direct reference to several of Parmenides's commands, all of which embody his fundamental thesis that nonbeing *is not*—thus it cannot be spoken or thought. Kirk, Raven, and Schofield describe the thesis: "Parmenides claims that in any enquiry there are two and only two logically coherent possibilities, which are exclusive—that the subject of enquiry exists or that it does not exist. On epistemological grounds he rules out the second alternative as unintelligible" (1983, 241). This principle inheres in numerous fragments and maxims: "You cannot recognize that which is not (for it is not to be done), nor could you mention it neither can you speak it" (DK 28b2; Barnes 1987, 132); "What there is to be said and thought must needs be: for it is there for being, but nothing is not" (DK 28b6; Kirk, Raven, and Schofield 1983, 247); "Never will this prevail, that what is not is: restrain your thought from this road of inquiry" (DK 28b7; Barnes 1987, 133); "That [being] came from what is not I shall not allow you to say or think—for it is not sayable or thinkable that it is not" (DK 28b8; Barnes 1987, 134). It is no coincidence that in the *Sophist* dialogue (232b–233c), after reinforcing the characterization of sophists as proliferators of contradiction [*antilogikê*], Plato quotes Parmenides: "Never shall this force itself on us, that that which is may not be; [w]hile you search, keep your thought far away from this path" (237b; N. White 1993, 25).[23] As these and other fragments attest, to Parmenides, "a world that is full of objective contradictions is full of negations and so of non-worlds. Such a view can be neither thought nor said" (Kerferd 1981, 71).

For Parmenides, speaking what *is not* is problematic, because to speak *that which is not* is to imply that *that which is not* in some way (even if only linguistically) *is.* To a modern reader, for whom language is not ensnared in *phusis*—for whom it names, indexes, references, and so on—to speak of *what is not* does not necessarily imply that *what is not* is. But language manifestly does not yet have this indexical and denominative function for Socrates and his interlocutors, and it is this nonindexicality of language that Protagoras's thought is identifying, playing with, and perhaps even exploiting. As the Eleatic Stranger in the *Sophist* puts it, "All these issues are full of confusion, just as they always have been. It's extremely hard, Theaetetus, to say what form of speech we should use to say that there really is such a thing as false saying or believing, and moreover to utter this without being caught in a verbal conflict" (*Soph.* 236e–237a; N. White 1993, 24). The verbal conflict results from the fact that merely to speak about *what is not* necessarily implies that in one way or another it *is.*[24] In other words, by denying that something *is*, one necessarily implies that it *is*. For this reason, Parmenides would say, "it's impossible to say, speak, or think *that which is not* itself correctly by itself. It's unthinkable, unsayable, unutterable, and unformulable in speech" (*Soph.* 238c; N. White 1993, 27).

To this Protagoras would respond that even Parmenides's pronouncement, which contradicts nonbeing, contradicts itself. Or, as the Eleatic Stranger puts it, "*That which is not* even confuses the person who's refuting it in just this way, that whenever someone tries to refute it, he's forced to say mutually contrary things about it" (*Soph.* 238c; N. White 1993, 27).[25] Where Parmenides claims that it is impossible to speak what is not, since what is spoken, by definition, *is*, Protagoras responds that "speaking *what is not* is not. The very phrase that speaks of nonbeing denies its own existence. By contradicting Parmenides, Protagoras affirms him, and by affirming him he contradicts him.

According to Schiappa, refuting Parmenides was the purpose of the man-measure doctrine (2003, 139). But the genius of Protagoras's thought-world is that he was able to inscribe Parmenides's ontology within Heraclitus's, even though the two were themselves contradictory, and produce out of the contradictory synthesis an epistemology that was as paradoxical as it was inescapable, and as coherent as it was contradictory. Parmenides insists that being is a monistic totality, in direct opposition to Heraclitus's insistence that being is a fungible flux of opposing forces. Parmenides insists that all becoming is really being, in direct opposition to Heraclitus's insistence that all being is really becoming. Protagoras exploits Parmenides's opposition to Heraclitus as a means of reducing it to the Heraclitean unity of opposites and theory of flux.[26] In Protagoras's hands, Parmenides, in contradicting Heraclitus, affirms the tension of opposing forces, and in contradicting the possibility of speaking of nonbeing, substantiates it.

As M. T. Thornton rightly describes it, "The important implication of the Flux doctrine for sensible particulars is not that they are too *fugitive* to be described, but that, whatever you say of them, the opposite will be equally true: they are never *unqualifiedly* such-and-such (152d6, cf. *Rep.* 479). . . . If everything were in a state of total flux, then there would be no significant way of linguistically designating either particulars or characteristics" (1970, 583–84). This perhaps should be stated more forcefully: If everything is in a state of total flux, and if all *phusis* is defined by the unity of opposites, then each individual *logos* is the full measure of *what is* at any given time, and its contradiction is not a contradiction but, ultimately, a further affirmation of the Heraclitean coextension of *phusis* and *logos*. By claiming that Protagoras's man-measure doctrine is self-refuting in the *Theaetetus*, Socrates's is indicating the inherent two-*logoi* encoded within it; by contradicting it, he demonstrates that Protagoras cannot be contradicted, just as nothing in *phusis* can ever fully overcome the tension of opposites that defines *what is*. The Protagorean inheritance of Eleatic and Heraclitean thought in the form of sophistic linguistics and paradoxical reasoning creates a rhetorical crisis. When one engages in a sophistic set-to with a contradictor, there is simply no way out of the verbal puzzles he or she creates. Socrates may be dissatisfied with the contradictions the doctrine leads him to conclude, but he nevertheless cannot overturn the doctrine.

Conclusion

All this amounts to the same end point for Cratylus, Hermogenes, Theaetetus, and Socrates: the investigations terminate in the Protagorean relativism that they seek to avoid, and an inability to offer a compelling and sound explanation for how it is that *logos* can ever be false. As the above analysis shows, the etymologies are offered as a dramatization of the consequences of presuming the plausibility of Cratylus's view that *onomata* are a product of *phusis*, and as such, a mechanism for accessing *phusis*. What results is not correct *onomata* or true *logos* but a radically unstable *phusis*. But their avoidance of Heraclitean flux in the form of linguistic conventionalism results in a different version of the same problem: Protagorean relativism is substituted for Heraclitean flux. When Theaetetus and Socrates engage directly with the man-measure doctrine as a way of overcoming the vicissitudes of Heraclitean flux, the best they can accomplish is to show that it is self-refuting, thus affirming the doctrine through its companion doctrines of two-*logoi* and the impossibility of contradiction.

The *Theaetetus* concludes with a final attempt to define knowledge that cannot merely be reduced to Protagorean perception or overthrown by contradiction. His definition of knowledge as "true judgment with a *logos*" (201d)—where true judgment without *logos* is not knowledge, and the things of which there is no *logos* cannot be known—is his final attempt to overcome the epistemic crisis of Protagoras's man-measure doctrine. Ultimately, this attempt is unsuccessful for the simple reason that he cannot devise an adequate definition of *logos* (*Tht.* 210a–b)—in other words, he is unable to construct a theory of language, speech, and rhetoric. The answer to the question that motivates the discussion in the *Theaetetus* (Socrates's complaint that he "can't get a proper grasp of what on earth knowledge really is. Could we manage to put it into words?") is a resounding no. It cannot be put into words precisely because words cannot (yet) be detached from the flux of *phusis*. It is no coincidence that the failure to develop an adequate theory of *logos* at the end of the *Theaetetus* is punctuated by Socrates's departure to face the charges against him; charges that will lead to his death, precisely because of his rhetorical failure to make himself seem to be what he is to those who would judge him.

What Socrates is fumbling for in these portrayals is an external frame of reference that will make it possible to measure, judge, and evaluate the comparative merit and truth of a given *logos*. As Marina McCoy has observed, the discussion of mathematics at the beginning of the *Theaetetus* serves as a rich analogy for what he is after:

> Theaetetus's work in mathematics perfectly mirrors the situation with respect to the discussion of knowledge as perception. Plato was well aware of the concept of the incommensurable, as he uses the term οὐ συμμέτροι to describe the mathematical problem at 147d; that is, he understood that certain lengths cannot be "grasped" or measured by a common term. Similarly, Plato sets side by side two approaches to understanding

> knowledge that also seem to be incommensurable. No common term can evaluate both the approaches of Theaetetus and Protagoras adequately, for their concepts of truth, wisdom, and knowledge are entirely different. (2005, 37)

They cannot find a common measure by which to judge true *logos* precisely because, as the end of the *Theaetetus* demonstrates, they cannot develop an adequate theory of *logos* that can overcome Protagoras's two-*logoi* method.[27] The result is that there is no "external epistemic measure by which to judge competing accounts or speeches" (Gonzalez 2014, 54), and there will not be one until Plato can develop a theory of *logos* that is adequate to differentiate between true and false speech. The most they could hope for is, as demonstrated in the *Euthydemus*, to win the acclaim of an audience that "praised them to the skies . . . laughing and clapping and cheering till they nearly wore themselves out" (303b; Rouse 1961, 417).

« 4 »

Sophistry without Measure, Dialectic without Rhetoric

The Interpretive Dispute in the *Protagoras*

In the previous chapter, we witness how in the *Cratylus*, the *Euthydemus*, and the *Theaetetus* Socrates attempts to gain escape velocity from the agnosticism and uncertainty that are provoked by Protagoras's man-measure doctrine, the related doctrines of two-*logoi* and the impossibility of contradiction, and the Heraclitean ontology implicit therein. Although the attempts fail, Socrates intuits at the end of the *Theaetetus* that the way forward lies in his ability to devise a theory of *logos* as such. While that goal was not obtained, the course was nevertheless set. Whereas the previous chapter defines the epistemic problem provoked by Protagoras's doctrines, this chapter illustrates the discursive effects of that problem, displayed in the *Protagoras*.

The *Protagoras* dialogue is set around 433 to 431 BCE, during Protagoras's lifetime and several years before the dramatic date of both the *Cratylus* and the *Theaetetus*. The main action centers on a debate between Protagoras and Socrates on the subject of whether or not virtue can be taught. In this way, the conversation works as a not-so-subtle evaluation and critique of the sophists' activities—the teaching of, among other things, virtue. The discussion that ensues depicts a competition for verbal victory disguised as, on

Socrates's part, an attempt to establish a dialectic method that is somehow distinguishable from the sophists' eristic and antilogical tactics. I focus this analysis on an often neglected aspect of the dialogue: Protagoras's and Socrates's rival interpretations of Simonides's poem. Their dispute illustrates the practice of dialectic in the absence of a theory of *logos* that might function as a science for measuring the comparative merit of their linguistic claims. In the absence of such a science, the poem can be made to mean anything and everything, and consequently, dialectic is indistinguishable from eristic and antilogic. The true stakes of this are not limited to petty poetic interpretations such as the one displayed in the *Protagoras*. If words can be made to mean anything and everything, then belief likewise will follow the "use and wont of language" manipulated by those "who drag words this way and that at their pleasure" (*Tht.* 168c; Levett 1990, 294). As though he were forecasting the effect of Gorgias's verbal sorcery, discussed in chapter 1, Socrates reminds those present for the dispute between Socrates and Protagoras that such seductive trickery "persuades the very best of the young men" in the most "powerful cities" (*Prt.* 316c; Beresford 2005, 14), infiltrating their politics with dangerous untruths.

In what follows, I define three sophistic practices of eristic, antilogic, and dialectic and explain how defining a proper method of dialectic—an overriding concern across numerous dialogues—works as a unifying but unrealizable goal for the conversation in the *Protagoras*. I then analyze the interpretation of Simonides's poem in the *Protagoras*. As I explain in the introduction, Cole contends that the analysis of written eloquence is an indispensible precondition of the development of a theoretical metalanguage that constitutes rhetorical theory. Although the analysis of Simonides's poem serves as an example of such an analysis, it fails to produce such a metalanguage, and it is this glaring absence of a theory of *logos* that, I argue, seals the fate of the discussion. Despite Socrates's insistence that their conversation follow a method of dialectical question-and-answer, the absence of rhetorical theory is tantamount to the absence of any fixed measure that might distinguish between true and false discourse. In this way, the dialogue illustrates the discursive effects of the epistemic problem defined in the previous chapter, and demonstrates how dialectic alone is insufficient for discerning between *logos alêthês* and *logos pseudês*. What must be developed is a method that is itself grounded in rhetorical theory, which might serve as an external measure that could extract dialectic from antilogic and eristic.

Antilogic, Eristic, Dialectic, and the *Protagoras*

In *The Sophistic Movement*, G. B. Kerferd explains how Plato, throughout his dialogues, consistently divides sophistic verbal activity into three activities: *antilogikê*, or "antilogic"; *eristikê*, or "eristic"; and *dialegesthai*, or "dialectic." Through repeated assessments of these three verbal practices, Plato attempts to refine his dialectic method by separating it from antilogic and eristic. His aim is to endow the philosopher with the art of dialectic and at the same time discard the eristic and antilogic of the sophists. Over the course of several dialogues, "by disciplining the practice of *dialegesthai* into an increasingly rule-governed event (*to dialegesthai*) in which the dialectician participates, he is able to transform the sophistic practice of dialogue into an Art—*hê dialektikê technê*" (Timmerman and Schiappa 2010, 34). In this way, the dialectic method of Plato comes to be what it is in contrast to both antilogic and eristic.

Plato refers to antilogic as the art of "causing the same thing to be seen by the same people now as possessing one predicate and now as possessing the opposite or contradictory predicate" (Kerferd 1981, 61).[1] We might think of this as Plato's own description of the rhetorical effects of the two-*logoi* doctrine. Where the practice of two-*logoi* manifests, it makes things appear one way at a given time and another, possibly opposite or contradictory way, at another time. We encounter this effect in the *Phaedrus*, for example, where Phaedrus's speech in praise of the best sort of lover in fact praises the nonlover. While one might be inclined to think of one who loves as the best sort of lover, the sophist through the art of antilogic can replace that view with its opposite.

Although, as Kerferd notes, Plato often uses *antilogic* and *eristic* interchangeably, he nevertheless distinguishes the problematic motivations of the speaker when he discusses eristic. Those who use eristic are determined to win a dispute or are concerned only with "seeking victory in argument" (Kerferd 1981, 62). In eristic, "concern for truth is not a necessary part of the art—victory in argument can be secured without it" (Kerferd 1981, 62). And while Socrates often himself practices a form of *antilogic*, the pattern that emerges across Plato's numerous uses of the terms *eristic*, *antilogic*, and *dialectic* reveals a desire to separate victory-oriented eristic from a truth-oriented discourse, which he calls *dialegesthai*. The real challenge, as Kerferd points out, is carving the distinction between antilogic and dialectic, since "it is possible for people without being aware of it to mistake antilogic for dialectic (*Rep.* 454a4–5). . . . Without dialectic the practice of antilogic is dangerous in the extreme" (1981, 63–64).[2] While Plato's routine prioritization of dialectic over other discursive methods is obvious even to a casual reader of the dialogues, it is less obvious how his definition of the practice is the result of an arduous extraction from other sophistic verbal practices, how it differs from those practices, and what, exactly, distinguishes dialectic as "the ideal method, *whatever that may be*" (R. Robinson 1953, 70).

Protagoras is an enormously important source for understanding how Plato meant to define his method of dialectic, given the prominence of the theme in this dialogue. Myles Burnyeat has observed that *dialegesthai* (the verb used to describe his dialectic method) appears far more frequently—thirty-two times—in the *Protagoras* than in any other dialogue.[3] Thus this is "Plato's most sustained treatment of the comparative merits of the many different forms of διαλέγεσθαι" (Burnyeat 2013, 419). Following the *Protagoras,* the second most frequent appearances of the term occur in the *Theaetetus* (twenty-one times), the dialogue that contains Plato's most direct treatment of Protagoras's thought. This simple fact indicates the crucial role Protagoras's thought played in provoking the need for a rigorous method of dialectic in the first place. The agnosticism that plagues Socrates in the *Theaetetus* makes a rule-governed discursive method a necessity. Without it, he has no means of overcoming the Protagorean epistemic crises or his own inability to distinguish between true and false speech.

Nevertheless, what emerges from the discussion portrayed in the *Protagoras* is a discursive method that is fundamentally indistinguishable from eristic and antilogic, despite repeated attempts on Socrates's part to separate dialectic from and prioritize it over other methods. The *Protagoras* depicts Socrates's failed attempts to redescribe "*dialegesthai* in such a way as to claim it as a legitimate philosophical practice and distance it from 'sophistic' practices . . . [of] eristic and antilogic" (Timmerman and Schiappa 2010, 34). In the same way that the flux of *phusis* and language "haunts the epistemological inquiries" (Tindale 2010, 31) in the *Theaetetus* and the *Cratylus,* antilogic and eristic haunt Socrates's dialectic in the *Protagoras.*

The dialogue depicts sophistic activity as much more than just eristic, antilogic, and dialectic. From the *Protagoras* dialogue, for example, we inherit the view that sophists charged wealthy clients high fees; that *orthoepeia*, or the "'correctness of names[,]' was something of a standard theme in sophistic discussions" (Kerferd 1981, 68); that display oratories, like Protagoras's "Great Speech" had an effect like magic on their hearers (de Romilly 1975, 66); and that "the appeal to poetry is a well-known sophistic procedure" (Kerferd 1954, 250). Plato's depiction of sophistic activity in the *Protagoras* dialogue leads to the widespread understanding that the practices of figures like Protagoras, Prodicus, and Hippias, who are characters in this dialogue, were defined by a victory-oriented eristic contest in which sophists overwhelmed their hearers with oratorical power, manipulated the poetic tradition, and quibbled over hairsplitting definitions. In brief, all the characteristics of sophistic activity that "Plato continually exploits as though they were the essentials" (Havelock 1957, 206)—and that would come to dominate the standard view of the sophists and their practices—are simultaneously present in this single dialogue.

At the same time, however, in this dialogue we witness Socrates employ and manipulate these very sophistic practices, especially in the portion of the dialogue in which Protagoras and Socrates offer competing interpretations of a poem by Simonides, often treated as an irrelevant detour or distraction from the supposed "main point" of the dialogue: the unity of virtues and whether or not virtue can be taught.[4]

The value of this section of the dialogue deserves reconsideration, but not because, as some have argued, it possesses some sincere philosophical content that is relevant to the central discussion of virtue.[5] Rather, I suggest it subtly displays how sophistic manipulation occurs when sophistic methods—including dialectic—operate independently of the methods supplied by rhetorical theory. Simonides's poem is an example of what Cole refers to as "written eloquence." As Cole posits, "Analytical metalanguage [i.e., rhetorical theory] can only develop on the basis of a close study and comparison of particular pieces of persuasive eloquence, and such close examination is only possible when these pieces of eloquence are available in written form" (1991, 112).[6] However, this analytical process that is necessary for the development of rhetorical theory does not always or inevitably result in rhetorical theory. Socrates and Protagoras's analysis of the written eloquence of Simonides's poem manifestly fails to produce a theoretical metalanguage—a failure made all the more apparent by contrast to the theoretical metalanguage of *mimêsis*, *onoma*, and *rhêma* that results from the analyses explored in the following chapters. In contrast to linguistic procedures highlighted in the *Republic* and the *Sophist*, the discussions of language and the meaning of words in the *Protagoras* do not result in a theoretical taxonomy. In place of a rhetorical metalanguage, there are "elaborate discussions of apparent synonyms" (Kerferd 1954, 253), "a ridiculous extreme of bad interpretation" (Gagarin 1968, 54), and a "distorting Socratic overlay" (Coby 1987, 100)—language games as opposed to language theory, in other words. These provide only temporary escape from Protagoras's oratorical power; they do not, however, provide an escape from the web of Protagorean epistemology and sophistic contradiction defined in the previous chapter. It is precisely this absence of rhetorical theory that makes it possible for Plato to portray Socrates's sophistic methods as an unmeasured—and unmeasurable—eristic and antilogical contest that manipulates language, including the language of the poetic tradition, for the primary purpose of achieving victory.[7] Taken together, these dialogues portray the stakes of Socrates's ultimate failure to overcome the problem of Protagorean epistemology and the man-measure doctrine: such methods can make a weak position strong and a strong position weak. When applied in public deliberations as opposed to private performances, the life of the polis is on the line.[8]

In what follows, I explain how sophistic verbal activities, including eristic, antilogic, and dialectic, are used and exploited in the *Protagoras*. Given the absence of a distinction between seeming and being that can overturn Protagoras's doctrines, Plato depicts a dialectic that is little more than victory-oriented discourse of ever-shifting postulates. Socrates's dubious analysis of the poem by Simonides serves as an example of written eloquence without rhetorical theory, and therefore also of dialectic without rhetoric, which itself is sophistic eristic and antilogic without measure.

Socrates versus Protagoras: Simonides's Poem in Its Dialectical Context

The *Protagoras* dialogue is set just before the outbreak of the Peloponnesian War, around 433–431 BCE, indicated by the remarks about the young Alcibiades's age—born in 451, he was just getting his first beard (309a–b). Athens at this time is at the pinnacle of its golden age of wealth and prosperity; but it is also on the brink of destruction. It is set immediately before the outbreak of the great plague of 430 that took so many lives, including the lives of many who are present in the dialogue.

The dialogue opens in the streets of Athens as a conversation between Socrates and an unnamed friend. His friend asks Socrates where he's been, and teases him about his amorous pursuit of the young and beautiful Alcibiades, but Socrates confesses that he has been dazzled by someone more beautiful and impressive even than Alcibiades, a foreigner from Abdera, "the greatest intellectual alive today" (309d; Beresford 2005, 6), Protagoras. His friend is eager and excited to hear all about it, so the two sit down together and Socrates begins to recount the interaction.

Earlier that day, he tells his friend, just before dawn, Socrates is awakened while he is still lying in bed by a loud banging on his door. It is his friend Hippocrates, in a frenzy to tell Socrates the news that Protagoras is in Athens, at Callias's house (we met Callias in chapter 1, in Xenophon's account of the party where Socrates disparaged the wasteful extravagance of perfumes). Hippocrates is frantic for Socrates to take him to Callias's and introduce him to Protagoras so he can convince him to give him lessons in exchange for money. It is too early to go to the house since dawn has not yet broken, so Socrates suggests they pass the time by pacing together in the courtyard of his house and wait for day to break.[9]

As they stroll in the courtyard, Socrates strikes up a conversation in his characteristic fashion. He asks, as though he doesn't already know, what people call Protagoras (311e). It is clear by Hippocrates's answer that this was a leading question: "A sophist, Socrates. People call the man a sophist" (311e, Beresford 2005, 8). Socrates responds by asking Hippocrates what he hopes to become by studying under Protagoras. The question piques Hippocrates's conscience; he blushes in response, and admits that he would be embarrassed to claim such a title for himself (311e–312a). Before we even arrive at Socrates's next question ("What is a sophist?"; 312c), we already have the distinct impression that the definition will be a negative one. Numerous sources from antiquity attest to the fact that, when this term began to see wide use during the fifth century BCE, its sense was not necessarily pejorative, and its positive or neutral meanings persisted alongside its negative ones well into the fourth century.[10] But throughout his works, "Plato attempted to confine the application of the term to the likes of Protagoras, Hippias and Prodicus, itinerant purveyors of, above all, the skills in persuasion that would be needed by a young man ambitious to succeed in democratic politics" (Denyer 2008, 74).

The discussion at 312c–313a follows almost identically the form of the conversation we witnessed at the outset of the *Gorgias*. Socrates asks Hippocrates what the object of the sophists' knowledge is, and Hippocrates speculates that it must be skilled speaking; but this leads only to the further question—speaking about what? This question is left unanswered for the time being, and its unanswerability is cause for concern, according to Socrates. Just as he does in the *Gorgias*, he expresses his dismay that the sophists teach skills in persuasive speaking without knowing whether the content of the persuasion is good or bad, right or wrong. But, just like a shrewd salesperson, "they'll claim it's all good, because they're selling it; and as a customer you don't know any better. . . . That's how it is with these people who deal in education, touring the cities like travelling salesmen, peddling their courses to anyone who wants them" (313d; Beresford 2005, 11).[11]

When Socrates and Hippocrates arrive at the house the servant opens the door and, upon seeing them, shouts, "'Oh no! Sophists! He's busy!' And with that he very keenly [slams] the door in our face, with both hands, as hard as he could" (314d; 12).[12] Socrates reassures the servant that they are not there to see Callias, that they are not sophists—rather, they are there to see the sophist Protagoras. In other words, they are not there to take Callias's wealth and impose on his hospitality and household, but to pay, and pay handsomely, for time with Protagoras.

When they are allowed in, they join an illustrious party, attended by no less than three sophistic celebrities (Protagoras, Prodicus, and Hippias) and some of the most elite Athenians of the day. In addition to Callias and his half-brother, Socrates also lists as members of the party Plato's uncle Charmides, two of Pericles's sons, Acumenus's son Eryximachus, Phaedrus of Murrhinous (the star of the *Phaedrus*), Androtion's son Andron, Pausanias from Cerameis, Adimantus Cepis's son, Adimantus Leucolophides's son, Alcibiades (Athens's most notorious bad boy and Socrates's longstanding crush), Critias Callaeschrus's son (another of Plato's uncles), Philomelus's son Philippides, and Protagoras's "most famous pupil": Antimoerus from Mende (315a; Beresford 2005, 13). As Socrates describes the scene to his nameless friend, Protagoras was walking back and forth in the colonnade, flanked by followers. As Protagoras paced up and down, turning at each end of the colonnade, his "chorus" (315b; Beresford 2005, 13) followed on either side, carefully staying out of his path by splitting down the middle, one half circling right and the other left, to rejoin him in his march each time did an about-face. Mirroring his description of Protagoras as a peripatetic Orpheus, Socrates describes Hippias of Elis as an enthroned Minos and Prodicus of Ceos as a reclined Tantalus. The former "was sitting there in his high-backed chair, passing out judgements" (315c; Beresford 2005, 13), while the latter was still in bed, "wrapped up in sheepskins and blankets (a huge pile of them, as far as I could see)" (315d; Beresford 2005, 13).[13] Socrates explains the sheer size of the group by noting somewhat pointedly that many of them were foreigners—"The people Protagoras gathers from the cities he passes through: he draws them with his spellbinding voice, like Orpheus, and wherever the voice leads, they follow, under his spell" (315a–b; Beresford 2005, 13).

From Orpheus to Minos to Tantalus, Socrates describes the scene as a descent from the outer reaches to the inner depths of the underworld. The spectre of death is reinforced by the inhabitants of this underworld: Athenian celebrities who will, in the span of only a few years, be killed either by the plague or the war that will shortly ensue. Callias himself is a symbol of Athens's prosperity and imminent decline: at the dramatic date of the dialogue, he is the wealthiest man in Athens, but, "by 387 he had, in spite of his dealings with Protagoras, the expert on household management (318e5) reduced his fortune to less than two talents (Lys.19.48); and he died (some time after 371: Xen., *HG* [*Hellenica*] 6.3.2) in penury, unable to afford the necessities of life" (Denyer 2008, 71). If Beresford is correct that "in effect, we have the whole world of Plato in one house" (2005, 45n23), then it is a world on the brink of utter destruction and demise.

Socrates and Hippocrates soon reveal the reason for their visit: to ask Protagoras what, exactly, is his expertise and what he teaches all those followers who crowd around him on all sides (318c–d). When Protagoras says that he teaches his students how to be responsible members of the polis and managers of their household affairs—virtuous citizens, in other words (318e)—Socrates is skeptical. He doubts it is possible to make someone good or virtuous by teaching them to be so (320b).

Protagoras offers to tell a story that will explain why it is that virtue can be taught. It is in an effort to offer this explanation that Protagoras gives the myth of Prometheus (320c–323c), perhaps the most famous portion of the dialogue. In it, Protagoras tells how in the creation of the world, the god Epimetheus, whose name translates literally to "thinks too late," distributed certain abilities and powers to all living things. To some he gave wings, others claws, others sharp teeth, and so on. The purpose of these abilities was to create a kind of balance of forces, so that none could decimate or outstrip the other. But, as his name indicates, he didn't think ahead or appropriately measure how many powers there were to distribute and how many creatures he would have to distribute these powers to. Because he worked haphazardly and without measure, once he arrived at the human, he had run out of abilities. The human would have been left naked and raw, if it hadn't been for the fact that Prometheus, who thinks ahead (or so the literal meaning of his name suggests), decided it would be best to steal from the gods fire and *technê* (321d). Their ability would not be borne on their bodies, but would be something external they could use. Zeus found out about the theft and punished Prometheus, but nevertheless endowed humans with the ability to learn virtuous uses of these and other *technai,* so that their own power might be kept in balance and they would not do excessive harm to one another. The upshot of the myth is the fact that "being good is something people can be taught" (328c; Beresford 2005, 30), and it's easy to find teachers for this because it only takes being "even just a little bit better at advancing someone toward being good" (328a–b; Beresford 2005, 29) in order to teach them.

Through Socrates's account of the speech and its effect on him, we witness secondhand Protagoras's oratorical power: "Protagoras, after this long and wonderful performance, broke off from his speech. And for quite some time I just sat there gazing at him, mesmerized, waiting for him to say something, longing to hear more! But once I realized that he really had entirely finished, it was as though I had to struggle to regain my senses" (328d; Beresford 2005, 30). Here we have the rare experience of seeing Socrates overpowered; not by the raptures of poetic ecstasy but by the *logos* of an oratorical expert. Even though he was initially dubious, Protagoras's verbal power overwhelms him, and Socrates's entire focus and objective seem to shift. At the end of the speech, he is driven to admit that, before Protagoras spoke, "I didn't think it was through other people's care and attention that good people become good people. But now I'm convinced" (328e; Beresford 2005, 30).

His conviction is short-lived, however. After a moment's recovery, he regains his critical distance. He claims to have a lingering discomfort with Protagoras's speech and good speeches in general, for the simple reason that "if you go and ask one of them some follow-up question, well, you might as well be talking to a book. They're incapable of answering you or of asking anything themselves. If you ask even some minor question following up on something they've said, they're like bronze bowls, which *bong* when you tap them, and go on and on bonging until you grab hold of them (328e–29a; Beresford 2005, 30).[14] This complaint, which indirectly defines the practice of dialectic, serves as a preface to the dialectical exchange (333c) that follows. The back-and-forth, question-and-answer between Protagoras and Socrates aims to address a question that is logically prior to whether virtue can be taught—Socrates seeks to inquire into the nature of virtue. Is it a composite or a whole, many or one? (329c).[15]

In the discussion that follows, however, the rivalry between Socrates and Protagoras, their mutual desire to win the assent and the acclaim of the audience, and Socrates's unvirtuous determination to set the terms for the discussion in a way that will play at once to his own strengths and his opponent's weaknesses, overtakes the professed subject of the discourse—whether virtue can be taught, and whether virtue is many or one. For example, Socrates claims that Protagoras began making a fuss about being questioned, and, he says, "I got the sense that Protagoras, by this point, was a bit prickly, and riled-up, and taking the questions in a ready-for-battle kind of way. So when I saw that was the mood he was in, I thought I'd better be careful and ask my next question very gently" (333e; Beresford 2005, 38). In describing Protagoras as "agonistic" in this way (333e), he indicates his rival's eristic motivations.

Socrates asks whether things are good insofar as they are good for humans, to which Protagoras responds, offering several examples, that many things are good which are not necessarily beneficial to people (333e–334c). This response, with its rapid litany of well-chosen examples, wins further acclaim from the audience—a mark of eristic victory. This, in turn, prompts Socrates to attempt to handicap his interlocutor as a means of securing his own victory: "When he'd said all that, the people who were there burst into rowdy applause; they thought it was a great speech. And I said, 'Protagoras, the fact is, I'm a bit forgetful, and if someone makes long speeches at me I tend to lose track of what it is we're talking about. . . . You've met someone who's a bit forgetful, so you've got to trim your answers for me, and make them shorter, if you expect me to keep up" (334c–d; Beresford 2005, 39). Even though Socrates still calls this exchange a "dialectic" (334d, 335a), it's clearly eristic for both Protagoras and Socrates. We as readers know the untruth of Socrates's response. Our eyes can scan the page above and easily see that Protagoras's speech was not very long at all, but the same length as the one Socrates has just given, explaining why he cannot absorb long speeches (335b–336b). Moreover, Socrates is claiming to be forgetful and therefore unable to follow Protagoras's long speeches; but we the readers know that the entire debate, including a verbatim report of the long speeches, is being recounted from memory. Socrates, witnessing the success of his speech with the people gathered at Callias's house, unsettled by their applause and adulation, is seeking through these false excuses a way to put a stopper in Protagoras's enchanting Orpheic voice, to keep Protagoras from claiming victory, and to claim victory for himself.

When Socrates asks Protagoras, for the sake of his faulty memory, to follow a shorter form of dialectical question-and-answer, Protagoras sees through his guile and exposes it for its true motivations: "So does that mean as long as *I* think they need to be, or as long as *you* think they need to be? . . . I've entered into contests of speech (*agôna logôn*) and argument with a lot of people before now, and if I'd always done what you're telling me to do—conducted the discussion (*dialegesthai*) on my opponent's (*antilegôn*) terms—I'd never have been thought any better than the next man and 'Protagoras' would never have become a household name throughout Greece" (334e–335a; Beresford 2005, 40; translator's emphasis). Socrates then adds petulance to deceit and manipulation. Because Protagoras does not capitulate to his demands about how *dialegesthai* (335b) should proceed, Socrates threatens to leave. The dialectic will be on his terms or on no terms at all: "I decided there was no point in my participating any further in the meeting" (335b; Beresford 2005, 40), and he rises to exit, offering a feeble excuse: "The fact is, there's somewhere I really must be going" (335c; Beresford 2005, 40). Again, the reader knows this excuse to be untrue: at the beginning of the dialogue, when Socrates encounters his unnamed friend just after leaving the company at Callias's house, he has nowhere else he has to be, thus he has the time to sit down with the friend to recount this story he is currently telling.[16] The party tries to stop him from departing, even grabbing his arm and his cloak, and they intervene in order to strike an accord between Socrates and Protagoras.[17] As they attempt to reach a compromise, even Alcibiades, who takes Socrates's side in the dispute, implies that Socrates's motives are duplicitous: he suggests that Socrates isn't very good when it comes to rousing speeches, but that he excels at dialectical question-and-answer (*dialegesthai*, 336b–c), and, as if to signal to the reader that our suspicions are true, denies any feebleness in Socrates's memory.

Ultimately, Socrates ignores all the proposed compromises, distorts the nature of Protagoras's objection to Socrates's requirement that his speeches be brief, and has his own way. Although Protagoras had earlier claimed they both should be able to answer the other's questions in whatever manner they thought most appropriate, Socrates portrays his position as though Protagoras simply wanted to go first with asking questions:

> Look, here's what I'm prepared to do to make it possible for us to carry on with the meeting and get some discussions [*dialogoi*] going—which is what you're all so keen on: if Protagoras doesn't want to answer questions, fine, let's have him ask some questions and I'll do the answering—and in the process I'll try to show him how I think someone who's answering questions should go about it. But then once I've answered as many questions as he feels like asking, *he's got to answer my questions in the same way*. And if, at that point, he doesn't seem very keen on giving answers that stick to the question, we'll all ask him together just the same thing as you're asking me—not to mess up the meeting. (338c–d; Beresford 2005, 44; emphasis mine)

This "compromise" position reflects no change whatsoever from Socrates's initial stance where he insisted that if the conversation were to proceed, it should be in the short, dialectic method of his preference. Protagoras, so as not to be the one to break up the discussion, relents: "Everyone thought that that was what we should do. So Protagoras, although he was very reluctant, found himself forced to go along with it: he would ask me some questions and then, once he'd had enough of asking questions, take his turn at answering mine—keeping his answers brief" (338e; Beresford 2005, 45).

It is in this context that the discussion of Simonides's poem begins. Although Socrates has repeatedly insisted that their discourse follow a dialectic method, it is a dialectic that cannot be detached from Socrates's eristic desire for victory. As the ensuing conversation reveals, these motivations drive Socrates to inflect his dialectic with the techniques of antilogic. In the following section, I examine how the eristic contest for victory between Protagoras and Socrates leads Socrates to produce antilogical interpretations of the poem rather than the sort of theoretical metalanguage that can work as an external measure to judge the veracity of their competing linguistic claims. Consequently, neither interpretation can be denounced as false.

Socratic Sophistry, Eristic, and Antilogic in the Interpretation of Simonides

When Protagoras assumes the role of questioner, he proposes that his discourse "will still be about the same thing you and I have been talking about—being good—but shifted to a poetic context" (339a; Beresford 2005, 45). He quotes part of a poem by Simonides:

> Really and truly good
> is a hard thing
> for a man to be [*genesthai*],
> I'll give you that—
> straight as a die,
> in hands and feet and mind,
> built without a single fault. (339b; Beresford 2005, 45; translation modified)

Before going any further, Protagoras asks Socrates whether he knows the poem well enough for their discussion to commence, or "do you want me to go through the whole thing for you?" (339b; Beresford 2005, 45). Socrates responds, "'No, no need,' I said. 'I know the song—it so happens it's a song I've devoted quite a lot of thought to myself'" (ibid.). Protagoras then implies that Socrates is missing something, and tells him, "You'd better take a closer look [*hora dê*]" (339b; Beresford 2005, 46).[18] This way of initiating the discussion establishes Simonides's poem as an example of written eloquence—it is a poem that is known by Socrates and Protagoras alike precisely because it has been available to them in writing. This availability naturally invites the kind of challenge Protagoras poses.

Nevertheless, Socrates declines the invitation to look at the poem again before Protagoras leads him to endorse explicitly the view (1) that "it's very well put together and makes perfect sense" (339b; Beresford 2005, 45) and does not contradict itself, and (2) that if it were to contradict itself, it would not be well put together or make perfect sense (339b). Once Protagoras gains these admissions from Socrates, he delivers another passage from the poem:

> But for me that Pittacus thing
> just don't quite ring—
> even though he is real smart—
> he says "bein' [*emmenai*] good is hard." (339b–c; Beresford 2005, 45–46)

Protagoras then has laid his trap, which becomes clear when he asks Socrates, "You realize this is the same person who's making both claims, this one and the one before? . . . So do you think the second claim is consistent with the first one?" (339c; Beresford 2005, 46). Socrates hesitates. He recounts to his friend that he stood by his original praise of the poem, but that he was beginning to feel uncertain about his initial position: "'Yes, I think so'—at that moment, mind you, I was beginning to suspect he might be on to something. 'Why?' I said. 'You don't think so?'" (339c; Beresford 2005, 46). Protagoras has Socrates right where he wants him—not only does Socrates fail to notice the contradiction, he stands by his earlier assertion that the passages conceal no contradiction.

Socrates is right to hesitate, as Protagoras's response makes clear. He lambasts Socrates: "How could you possibly think someone who made both these claims was being consistent?" (339d; Beresford 2005, 46). Simonides gives his own view first—that it's hard to be good. But then, a few lines down, he criticizes Pittacus for saying the same thing. Consequently, Protagoras notes, there must be a contradiction: "Somewhere, either with the first claim or with the second, he's not speaking rightly!" (339d; Beresford 2005, 46; translation modified).

For the third time in the dialogue, Protagoras's skill seems to have overwhelmed Socrates. He has forced Socrates's hand, tricking him into claiming that the poem was noncontradictory and well put-together, then getting him to reinforce that claim, only to point out a contradiction by lifting two passages from the poem and placing them side by side, that the poem claims both that being good is hard and that Pittacus was wrong to say that being good is hard. It is clear from this discussion that it is no longer about its apparent subject—being virtuous or good; rather, both Socrates's and Protagoras's aim is to defeat his opponent. This is much more than a simple change of genre, as Protagoras claimed it was (339a). Behind the subject of the investigation and the dialectical exchange is an ulterior desire for eristic victory.

Once again, Socrates finds himself on his back foot due to Protagoras's success. Protagoras's speech, Socrates recalls, "got him a big round of applause from a lot of the people in the audience. And as for me, at first I felt like I'd taken a punch from a champion boxer—everything went black! my head was in a spin!—with him making his point and then the rest of them heaping on the applause. But then—and between you and me the idea was to give myself a little time to think about what the poet might be saying—I turned and called to Prodicus" (339d–e; Beresford 2005, 46). This is an unusual moment in the Platonic corpus not only because we witness in Socrates naked insincerity and duplicity, but also because he so unashamedly and candidly admits to feeling he'd been beat, to envying the applause and adulation the crowd was giving Protagoras, and to buying time so that he could strike back.

After gabbling and stalling, he attempts to recover from Protagoras's blow by offering an antilogical interpretation of Simonides's poem. In particular, Socrates relies for his argument on hairsplitting delineations of definition and verb tense, a method attributed to Prodicus precisely because of this portrayal (Kerferd 1954, 253–54). After gathering his wits, Socrates strikes back, doubling down on his assertion that it's a good poem that contains no contradiction because it contains a difference between "being" and "becoming." Simonides is not contradicting himself, Socrates reasons, because he uses a different verb in the two passages Protagoras has referenced. He turns to Prodicus for assistance and asks, "Do you think that *becoming* is the same thing as *being*, or different?" Prodicus agrees that they are different. Simonides states his own view that "it's a hard thing for a man to *become* [*genesthai*] really and truly good." Simonides then criticizes Pittacus for saying that "*bein'* [*emmenai*] good is hard." Thus, Socrates concludes, "if being isn't the same thing as becoming, then Simonides isn't contradicting himself after all" (340b–c; 2008 47). In this counterinterpretation, Socrates has caused the same poem to appear in a contradictory manner to the audience—the basic function of sophistic antilogic.

Following Ulrich von Wilamowitz-Moellendorff (1898), it has long been widely agreed that this distinction between being and becoming is an erroneous opposition between *emmenai* and *genesthai.* Socrates attempts to inflect them with a different meaning by defining *genesthai* as "becoming" in order to exaggerate a contrast between the two terms. Rather, both verbs simply meant "to be."[19] His interpretation, therefore, amounts to (in the words of one critic), "violent transgressions of Greek syntax and idiom" (Carson 1992, 112), resulting in the outcome that "Socrates appropriates the poet's poem by stepping over the poet's will as if it did not exist" (Carson 1992, 122).[20] Socrates turns to Prodicus to develop this erroneous definition, a dramatic development that contributes to the later perspective that Prodicus was known for precisely this technique.[21] As this discussion demonstrates, the technique of sophistic *orthoepeia* is the raw material of antilogic. Through his slippery, "perverse" (Denyer 2008, 155) distinction between being and becoming, *emmenai* and *genesthai,* Socrates turns Protagoras's postulate on its head just as Protagoras had turned Simonides's poem on its head.

Socrates's antilogic doesn't end here. Protagoras points out, through more antilogic, that Socrates's interpretation creates a more serious problem than the one he was trying to solve, since "the poet would have to be exceptionally stupid to claim that to *keep* being good is something so trivial, when in fact it's the most difficult thing there is" (340e; Beresford 2005, 48). Again, Socrates antilogically twists out of his grasp. He claims that this was not what he meant. He shifts his position, saying what Simonides must have meant was that "*becoming* good is hard . . . hard, but possible—bein' good, on the other hand, is *impossible*" (344e; Beresford 2005, 54; emphasis translator's). To review, Socrates has contradicted Protagoras's first interpretation—that Simonides means being good is difficult and Pittacus is wrong to say being good is difficult. He likewise contradicts his own contradiction—that becoming good is difficult and Pittacus is wrong to say that being good is difficult since it's easy. Now, Socrates interprets Simonides as saying that becoming good is difficult, but Pittacus is wrong to say that being good is difficult, since it's not difficult it's impossible.

He continues in this vein of faulty reasoning to 347a, quoting other lines from Simonides's poem and offering similarly dubious readings. He explains Simonides's overall purpose in his poem as though it were itself a sophistic exercise in *orthoepeia*, since the poet is "clearly reprimanding Pittacus for not knowing how to make accurate semantic distinctions" (341c; Beresford 2005, 49). In order to back this claim, he suggests that Pittacus's saying, which Simonides quotes, is a classic example of "Spartan-style pithiness" (343b; Beresford 2005, 51). On this point he develops another sophistic style of reasoning that deliberately and explicitly makes a strong case for the weak view that Crete and Sparta, the least philosophical and most militaristic civilizations in the Greek world, have the longest and richest philosophic traditions. Socrates claims that this is only unknown to most people because they keep it such a well-guarded secret. It's their secret but deep love of philosophy, according to Socrates, that accounts for the effectiveness of their laconic mode of address, characterized by "unforgettable quips . . . dense and tightly packed—something that makes the person he's talking to suddenly look no smarter than a child" (342e; Beresford 2005, 51). The secret Spartan philosophical tradition, he claims, was actually behind some of the greatest Greek thinkers: Thales, Pittacus, Solon, and many others were, implausibly, acolytes of the laconic school (343a).

This explanation is yet another demonstration of sophistic interpretation—which, for the sake of diversion, display, and, in Socrates's case, eristic victory, aims to offer an *antilogos* that can make what is unlikely seem likely, or make a weak, improbable argument into a strong, probable one. Socrates employs the Protagorean strategy of making the weaker argument stronger than its opposing *logos*. As Schiappa summarizes this principle, it is "best understood as companion to the two-*logoi* fragment. Of the two *logoi* in opposition concerning any given experience, one is—at any given time—dominant or stronger, while the other is submissive or weaker. Protagoras claimed to teach the ability to make the weaker *logos* stronger; that is, to challenge the relationship of the stronger and weaker between conflicting *logoi*" (Schiappa 2003, 107).[22] Socrates claims that the least philosophical people are actually the most philosophical, in the same way that a sophist might, for example, "eulogize some miserable donkey as if it were a horse" (*Phdr.* 260c; Waterfield 2002, 47) or praise the nonlover as the best lover (*Phdr.* 230e–234c). Despite the dialectical form their discourse follows—the form that Socrates insists from the beginning their discussion must take—dialectic is indistinguishable from antilogic and eristic.

Neither irrelevant parody nor a sincere philosophic consideration of virtue could be the purpose of the interpretation of Simonides. If there is any relevance whatsoever of Socrates's candid admission that he was using whatever means he had available to him to keep Protagoras from winning the debate, the interpretation he offers is neither a parody nor a vehicle for sincere philosophical content, but a dramatic demonstration of Socrates's willful use of those available means of persuasion.[23]

Ultimately, Socrates concludes his sophistic display by denouncing poetic interpretation as a worthless activity—even though it's the very activity he's just engaged in. Charles Griswold suggests that "through his elaborate if forced exegesis of Simonides, Socrates has shown that he can outdo Protagoras at his own game, and . . . has declared that the game is not worth the candle" (1999, 289). And, as Griswold rightly points out, he "dismisses the exegesis of verses on the grounds that it is impossible to decide ultimately whose interpretation is right" (1999, 291). This impossibility stems from the fundamental fact that, as the foregoing dialectical exchange demonstrates, there is no external measure to judge the competing linguistic claims of the antilogical exercise. Given the demonstration we've just observed, any number of interpretations would be possible. If Hippias, Prodicus, Protagoras, or anyone else present at the party were to use the same method—inventing spurious definitions for words and false explanations that reverse the previous postulate—they would be able to make Simonides's poem say anything and everything precisely because, as they themselves acknowledge, they lack a science for measuring comparative claims that are strictly linguistic. In the absence of such a science, the sophistic methods of wordplay and improvisation expand and multiply meanings, rather than contract and reduce them; consequently, both Socrates and Protagoras force out of the poem new meanings and attempt to convince the hearers that those innovative meanings were there all the time, lurking just under the surface.

As Socrates describes it, the poets "can't be asked anything about what they're saying, and usually when people bring them into a discussion you get some people saying the poet means one thing, and others saying he means something else, when really they're discussing something they have *no way of proving one way or the other*" (347e; Beresford 2005, 59; emphasis mine). He has just demonstrated the truth of this: Socrates is able to make Simonides mean whatever he wants him to mean because he can quote him from memory, detach words from their contextual arrangement within the poem, focus attention only on those sections that would seem to support his position (344b, 344e, 345c–d, 346c–e), and supply new meanings and false explanations for the terms and concepts that don't. According to such a method, there is no limit or measure to what Socrates, or any other sophist, can force Simonides to mean.[24] His poem is little more than raw material that can be contorted to display the interpreter's cleverness.[25] This display is not only a parody of sophistic methods; it is a demonstration of the epistemic crisis of Protagorean thought according to which any and every postulate can be contradicted, including the contradiction, because language can be made to mean anything a winning argument determines it means.

We're given every possible reason to be extremely dubious if not downright distrustful of Socrates when he finally says:

> "You really mustn't think," I said, "that I have any aim in asking you all these questions beyond a simple desire to investigate; to investigate all aspects of being good, especially what on earth being good exactly is. And that's because I'm sure that getting clear on that would be the best way to get to the bottom of the problem you and I have had this long, drawn-out discussion over—whether or not being good is something people can be taught—with me claiming it isn't and you claiming it is." (359e–361a; Beresford 2005, 79)

These lines ought to be unsettling for anyone who aims to exonerate Socrates or views him as a mouthpiece for Plato's doctrine. Given what has come before, Socrates's claims of sincerity are worse than an outright lie—they are an eristic ploy to gain the trust of the audience at Callias's house by claiming not to be behaving eristically.

Conclusion

It is no coincidence that the dispute with Protagoras in this dialogue and the struggle with Protagoras's doctrines in the *Theaetetus* close on such a similar note. The *Protagoras* closes with Socrates articulating the need for a fixed standard of measurement for their contrasting *logoi*, and the *Theaetetus* closes with him articulating the need for an explicit theory of *logos*. Just as in the *Theaetetus*, Socrates's attempt in the *Protagoras* is unsuccessful.

At the end of the *Protagoras*, Socrates (again) proposes dialectic (*dialegesthai*; 347e–348c) as a remedy for their unlimited and unmeasured interpretation. He promises that dialectic—not literary interpretation—would allow them to "just engage with one another through their own ideas, making their own claims, and testing and defending them in turn. . . . I think we should shelve the poets and make our claims to one another on our own, through our own ideas, investigating the real world and examining *ourselves*" (348a; Beresford 2005 59; emphasis translator's). But we are meant to be dubious of this promise, and not only because Socrates quotes Homer immediately after denouncing poetic interpretation (348c–d).

We are meant to distrust the promise of dialectic precisely because it is the same method that Socrates has insisted they use from the beginning, because their use of dialectic does nothing to stem Socrates's unvirtuous interpretation of Simonides, and because even after they strip their dialectic method of all poetic interpretation, Socrates's eristic motivations and antilogical techniques persist unreformed. As the remainder of the dialogue demonstrates, despite the fact that they agree to go back, as it were, to the "original questions . . . to start again from the beginning" (349a; Beresford 2005, 60), and to consider the question of virtue without the ancillary discussion of poetry, Socrates carries on in his eristic striving. In the discussion of various virtues ("knowledge," "good sense," "bravery," etc.), pleasure, pain, good, and bad in the second half of the dialogue (349b–360e), he misrepresents Protagoras's views (349d), affirms the consequent (350c), uses a fallacy of four terms (350d–e), and equivocates over the terms *pleasure*, *pain*, *good*, and *bad* (355c–356a). In both the dialectical discussion of Prodicus's poem and the one that follows, Socrates aims to score eristic points against Protagoras (359a), to quibble over definitions (359c–e), to twist Protagoras's words (359e), and, finally, to defeat Protagoras over a minor point, a passing remark about bravery, and then rub his nose in his defeat (360d).[26] The consequence of these antilogical techniques is that, by the end of the dialogue, Plato has made Socrates defeat his own position taken up in the *Gorgias* (here assumed by Protagoras) and assume instead the position of Callicles.[27] Plato does not allow this to escape our notice, pointing out how Socrates ends the dialogue the way Protagoras began it, whereas Protagoras ends where Socrates began (361a–c).[28] Socrates and Protagoras alike end up in antilogical positions, driven to embrace views they do not hold because of the way the eristic contour of their dialectic has shaped their *logos*.

Although Socrates admits the question hasn't been answered and must be investigated again (361c), this dialogue is not, in fact, aporetic, since its professed goal (determining whether virtue can be taught) is not the actual goal. The actual goal is defeating Protagoras, as is made apparent by many dramatic markers in the text. Just as in the *Euthydemus*, their discourse ends not in a discovery of *logos alêthês* but in applause. Socrates claims that Simonides, "who had philosophical pretensions of his own, realized that if he could knock down this saying, like someone knocking out a world-famous wrestler, and get the better of it, he'd win that kind of fame himself among his contemporaries." In the same way, Socrates in the *Protagoras* engages in "a deliberate ploy to knock [Protagoras] off [his] perch" (343b–c; Beresford 2005, 51; translation modified) in order to win the acclaim of those in attendance. The investigation ends in a stalemate of *antilogos*: "Protagoras is eager to bring this humiliating experience to a close, without having to undergo the further humiliation of openly contradicting either what he said previously or what now seems to have been proved" (Denyer 2008, 201; 360d13).

Nevertheless, Socrates proposes a solution in passing: "You've just got to be a kind of expert at weighing things up" (356b; Beresford 2005; 71). As Francisco Gonzalez has pointed out, this is without a doubt an allusion to Protagoras's man-measure doctrine: Socrates is implying that "if there existed an external epistemic measure by which to judge competing accounts or speeches, disputes about what is good could be settled without any recourse to that type of dialogue in which we must, in the words of a passage from the *Republic* (348a–b), be both advocates and judges" (2014, 54).

Forecasting his struggle with Protagoras's doctrines in the *Theaetetus*, Socrates acknowledges that such a standard of measurement must be independent of how things might be made to appear through clever argumentation: "Think—wouldn't appearances [*phainomenou*] mislead us . . . ? Measuring know-how [*metrêtikê technê*], on the other hand, would cancel out the effect of those appearances [*phantasma*]; it would show us the truth, allow a person's soul to remain calm, and settled, and fixed on reality—it would save our lives" (356d–e; Beresford 2005, 72).

The myth of Prometheus demonstrates what is at stake for lacking such a science of *logos*. In the same way that Prometheus stole the fire and the *technê* of the gods, Socrates descends into the underworld in order to steal the linguistic techniques of the godlike Protagoras. But as both the myth and Socrates's discourse demonstrate, this does not correct the error of failing to think ahead in the first place, or right the problems that are incurred by failing to use the proper technique in the proper way and at the proper time, which, in the case of verbal debate, later rhetorical theories would dictate. Just as people armed with fire and *technê* "soon came up with words for things and formed articulate speech and invented shelters, clothes, shoes and bedding, and worked out how to grow their own food" (322a; Beresford 2005, 21), so Socrates—armed on the fly with sophistic ability—is able to invent new meanings for the poem and innovate its content. Nevertheless, just as the people in the myth who, because of the incomplete and partial nature of their technical know-how, end up ruining themselves and one another with their unskillful applications, so Socrates ruins his own integrity by haphazard and unskillful applications of sophistic methods. Dialectic is simply not enough, as the end of the dialogue illustrates. What is needed is, in the moment of disagreement and unresolved debate, a method for weighing the rival linguistic claims of pleasure and pain, greater and lesser, bigger and smaller, near and far, long term and short term. In the absence of such a linguistic method, Socrates's dialectic cannot help but sink to sophistry.

Although the standard view is that "Plato does not take on Protagoras and his ideas because he is a sophist. Rather, [Plato] opposes the sophist *because of his ideas*" (Beresford 2009, 187), these two oppositions are not mutually exclusive. In the *Protagoras* as in the *Gorgias*, Socrates takes offense at the sophists' infiltration of Athenian political life because they go about "touring the cities like travelling salesmen, peddling their courses to anyone who wants them." In the process, they break up the traditional order and disrupt received wisdom. Plato even puts this view in the mouth of Protagoras:

> If a man is an outsider, and comes into large and powerful cities, and persuades the very best of the young men in those cities to give up spending their time with anyone else, family or friends, young or old, and to spend their time with him alone, so as to better themselves under his influence . . . well, a man who does that for a living has to watch his back. It can cause a lot of resentment, and hostility, and ill will. (316c–d; Beresford 2005, 14)

Socrates again describes the activities of the sophists during his trial: people like Gorgias, Protagoras, Hippias, and Prodicus are "perfectly capable of going into any city and actually persuading the young men to leave the company of their fellow citizens, with any of whom they can associate for nothing, and attach themselves to him, and pay money for the privilege, and be grateful into the bargain" (*Ap.* 19e–20a; Tredennick 1961, 6). The sophists detach the native sons of every town—and most important, the native sons of Athens—from their traditional network of friends and relations and fellow citizens. The native sons are stripped from their community in the same way that the dead are stripped from their families and loved ones. If the sophists "can reduce the reputation of these [philosophers], and make them of no account, they will win the prize of undisputed victory in public opinion as men of wisdom" (*Euthyd.* 305c–d; Rouse 1961, 419). The consequence of their victory has wide-ranging effects: in a democracy, the persuaded public opinion determines the fate of the polis as such. It is for this reason, perhaps, that Socrates suggests that the practice of sophistic antilogic and eristic contest should remain an exclusively private matter. He recommends that the followers of Protagoras, Euthydemus, and Dionysodorus "take care not to speak before a crowd" and never "argue with anybody else" aside from their private, fee-paying students (*Euthyd.* 304a–b; Rouse 1961, 417), lest others learn these tricks and exploit them as "frontiersmen between philosophy and politics" (*Euthyd.* 305c; Rouse 1961, 419).

The descent into the underworld seen at the outset of the dialogue serves as an apt analogy for this itinerant fellowship that destabilizes traditional relations and affiliations through its victory-oriented verbal arts. The sophists of fifth-century Athens use those arts with an eye toward winning verbal contests and teaching others to do the same. When that practice passes from the private to the public realm—from Callias's house to the assembly, as it were—it breaks relationships and dissolves the ties of family and community, not unlike death itself. This analogy only intensifies the criticism in the

Gorgias dialogue, where Plato blames above all the sophists for the death and destruction that would visit Athens through the plague and the war.

The dialectic displayed and thematized in the *Protagoras* and the *Theaetetus* is unable to separate honest from dishonest discourse, truth from falsity, perception from knowledge, seeming from being, or philosophy from sophistry. Rather, as becomes apparent in the contrasting textual interpretations displayed in these dialogues with those displayed in the *Phaedrus* and the *Republic*, the examination of the rhetorical elements of written eloquence—its arrangement, proof, purpose, methods, and language—and the development of a theoretical taxonomy to define that language are necessary for placing proper limits on the available range of interpretations. And it is only through this development of a theory of *logos*—rhetorical theory—that Plato is ultimately able to distinguish between seeming and being, and between true and false. Socrates's attempt in the *Theaetetus* to develop such a theory by giving an account of what *logos* as such is sets the direction for how dialectic must proceed if it is to be successful. Although this attempt is unsuccessful in the *Cratylus* and the *Theaetetus*, it is revisited on the following day in the *Sophist* dialogue by Theaetetus and the Eleatic Stranger while Socrates is away hearing the charges that have been brought against him.[29]

« 5 »

The Rhetoric of *Mimêsis*

Sophistic Imitation and Seeming in the *Republic*

Throughout his depictions of Protagoras himself, as well as Progatoras's doctrines and their epistemic consequences, Plato demonstrates a profound determination to develop a theory of *logos* capable of distinguishing between true and false speech (*logos alêthês* and *logos pseudês*) predicated on a deeper distinction between truth and its appearance or being and seeming. These attempts proceed in fits and starts in the *Protagoras* and the *Theaetetus*, where "Heraclitus and the Sophists make an infernal racket" (Deleuze 1995, 127), and only come to fruition in the *Republic* and *Sophist* dialogues. There, Plato's rhetorical theories of *mimêsis*, *onoma*, and *rhêma* capacitate the distinction that elsewhere is sought inconclusively. This chapter examines the first of these terms—*mimêsis*—to illuminate how, as a rhetorical theory, it forges a nascent but unfinished distinction between true and false speech. Between books 3 and 10 of the *Republic*, Plato develops two altogether new senses for the term, based on Socrates's analysis of Homer's written eloquence. These senses reinterpret *mimêsis*, which simply meant "imitation", as a kind of language (book 3) and as a kind of falseness (book 10). Although the theory of *mimêsis* does not fully delineate what constitutes false speech, it paves the way for Plato to do so in his *Sophist* dialogue.

Plato's *mimêsis* is not typically read as an important concept for the development of rhetoric or rhetorical theory in Plato's thought; indeed, the *Republic* itself is seldom considered in discussions of rhetoric and Plato.[1] This oversight exists in spite of numerous obvious parallels, most likely deliberate, between the *Republic* and the dialogue explicitly devoted to the consideration of rhetoric, the *Gorgias*. Scholars have observed, for example, that the *Gorgias* is second only to the *Republic* in its influence over politics in the West (Wardy 1996, 56). Moreover, the "unspoken theme" (Saxonhouse 1983) of the *Gorgias*—the politics of Athens and the question of justice—is the spoken theme of the *Republic*. Both dialogues contain temporal references that suspend the dramatic action over the entire course of the war with Sparta (Nails 2002, 324–27). In fact, the two dialogues mark the primary places where Plato develops a set of political views, one more "equalitarian" and the other more "totalitarian" (Popper 1963, 93). Also, the two dialogues begin in similar circumstances. In the *Gorgias*, Socrates and Chaerephon are invited into an unnamed person's house who, we infer, is wealthy, given his means to entertain the wealthy and famous Sicilian sophist Gorgias and throw a feast in his honor. The *Republic* begins similarly, with an account of Socrates being invited into the home of the wealthy Sicilian Cephalus and his son Polemarchus, who are throwing a feast during the festival celebrating the Thracian goddess Bendis in the port of Piraeus, just outside of Athens. Even more specifically, identical themes appear in both dialogues. Both directly address and attempt to define concepts of goodness and justice; both present a myth of the afterlife; both question whether verbal skill—poetic or rhetorical—is backed by knowledge; both confront the status of verbal arts as *technê*; both present a chain of being that ranks the philosopher relative to (among others) poets and sophists; and both consider the political consequences of a city's profligate acquisitiveness. Despite these and other similarities, the *Republic* contains no explicit discussion of rhetoric.

This fact alone is puzzling. Since the centerpiece of the *Republic* concerns the education and training of the city's guardians, it is remarkable that the educational programs of the sophists, including their arts of rhetoric, are conspicuously absent from the dialogue.[2] Where we might expect such a discussion—in the portions that deal most directly with education—we find instead Socrates's protracted discussion of poets, poetry, and, above all, *mimêsis*, "that most baffling of all words in his philosophic vocabulary" (Havelock [1963] 1998, 20). It is a term that has long held a place of profound importance and influence in almost every mode of humanist inquiry aside from rhetoric, including but not limited to literary theory, performance theory, theories of art, not to mention philosophy.[3] *Mimêsis* is commonly viewed first and foremost as an important key term in Platonic literary theory and the early history of aesthetic theory, a presumption that has proliferated attempts either to redeem or dismiss Plato's disparaging remarks on poets and artists. The persistent question "How are we to make sense of the criticism of poetry in the tenth book of the *Republic*?" has plagued "the finest of scholars from antiquity to the present" (Mitscherling 2009, 20).[4] The role of Socrates's rhetorical criticism—that is, the production of a theoretical vocabulary through the analysis of a model of written eloquence—in the emergence of the key concept of *mimêsis* has not yet been brought to bear on these scholarly investigations.

For figures like Gilles Deleuze, Jacques Derrida, and others, Plato's concept of *mimêsis* is much more than a critique of art and artists. It is hegemonic in the history of ideas, forming the very architecture of metaphysics in the West and the blueprint by which Platonism would come to dominate (if not "blight") the whole history of Western philosophy, wherein *what is* is defined precisely as that which is set apart from the thing that imitates, represents, or otherwise comes after (and is therefore secondary to) *what is*.[5] As Derrida memorably framed the problem: "This order will appear to be contested, even inverted, in the course of history, and on several occasions. But never have the absolute distinguishability between imitated and imitator, and the anteriority of the first over the second, been displaced by any metaphysical system.... All these derivative oppositions send us back to the same root" (Derrida 1981b, 192). It is in no small part the aim of Deleuze's masterwork *Difference and Repetition* to overcome this blueprint for thought so that difference may be grasped for itself outside the frame of *mimêsis*. The task of philosophy—"eliminating all presuppositions" (1995, 129)—cannot be carried out if it does not overcome the deeper presuppositions regarding what constitutes thought as such. Thought as such, Deleuze insists, is a by-product of "the discourse of the representative." According to this discourse, which dominates Western philosophy, "thought has an affinity with the true; it formally possesses the true and wants the true" (1995, 131). The "discourse of the representative" and thought's "affinity with the true" are the unequivocal by-products of Plato's important distinction "between the original and the image" (1995, 126). In other words, Deleuze regards Plato's theory of *mimêsis* as the seminal formulation of the structure of thought itself in the West.

Despite the unequivocal prioritization of Plato's *mimêsis* in the history of ideas, it has yet to be understood how, precisely, methods of fifth- and fourth-century BCE rhetorical theory informed this theory, how that theory was implicated in Plato's larger fixation on routing the sophists, and what this might indicate about the range of applications for Plato's theory of *mimêsis*. My analysis of *mimêsis* qua rhetorical theory indicates that the concept alone is incomplete as a template of Platonist metaphysics. Rather, the *mimêsis* of the *Republic* is a partial theory of *logos*, a partial definition of falsehood, but not a complete definition of false *logos* as such, and therefore is not (yet) a complete structure of thought that bears its full "affinity with the true." Interpretations of Plato's *mimêsis* must be extricated from the metaphysical speculations of the middle books of the *Republic*, since, I argue in this chapter, numerous indicators in the text suggest their incompatibility. I propose that interpretations of Plato's *mimêsis* should be detached from the middle book's analogies of the sun, the line, and the cave, which are among the most important source materials for Plato's so-called metaphysics and his theory of the Forms. I argue instead that *mimêsis* ought to be interpreted in conjunction with Plato's theories of *onoma* and *rhêma*, which Plato explicitly links to the *mimêsis* of the sophists in the *Sophist* dialogue. Together, they constitute a complete theory of false *logos* and, as such, a means of overcoming the influence of the sophists.

In this chapter, I suggest that Plato's theory of *mimêsis* is developed first and foremost as a rhetorical theory that attempts to distinguish between two different types of language, which Socrates identifies through the explicit analysis of Homer's "written eloquence" (Cole 1991, 112). In the first section I define this nascent rhetorical theory, which begins in books 2 and 3, and show how Plato transforms the meaning of the term from its common understanding (imitative actions or ways of sounding or speaking) to an uncommon meaning (imitative language). In the second section I explain how Plato then further stretches the meaning in book 10 from *mimêsis*-as-language to *mimêsis*-as-such, which includes any kind of copy-making. In the latter case, he uses *mimêsis* as the foundation for his understanding of falsehood, which will be more fully developed in the *Sophist*. In the third section I address an important barrier to properly comprehending Plato's rhetorical theory of *mimêsis*: namely, the barrier of the middle books. The application of the metaphysics of the middle books to the theory of *mimêsis* is perhaps among the most entrenched interpretive axioms that dictate Plato's theory of *mimêsis*. Critics almost ubiquitously presume that Plato's analogies of the sun, the line, and the cave function as an interpretive lens for *mimêsis* (and vice versa). I suggest that these analogies should be understood as having a related but nevertheless a distinct aim from Plato's rhetorical theory of *mimêsis*. While Plato's rhetorical theory of *mimêsis* was indispensible for the development of Plato's metaphysics, it was not (yet) founded on it, and it was not alone sufficient for its foundation.

Mimêsis as Language

There is a longstanding debate over the inconsistent use of the term *mimêsis* in the *Republic*. In brief, as several scholars have noted, Plato seems to use the term *mimêsis* in profoundly different senses in the early (books 2–3) and late (book 10) discussions of poetry, as well as in other dialogues such as the *Laws* and the *Cratylus*.[6] In the first discussion, *mimêsis* is confined to poetic language, while in the second discussion it encompasses not only pictorial images but all forms of representation. I suggest that the two senses are not as far from each other as they may seem, given that the latter sense is made possible only through the method of rhetorical critique executed in the former. In books 2 and 3, Socrates links *mimêsis* to the language of the poets, which as I demonstrate was an innovative and irregular application of the word. It is only after Socrates breaks new ground with this meaning that he is able to consider *mimêsis* in the context of other forms of "making," or *poiêsis*.

Undergirding both discussions is the same overriding concern with falseness that haunts Socrates's considerations of Protagoras and his doctrines in the *Protagoras*, the *Theaetetus*, the *Cratylus*, and the *Euthydemus*. In the first treatment of *mimêsis*, Socrates introduces the topic of the guardians' education, and returns yet again to his abiding concern over *pseudos logos*. He splits education into two categories: gymnastics for the body and music for the *psychê* (376e). Musical education includes speaking [*logous*], which can further be divided into true and false speeches or tales [*logôn de ditton eidos, to men alêthes, pseudos d' heteron*] (376e). Because in early education "we start by telling children stories which are, by and large, untrue [*pseudos*], though they contain elements of truth [*alêthê*]" (377a; Waterfield 2008, 71), Socrates wants to begin their conversation by considering the work of the story-makers [*muthon poiêsôsin*].

This is a new context for Socrates's ruminations on false speech, as his interlocutor Adeimatus's bewilderment dramatically confirms (377a–d). As we have seen, where Socrates struggles with Protagorean thought in other dialogues, interlocutors readily admit that there is such a thing as false speech, and they automatically associate falsehood with lies, incorrect postulates, or contradictions; but they nevertheless struggle to define what precisely makes those postulates and contradictions false. In this case, by contrast, Socrates introduces a new line of attack by considering the stories of Homer and Hesiod, and makes the radical suggestion that these grand works—the very repository of Greek custom, ethics, and the unequivocal "political and social necessity . . . of the 'best Greek polities'" (Havelock [1963] 1998, 125)—might just have been little more than "untrue stories" (377d; Waterfield 2008, 72), and Homer might just have used "written words to give a distorted image of the nature of the gods and heroes, just as a painter might produce a portrait which completely fails to capture the likeness of the original" (377e; Waterfield 2008, 72). Socrates proposes they consider those stories with the understanding that they will "accept any good story they write, but reject the others" (377c; Waterfield 2008, 71).

Socrates's discourse at this point is a demonstration of what Thomas Cole describes as "the rhetorician's preoccupation with controlling the medium of transmission" (1991, x). This preoccupation is possible only, Cole contends, through the availability of a "written eloquence"—"that is, a body of prose texts which might be read or delivered verbatim and still suggest the excitement, atmosphere, and commitment of a spontaneous oral performance or debate. . . . Without such texts there would have been no satisfactory data base on which to conduct the detailed, precise analysis of the verbal medium that is characteristic of rhetoric" (1991, x). Through an analysis of written eloquence—an examination of texts outside of the context of their performance—the analyzer is able to develop an "analytical metalanguage" to describe the devices that inhere in the language and that function as "general principles governing the use of discourse" (Cole 1991, 92). Socrates's and Adeimantus's discussion of Homer proceeds in precisely this manner: it is an analysis of the verbatim text of the *Iliad* from which they derive the analytical metalanguage of *mimêsis* that implicitly governs the discourse.

Their analysis of Homer's eloquence is guided by the desire to root out falsehood, but it is apparent from their discussion that this does not refer to stories that simply did not happen, or what we would now call "fiction." Rather, Socrates wants to root out what he calls the "true falsehood" [*alêthôs pseudos*]: "the state of not-knowing caused by falsehood in the *psychê*. I mean, a spoken lie is only an imitation [*mimêma*] and subsequent reflection of the mental condition" (382b–c; Waterfield 2008, 78; translation modified). It is this state of epistemic deception that Socrates wants to purge from poetry, and as his analysis reveals, doing so requires consideration of the actual words of the poem.

Plato does not allow the writtenness of the text to escape our notice. From 379d to 393a, Plato has Socrates provide nearly forty exact quotes from Homer. He critically analyzes how words of the poem exert profound power over the hearers, how they work their way into the hearers' *psychê* in a way that is "ineradicable and permanent" (378d; Waterfield 2008, 73). They reproduce their own psychic nonknowing in the hearer by provoking physical and psychological effects—effects like cowardice, fear, despair, sexual desire, greed, and other strong psychic responses. For this reason, Socrates suggests, "We'll implore Homer and the rest of the poets not to get cross if we strike [*diagraphômen*] these and all similar lines from their works. We'll explain that it's not because the lines are not good poetry and don't give pleasure to most people; on the contrary, the better poetry they are, the more they are to be kept from the ears of children and men who are to be autonomous and to be more afraid of losing this freedom than of death" (387b; Waterfield 2008, 80–81). These references to "striking lines," verbatim quotes, and the critical distance of the analysis all explicitly indicate that Socrates is thinking of it as a written text.[7]

It is this account of the psychic dangers of poetry, another (albeit different) effect and manifestation of false speech, that frames the question of *mimêsis*. And yet Socrates's turn to the language of poetry in this context is thoroughly disorienting to his interlocutor. When Socrates proposes, "The next thing we should look at, in my opinion, is diction [*lexis*]. Then we'll have considered not only what is said but how it's said [*a te lekteon kai hôs lekteon*]" (392c; Waterfield 2008, 87; translation modified.), Adeimantus responds with utter confusion. He says, "I don't understand what you're getting at here" (392c–d; Waterfield 2008, 87). Adeimantus's response indicates dramatically that thinking of poetry as "a way of speaking" [*hôs lekteon*] is disorienting and does not naturally fit with the lived poetic experience.

It is in an effort to clarify this misunderstanding for his interlocutor that Socrates draws the famous distinction between *diêgêsis* and *mimêsis*: "Isn't everything said by storytellers or poets . . . pure narrative [*diêgêsei*], an imitative narrative [*mimêseôs*], or both?" (392d; Waterfield 2008, 87–88; translation modified). What to a modern reader is a longstanding truism of literary theory—the distinction between narration and discourse—is for Socrates's interlocutor so novel a concept that it can scarcely be grasped:

"I'm still finding this very obscure" (392d; Waterfield 2008, 88), Adeimantus rejoins. His confusion both indicates and emphasizes that Socrates's proposal to consider the poets' words not as a performed life-world, or even as words and phrases, but as a particular way of using words, language, and diction in itself marks a new and unfamiliar concept of what poetry is and can be.[8] It is not merely tales that are false or performances that evoke strong emotion to create a state of epistemic deception; rather, it is a certain manner of using language—a technique that can be defined through an empirical study of language *as* language.

There is no consensus over whether Socrates's discussion of *mimêsis* in book 3 constitutes a standard or unusual sense of the term. *Mimêsis* was a rare topic in the literature prior to Plato, and it is only with Plato that it is theorized explicitly for the first time (Halliwell 2002, 122). An analysis of the prior literature indicates that earlier uses cannot fully account for Plato's use of the term in his critique of poetry.[9] Where the verb *mimeisthai* ("to imitate") and its cognates appear in the early literature, it refers to a general practice of following or emulating the example of a model, such as when a child's speech patterns or gestures simulate or reproduce a parent's voice or body. The most common uses for the term had to do with neither poetry (book 3) nor painting and visual arts (book 10) but with the general concept of following an example or precedent, either good or bad, of an ancestor, a god, a tyrant, a culture, a teacher, a leader, and the like.[10] In other words, the common meaning of the term should not be an unusual description of the performance of a poet who simulates the voice and body of other people. Alexander Nehamas offers several examples to illustrate this compatibility. He cites the *Hymn to Delian Apollo* (l.163), according to which the Delian maidens "know how to *imitate* the voice and dance of all people" (Nehamas 1982, 56). Similarly, Aeschylus uses the term to refer to imitating the sound of a voice: "We will put forward a Parnassian accent, imitating the sound of the Phocian dialect" (Nehamas 1982, 56; *Cho.* l.564). These and other examples (Hdt. 4.16; Thuc. 1.95.3; and Democr. DK B39; Nehamas 1982, 56–57) illustrate that the activity of sounding or behaving like another person were common uses for *mimeisthai* and related terms. Since these activities could easily be ascribed to poetic performance, it should not be disorienting to Plato's audience or Socrates's interlocutor to discuss *mimêsis* in the context of a poetic performance. In addition to those supplied by Nehamas, several other examples similarly concur that the terms referred to sounding like (Pind., *Pythian Ode* 12.1) or adopting the mannerisms of a person or animal (Thuc. 7.63.3; Eur., *Rhe.* 201) in ways that might accurately describe what the poet does in the execution of a poetic performance.

Socrates's first discussion of poetry-as-imitation, beginning at the end of book 2 and stretching into book 3, causes such confusion for his interlocutor Adeimantus because Socrates is not using the term to refer to the poet's performance but to how he uses language (*hôs lekteon*) in the poetry itself. In his theory of *mimêsis*, Plato treats the text of Homer as though there were an "absolute separability of a speaker's message from the method used to transmit it" (Cole 1991, 12). It is this separability that poses such an intellectual difficulty for Adeimantus. Homer, by Plato's rendering, is not merely transmitting a "'non-rhetorical' . . . message and nothing more: a story plainly told" (Cole 1991, 12). Rather, Homer's discourse is shaped by a theoretical distinction between *diêgêsis* and *mimêsis*, or narration and discourse. Homer's discourse in this sense is rhetorical: his use of *mimêsis* ensures that his "message is better received . . . or more eagerly acted upon because this speaker moves his hearers" (Cole 1991, 12–13) through his deployment of mimetic discourse.

This can be seen in Socrates's analysis of the actual words of the *Iliad*. In the same way that, in the *Phaedrus* dialogue, Socrates reads the first lines of Phaedrus's speech to initiate his critique, here again he begins his critique of Homer by quoting the first lines of the *Iliad*:

> You know the very beginning of the *Iliad*, where Homer has Chryses ask Agamemnon to release his daughter and Agamemnon gets annoyed, and Chryses doesn't get his way and so calls on his god to curse the Greeks? . . . Well, as you know, Homer starts by speaking in his own voice and doesn't try to lead us astray by pretending that anyone else is the speaker; this goes up to the lines "He implored all the Greeks, but especially their leaders, the two sons of Atreus" [*Il.* 1.15]. Next, however, he speaks in Chryses' voice and tries his very hardest to make us believe that it isn't Homer who is speaking, but the old priest. And the same method of composition is employed throughout nearly all his narrative of events in Troy and Ithaca and in the *Odyssey* in general. (392e–393b; Waterfield 2008, 88)

Socrates has divided Homer's discourse into two types: "speaking in his own voice" and "speaking in Chryses's voice." He then uses this simple division to propose a theoretical division between the two types of language through which Homer transmits his story:

> When he assumes someone else's voice to make a speech, don't you think that on those occasions he does his very best to adapt his own style to whoever he tells us is about to do the talking? . . . Now, to adapt oneself—one's voice or one's appearance—to someone else is to imitate [*mimeisthai*] that person, isn't it? . . . So this turns out to be a case of Homer and the rest of the poets composing their narrative [*diêgêsin*] through imitation [*mimêseôs*]. (393c; Waterfield 2008, 88; translation modified)[11]

In his attempt to show Adeimantus his meaning, Socrates attaches the poet's performative imitation in voice and body—the common sense of the term—to the actual words and lines of Homer's poem. Given the common use of the verbal root of *mimêsis* to describe the work of poets and actors who conform their speech and their behavior so that they sound like and imitate another person, we must infer that what is meant to be confusing for Adeimantus is not that he refers to the *poet's imitative performance*, but to the form of the *poet's language* (*hôs lekteon*).

By drawing Adeimantus's attention away from the poet's voice and performance and to the language itself (not to what's said but how it's said [392c, 394c]), Socrates is emphasizing in a novel way how the powerful effect of poetry stems from a material, empirical source: the form of the poets' *language* as such. It arises from a certain type of diction that can be distinguished from other sorts of diction: *mimetic language* as opposed to *mimetic actions*, and discourse as opposed to narrative. When a poet imitates, he does so through recourse to a kind of language that can be bracketed from other kinds of language. What has happened, in effect, is that Plato has called our attention away from the performing poet and toward the strategic form of his verbal text. It's not just any language but the language of *mimêsis* that poses the most psychic dangers for those who hear it (394e–396e)—it has a particular ability to invade the *psychê* and reproduce the psychic state of the person being imitated. When the poet, standing before his audience, "does all that he can to make us believe that he is not Homer, but the aged priest Chryses himself" (393b; Waterfield 2008, 88), his hearers believe him, and it is in that state of deep credulity that those strong feelings of pity, fear, anger, and so on, invade the hearers' *psychê*. A person of bad character would not see the psychic harm that imitative poetry might do, Socrates explains. On the contrary, "the less good he is, the less he'll be inclined to omit any of the narrative and regard anything as degrading. We'll end up with someone who's prepared to imitate anything and everything, and to do so seriously and publicly" (397a; Waterfield 2008, 93; translation modified). It will not be made clear until later—in book 10 and in the *Sophist*—why this willingness to "imitate anything and everything . . . seriously and publicly" is so very dangerous. In this description, Plato means for us to be thinking of the dangers not of poetry but sophistry, as will be made clear.

The pedagogic technique that Socrates uses here is the same one that would develop the very "repertory of what later came to be called rhetoric": the "systematic collection of precepts" based on an analysis of written eloquence and "the single most important vehicle of rhetorical instruction" (Cole 1991, 80–81). The teacher of eloquence is bound to offer examples of good oratory, but cannot necessarily offer the analytical metalanguage to explain how it is effective or why: "Something rather different and more complex is involved when one is recording, not the art itself, but the concepts and principles on which it is based" (Cole 1991, 91). Plato's metalanguage of *mimêsis* is accounting for a phenomenon of discourse that had not yet been named, and denominating the poet's profound power to control the psychic fate of his hearers.[12] Adeimantus's confusion may be accounted for by the fact that this term instantiates precisely this sort of complex, sophisticated, theoretical taxonomy. It does not refer to the practical activity of imitating, acting like, or sounding like another person. Instead, it is a term of art, intended to theoretically define a linguistic function that heretofore had not been given a name.[13]

Mimêsis as Falseness

When Socrates brings the conversation back around to poetry and *mimêsis* in book 10, his idiosyncratic use of *mimêsis*, developed through his discussion of Homer in books 2 and 3, undergoes further transformation. In fact, the contrast is so stark that some suggest the prior discussion of *mimêsis* is entirely irrelevant to the later one.[14] Whereas in book 3 the term is localized to a particular type of diction or way of using language that signals a poet's dramatic impersonation, in book 10 it enlarges to a "wider sense. . . . The nearest English word is 'representation'" (Cornford 1941, 323). As I discuss below, it is this wider sense that becomes problematically "universal in scope and indeterminate in application" (Golden 1975, 120).[15] In this section, I examine the hidden link between the two definitions of *mimêsis*: the double meaning of *poiêsis*, which refers both to poetry and to made things. I argue that Socrates exploits this double meaning so that he can define *mimêsis* as both a form of language and a manifestation of falseness. He drops several hints in this discussion to suggest that the sophists are never far from his mind; the loose affiliation of imitation, language, falsehood, and the sophists only hinted at here will culminate in the final denunciation of the sophists in the *Sophist* dialogue.

To commence the second discussion of *mimêsis,* Socrates summarizes the previous conversation with Adeimantus as though they had concluded they would totally ban any imitative poetry from their ideal community. He reasons that "its total unacceptability is even clearer, in my opinion, now that we've distinguished the different aspects of the *psychê*. . . . This whole genre of poetry deforms its audience's minds, unless they have the antidote [*pharmakon*], which is recognition of what this kind of poetry is actually like" (595a–b; Waterfield 2008, 344; translation modified). This preface to the discussion unequivocally indicates that Socrates views the second discussion of *mimêsis* as though it were (1) confluent with previous discussion of *mimêsis* as imitative language; (2) disjointed from the middle books' discussions of goodness, morality, and the different aspects of the *psychê*; and (3) intended to raise self-conscious understanding of how *mimêsis* deforms the *psychê,* such that there might be an antidote against that deformation. The disjunction of the final discussion of *mimêsis* from the middle books is emphasized by the abrupt manner in which Socrates changes the topic of discussion—an abruptness that has led several scholars to view the tenth book as a later addition, or at least as evidence of sloppy writing on Plato's part.[16] I suggest, by contrast, that these three points are hermeneutic indicators that Plato wants his readers to uncover the unapparent link between the two discussions of *mimêsis,* to avoid the misleading similarities between *mimêsis* and the middle books, and to consider what, precisely, an awareness of *mimêsis* is intended to provide an antidote for.

Socrates revisits the subject under the auspices of seeking a broader definition not of *mimêsis*-as-language, but of *mimêsis*-as-such. This is a signature move, "a typical Socratic request for a unitary definition" (Halliwell 1988, 108), not unlike what is displayed in the *Gorgias,* the *Protagoras,* and the *Sophist* where Socrates seeks unitary definitions of *rhêtorikê* and *sophistîkê.* To reinitiate the conversation, Socrates asks Glaucon, "Can you tell me what *mimêsis* basically is? You see, I don't quite understand its point myself" (595c; Waterfield 2008, 345; translation modified).

In order to develop a general concept of *mimêsis* that is not tied to a particular example of mimetic language, Socrates turns—on the basis of the phonetic relationship between "poetry" and "making" (*poiêsis*)—to everyday objects or "made things": "Shall we get the enquiry going by drawing on familiar ideas? Our usual position is, as you know, that any given plurality of things which have a single name constitutes a single idea [*eidos*]. . . . Would it be all right with you if we said that there were, for instance, lots of beds and tables?" (596a–b; Waterfield 2008, 345, translation modified).[17]

This turn may seem disorienting to us, given that beds and tables seem entirely irrelevant to poetry, but to a Greek-speaking reader of Plato, there would have been a natural connection between things like beds and tables and what we would now call poetry—a point that is perhaps demonstrated by the fact that Glaucon expresses no confusion over the matter.[18] Our terms for *poetry* and *poets*, which it is well known are derived from the Greek terms *poiêsis* and *poiêtês*, would not have seemed to Glaucon conceptually estranged from beds and tables, since *poiêtês* and *poiêsis* would have referred more immediately to craftsmanship and the general concepts of creating, making, and doing, things that are made, and people who make things—things like beds and tables, as well as poems. Socrates's unusual affiliation between *mimêsis* and the *poiêsis* of Homer has cleared the way for him to consider connections between *mimêsis* and *poiêsis* generally.

Beds and tables serve as good examples of *poiêsis*, he explains, because they are made objects: "The manufacture of either of these items of furniture involves the craftsman [*dêmiourgos*] looking to the type [*idean*] and then making [*poiei*] the beds or tables (or whatever) which we use. The point is that the type [*idean*] itself is not manufactured [*dêmiourgie*] by any craftsman. How could it be?" (596b; Waterfield 2008, 345). In this example, Plato uses "to craft" (*dêmiourgein*) and "to make" (*poiêsein*) interchangeably, indicating that the analogy to beds and tables is relevant to their earlier discussion because of the double meaning of *poiêsis*, which refers both to poetry and to any made thing. In the second discussion, Socrates introduces the concept that behind these particular made things (bed_1, bed_2, bed_3, etc.) is the idea_{bed}. The idea is the very thing that links together and defines these diverse items *as* beds. The idea is beyond the reach of making.[19]

Socrates then introduces a hypothetical craftsman who could make not only a bed or a table, but any material thing on earth—a description that evokes both his earlier description of the dangerous imitative poets and, it just so happens, the marvelous sophists:

> There's another kind of craftsman too. I wonder what you think of him. . . . He makes everything—all the items which every single manufacturer makes. . . . It's not just a case of his being able to manufacture all the artefacts there are: every plant too, every creature (himself included), the earth, the heavens, gods, and everything in the heavens and in Hades under the earth—all these are made and created by this one man! . . . Don't you realize that you yourself could, under certain circumstances, create all these things? (596b–d; Waterfield 2008, 345–46).

To explain how the craftsman could accomplish such a feat, Socrates introduces the infamous analogy to mirrors and paintings, which will fill out his ultimate definition of *mimêsis*. The quickest way to accomplish this kind of omnipotent manufacturing, he says, "is to get hold of a mirror and carry it around with you everywhere. You'll soon be creating everything I mentioned a moment ago—the sun and the heavenly bodies, the earth, yourself and all other creatures" (596d–e; Waterfield 2008, 346).

The similarity of the descriptions at 397a and 596b–d is neither incidental nor accidental. Plato is hinting that we as readers ought to connect these descriptions of the all-powerful imitator to the sophists: he even has Adeimantus respond to Socrates's description of a craftsman who could make anything by exclaiming, "An altogether wonderful sophist!" (596d; my translation); almost immediately following this, Socrates explicitly compares Homer to the sophists Protagoras and Prodicus (600c–d).[20] It is not yet clear why he is subtly linking *mimêsis* to the work of the sophists. The parallels are a literary foreshadowing that the rhetorical theory of *mimêsis* will be a critical tool in Plato's final siege on sophistry in his *Sophist* dialogue.

When Glaucon points out that this kind of *mimêsis* would merely be producing the *appearance* (*phainomena*, 596e) and not the things themselves, Socrates admits, "That's a good point. . . . I mean, that's presumably the kind of craftsman a painter is. Yes?" (596e; Waterfield 2008, 346). It is only at this point that Socrates finally and explicitly attempts to explain the relationship between this example and the definition of *mimêsis* he is seeking: "Now, what about this imitator we're trying to understand? Shall we see if these examples help us? . . . Well, we've got these three beds. First, there's the real one, and we'd say, I imagine, that it is the product of divine craftsmanship. . . . Then there's the one the joiner makes. . . . And then there's the one the painter makes" (597b; Waterfield 2008, 347; translation modified.). God, he concludes, makes *the* bed, the craftsman makes *a* bed, but the painter makes *no* bed because, as Glaucon puts it, "the most suitable thing to call him would be an imitator of the others' creations" (597e; Waterfield 2008, 348; translation modified). Socrates responds that the term *imitation* must be reserved for "things which are, in fact, the third generation away from *phusis* [*phuseôs*]" (597e; Waterfield 2008, 348; translation modified). He then applies the definition back to poetry: "The same goes for the tragic playwrights, then, since they're imitators: they're the third generation away from the throne of truth [*basileôs kai tês alêtheias*], *and so are all other imitators*" (597e; Waterfield 2008, 348; translation modified, emphasis mine). Here we have arrived at a notion of *mimêsis*-as-falseness, but we do not yet see how this notion of falseness might assist Socrates's other inquiries into *pseudos logos*.

The outcome of these two discussions is this: in the first discussion, Plato has, in a novel move, attached the ancient concept of *mimêsis* to a certain technique of language used by the poets. On the basis of a double meaning for *poiêsis*, he has cleared a path for himself to introduce further associations between *mimêsis* and other forms of *poiêsis*. These associations give him the interpretive room he needs to be able to define *mimêsis* as a form of falseness—it is removed from both truth and nature. In short, he has executed crucial spadework for the developments to come: he has defined *mimêsis* as a form of language and as a form of falseness, and he has subtly associated both with the activities of the sophists. All that remains is for him to graft these three notions into a single definition, and he will have defined the sophists as cultivators of false language. This is the exclusive goal of his *Sophist* dialogue.

The Dubious Metaphysics of *Mimêsis*

The analysis above supplies scant evidence for a metaphysical interpretation of Plato's *mimêsis*. Is the "idea" in the craftsman's head really an eternal, metaphysical form? Is this incessant copy-making truly the bottom part of the "hierarchies of a representative theology" (Deleuze 1995, 265)? Whence the unassailable metaphysics of *mimêsis*? Richard McKeon describes the subordination of imitation by means of an implicit metaphysics, which has long inflected interpretations of Plato's use of the term:

> In its expansion and contraction, the word "imitation" indicates the lesser term of the proportion of being to appearance: if God is, the universe is

> an imitation; if all things are, shadows and reflections are imitations; if the products of man's handicraft are, his representations of them are imitations. If imitation is to be avoided, it is because of the danger of imitating, through error, ignorance, or falsehood, that which is not or that which is less than it might be or is less than that which imitates it. (1951, 154)

In other words, the term *mimêsis,* although initially developed as a rhetorical theory, ultimately gives way to a metaphysical distinction between being and seeming, truth and appearance, reality and its imitation. How? And why?

In this section I briefly summarize reasons for the view that the metaphysical definition of *mimêsis* is too hastily "transcendentalized"—a point that has been elaborated by Stephen Halliwell in his 1988 commentary on the *Republic* 10. I summarize Halliwell's interpretation and offer additional textual analysis in support of that interpretation. While it is accurate to suggest that Plato's final definition of *mimêsis* casts significant doubt on appearances, the full-fledged transcendentalization of *mimêsis* relies on a problematic conflation of the so-called "metaphysics" of the middle books of the *Republic* (especially the analogies of the sun, the divided line, and the cave) and the definition of *mimêsis* offered in book 10. Despite structural and lexical parallels, these concepts should not be collapsed, given the fact that, on the one hand, the rhetorical purposes of these two sections of the text are so strikingly different from each other, and, on the other hand, the tentative and incomplete nature of the analogies renders them inapplicable to the theory of *mimêsis.* By dissociating Plato's *mimêsis* from his metaphysics, I clear the way for its association with *onoma* and *rhêma,* which I discuss in the following chapter, and for its proper understanding as a theory of rhetoric.

Halliwell notes that in the second discussion, "mimesis is now judged to be *inherently* false or fake, rather than simply capable of conveying falsehoods" (1988, 5), and, he contends, this full indictment of *mimêsis* gains its gravitas from the metaphysics developed in the intervening books. He argues that, although the whole passage at 598 and following is structurally reminiscent of the subordination of images in the metaphor of the "divided line" (book 6.509d) and the opposition of shadows and reality in the allegory of the cave (book 7), these parts of the text should not be conflated into a seamless whole. The discussion of *mimêsis* in book 10 may "echo those earlier sections," but its terms are "adapted from . . . the metaphysics of the middle books" (1988, 118) and not a reproduction or continuation of the discourse. Halliwell's point is that this apparent similarity should not be mistaken for a unified discourse. *Mimêsis* is not, he argues, an extension of those analogies.

In book 5, Socrates defines the task of the philosopher as an endeavor to "transcend" the vagary, contingency, and deficiency of the "plurality of manifestations" that "appear all over the place, as they become associated with actions and bodies and one another" (476a; Waterfield 2008, 196), and to seek instead "the thing itself," apart from its material manifestations (476b). Echoing his other struggles against Heraclitean atomism, he laments that manifestations are always in flux, and consequently can't be "what really is" [*ho estin*] (507b; Waterfield 2008, 233). The allegories of the sun, the divided line, and the cave are Socrates's metaphorical attempts to give an account for *what is*; in this way, metaphorical reasoning is intended to fill the gap where a science is wanting.

The analogies are offered in response to Glaucon's request in book 6 that Socrates provide a direct definition of goodness, without relying on particular manifestations of good things that are themselves in a process of becoming and flux (507d). Socrates admits that he is incapable of offering such a definition—seeking a unitary definition of the ultimate moral and epistemic category is not quite as simple as seeking a unitary definition of *rhêtorîke* or *mimêsis*. He hedges: "I'm afraid it'll be more than I can manage. . . . What I suggest, my friends, is that we forget about trying to define goodness itself for the time being. . . . However, I am prepared to talk about something which seems to me to be the child of goodness and to bear a very strong resemblance to it" (506d–e; Waterfield 2008, 233). In this description, Socrates explicitly lays out that what follows is only a metaphorical discussion of goodness—the ultimate aim of all knowledge and morality. Because he cannot define so vast a topic, he must resort to a comparative analysis.

It is only in a metaphorical discussion—not a direct or literal definition—of what goodness is as such, that Socrates presents the analogies.[21] The sun is meant to be like goodness because, in the same way that goodness is that ineffable thing that makes it possible for people to be moral and to have knowledge, the sun is the very thing that makes human perception possible: "Even if a person's eyes are capable of sight, and he's trying to use it, and what he's trying to look at is coloured, the sight will see nothing and the colours will remain unseen, surely, unless there is also present an extra third thing which is made specifically for this purpose. . . . It's what we call light"

(507d–e; Waterfield 2008, 234). In the same way that the light of the sun facilitates vision so that things might be seen, so goodness facilitates knowledge and morality: "The eye's ability to see has been bestowed upon it and channeled into it, as it were, by the sun. . . . So the sun is not to be identified with sight, but is responsible for sight and is itself within the visible realm" (508b; Waterfield 2008, 235).

At this point, Socrates makes the analogy's comparative function explicit and shows how it supplies an indirect definition of the good in itself. It is necessary to quote the passage at length to indicate precisely how far Socrates goes to insure that the components of his analogy do not get confused with one another.

> The sun is the child of goodness I was talking about, then. . . . It is a *counterpart* to its father, goodness. As goodness stands in the intelligible realm to intelligence and the things we know, so in the visible realm the sun stands to sight and the things we see. . . . When our eyes are directed towards things whose colours are no longer bathed in daylight, but in artificial light instead, then they're less effective and seem to be virtually blind, as if they didn't even have the potential for seeing clearly. . . . But when they're directed towards things which are lit up by the sun, then they see clearly and obviously do have that potential. . . .
>
> Well, here's how you can think about the mind as well. When its object is something which is lit up by truth and reality, then it has—and obviously has—intelligent awareness and knowledge. However, when its object is permeated with darkness (that is, when its object is something which is subject to generation and decay), then it has beliefs and is less effective, because its beliefs chop and change, and under these circumstances it comes across as devoid of intelligence. . . .
>
> What I'm saying is that it's goodness which gives the things we know their truth and makes it possible for people to have knowledge. It is responsible for knowledge and truth, and you should think of it as being within the intelligible realm, but you shouldn't identify it with knowledge and truth, otherwise, you'll be wrong: for all their value, it is even more valuable. In the other realm, it is right to regard light and sight as resembling the sun, but not to identify either of them with the sun; so in this realm; so in this realm *it is right to regard knowledge and truth as resembling goodness, but not to identify either of them with goodness, which should be rated even more highly.* (508b–509a; Waterfield 2008, 235–36; emphasis mine)

Socrates cannot offer a unitary definition of goodness, truth, and knowledge as such, so he suggests instead that they are *like* the sun, which illuminates all things so that they can be seen. In the same way that the sun brokers visibility (it makes sight possible and illuminates the things we see), goodness brokers intelligibility (it makes intelligence possible and illuminates the things we know). Likewise, an absence of sunlight makes things less visible, to such a degree that diminished or artificial light is indistinguishable from an impaired visual ability. In the same way, an absence of goodness makes things less knowable to such a degree that mistaking becoming for being is indistinguishable from impaired intellectual faculties.[22]

Immediately following "the simile of the sun" (509c), Socrates offers the metaphor of the divided line. As is made apparent in the dialogue, this metaphor is not independent but subordinate. That is to say, it is not a separate metaphorical definition of goodness and *what is*; rather, it is an augmentation of the previous analogy—an analogy within an analogy. Socrates proposes to convert the metaphor into, not incidentally, a geometric model: he invites Glaucon to picture the two terms of the previous analogy—the sun itself and the visible realm that the sun illuminates—"as a line cut into two unequal sections, and following the same proportion, subdivide both the section of the visible realm and that of the intelligible realm" (509d; Waterfield 2008, 237).[23]

An ambiguity arises in this metaphor when Socrates moves on to describe the divisions in the intelligible realm. At this point, Socrates no longer is using the concept of sunlight, visibility, and illumination as an analogy to explain goodness, what is, and knowledge of what is. Rather, the *phoros* of the analogy (light) collapses into its theme (goodness and knowledge of *what is*). In the original analogy of the sun, the faculty of sight (A) is to the the sun (B) just as the knowledge and morality (C) are to the good (D).

sight : the sun
{A} {B}
::
knowledge / morality : the good
{C} {D}

In the divided line, by contrast, Socrates, somewhat carelessly, transposes the two sides of this comparison onto a linear model, divided into four segments:

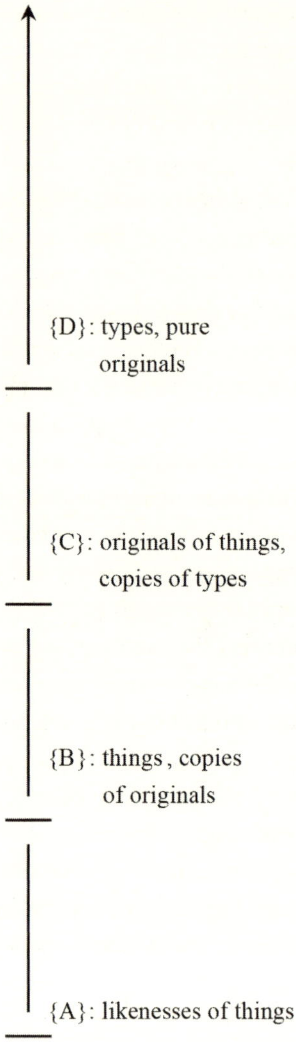

These four divisions of the line demarcate distinct zones of relative clarity and unclarity. The lowest bracket in the visible segment of the line (A) is made of "likenesses" [*eikôn*], including things like "shadows" and "reflections" [*skias* and *phantasma*], such as those that appear on the surface of water.[24] The second part of the visible segment of the line (B) consists of the things that the images in the lowest segment (A) are likenesses of: "all the flora and fauna there are in the world, and every kind of artefact too" (510a; Waterfield 2008, 237). Socrates explains the content of the lower segment of the intelligible realm (C) not as though it corresponds analogically to an element of the visible realm, but as though it were on an unbroken continuum with the visible realm. The lower segment of the intelligible realm (C) uses "those former originals as likenesses" (510b; Waterfield 2008, 238). That is, the "originals" in visible segment B serve as the "likenesses" of the first section of the intelligible segment C. Once the visible originals are taken as intelligible likenesses, one might "travel to a starting-point where nothing needs to be taken for granted, and it has no involvement with likenesses, as before, but makes its approach by means of types alone, in and of themselves" (D) (510b; Waterfield 2008, 238).

Chaïm Perelman and Lucie Olbrechts-Tyteca have analyzed the argumentative effect of the transformation from analogy to example or illustration: "In the ordinary course [of an analogy], the *phoros* is better known than the theme of which it should clarify the structure or establish the value, either its value as a whole or the respective value of its components" (1969, 373). In this case, as Socrates has made clear, the theme of the analogy—goodness—is obscure and indescribable, so he establishes the *phoros* of the light of the sun and the things it illuminates as a way of making that less obscure and more describable. The divided line inscribes the theme and *phoros* of the analogy within the same geometric model: "When the two relations encountered belong to the same sphere, and can be subsumed under a common structure, we have not analogy but argument by example or illustration" (Perelman and Olbrechts-Tyteca 1969, 373). In this case, the elements of the divided line, which were introduced as an analogy for goodness, now become a model for goodness and knowledge as such, defined by the example of visibility and perception. Socrates's indirect definition of *what is* has been transformed from a two-term analogy to a single-term definition. The visual models and diagrams, which are the originals of the visible realm, can no longer function analogically as an explanation of *what is* because they now are themselves the likenesses of the intelligible realm. *What is* is not analogically defined by what is seen; rather, the likenesses of *what is* are "those very things which are themselves the originals of a lower order" (511a; Waterfield 2008, 239). In effect, Socrates obscures the distinction between analogizing goodness and illustrating it, making the rhetorical purpose of the divided line unclear.[25]

The final and most famous analogy of the cave is introduced in a context similar to the previous one: in the same way that the divided line was introduced as an elaboration of the analogy of the sun, the cave is an elaboration of the analogy of the line. The metaphorical correspondence between the visible and the intelligible, converted into a relation of subordination in the definition of the divided line, is transferred back into a metaphorical correspondence in the allegory of the cave.[26] Again, Socrates explicitly reminds Glaucon that this is an analogy of an analogy: "You should apply this allegory as a whole, to what we were talking about before. The region which is accessible to sight should be equated with the prison cell, and the firelight there with the light of the sun. And if you think of the upward journey and the sight of things up on the surface of the earth as the mind's ascent to the intelligible realm, you won't be wrong" (517a–b; Waterfield 2008, 243–44).

If the rhetorical purpose of these three illustrations is to provide an indirect account of goodness and knowledge, then we are forced to note that the relationship of this section of the dialogue to the two discussions of *mimêsis* that bookend it is tenuous at best. One reason for their mutual irrelevance is their difference in topic. The discussions of *mimêsis* do not concern goodness and knowledge, but poetic language and what imitation as such is. Furthermore, Socrates's lack of clarity on whether he is analogizing goodness and knowledge or defining it—which, given numerous indicators in the text, can only be intentional on Plato's part—makes any seamless application of the analogies to the theory of *mimêsis* (or vice versa) problematic. Finally, it must not escape our notice that while the second discussion of *mimêsis* defines a form of falseness that is at least partially predicated on deceptive appearances, the analogies of the middle books are deeply reliant at every level on sight and seeing to capacitate any form of true knowledge. As Nicholas Smith has pointed out, "Some scholars have been seriously troubled by the notion that images of any kind could be included among the knowables" (1996, 30). But this is troubling only if we presume that Plato's analogically inconsistent nesting dolls and the theory of *mimêsis* are interanimating. If we give the allegory of the cave the final word (as Plato does in this portion of the dialogue), it must not escape notice that vision is the mode of knowing on the surface of the earth illuminated by the blazing light of the sun just as it is the mode of conjecture in the depths of the cave illuminated by firelight. On the surface, knowing is represented as seeing. Socrates explains:

> It's my opinion that the last thing to be *seen*—and it isn't easy to see either—in the realm of knowledge is goodness; and the sight of the character of goodness leads one to deduce that it is responsible for everything that is right and fine, whatever the circumstances, and that in the visible

> realm it is the progenitor of light and of the source of light, and in the intelligible realm it is the source and provider of truth and knowledge. And I also think that the *sight* of it is a prerequisite for intelligent conduct either of one's own private affairs or of public business. (517b–c; Waterfield 2008; 244, emphasis mine)

The point here is that even in the avowedly most "metaphysical" aspects of the *Republic*, where being arguably is elevated to a supersensory realm, which "*logos* grasps by itself by the ability to practice dialectic" (511b; Waterfield 2008, 239), appearance and seeming are not and cannot be fully stripped from being and *what is*. Socrates's inconsistency—his vacillation between metaphor and definition and his consequent equivocation about appearance and visiblity—makes it impossible to fully relegate appearance to "mere seeming" or to fully interpret *mimêsis* through the lens of the sun, the line, and the cave. Although the metaphor of the divided line moves away from allegory and toward a literal definition, according to which visibility, appearance, and sight are literally subordinated to intelligibility, the simile of the sun and the allegory of the cave rely so heavily on visibility and appearance to define intelligibility that they problematize that subordination. Here, in one of the most crucial episodes of Plato's metaphysics, change and becoming, not appearance and seeming, are set in unequivocal opposition to *what is*: the *psychê* must turn "away from the world of becoming, until it becomes capable of bearing the sight of real being and reality at its most bright, which we're saying is goodness. . . . That's what education should be" (518d; Waterfield 2008, 245).

If the lowest segment of the divided line (A) were identical to imitations of the painter and poet, if the visible models for those likenesses (B) were identical to the beds, tables, and everything else that the painter imitates, and if the intelligible realm (C and D) were identical to the idea that the craftsman has in mind when he makes the bed or the table, then it might naturally lead one to make presumptions about, as it were, "the metaphysical argument of Book X" (Cain 2012, 189). If we conflate these aspects of the *Republic*, *mimêsis* might just be, as McKeon puts it, "the lesser term" of the metaphysical distinctions between being and appearance, things and their shadows or reflections, God and the universe (1951, 154). But the overall context of these two portions of the text strains against such a conceptual overlap. One is an attempt to construct, through analogies, an indirect definition of goodness and what is. The other is an attempt to construct, through examples, a unitary definition of *mimêsis*. These distinct purposes resist conflation.

Furthermore, as Halliwell rightly argues, "the language of 'simulacra' (*eidola*) and 'apparitions' (*phantasmata*) is loosely reminiscent of the spirit of the Divided Line and the Cave" (2002, 57), but it cannot be equated with the latter because the terminology is so conspicuously different. In the example of the divided line, Plato uses the term *phantasmata* to refer to "reflections," which are one subset of "likenesses" (*eikôn*) along with their counterpart "shadows" (*skia*). While it is true that the term *phantasmata* also appears in the discussion of *mimêsis* in book 10, it refers explicitly to the work of mirrors and painters (598b, 599a), and not to the imitative function of poets. The mimetic function of poetry, which Plato terms *eidôlon*, is not itself a *phantasma*. The fact that Plato used such strikingly different vocabulary to discuss such similar, or seemingly similar, concepts in the same work is a compelling reason not to conflate these two portions of the text; to do so would be to obscure the very distinctions Plato painstakingly cut. The vocabulary that "belongs to a general Platonic idiom of ontological hierarchy (between 'original' and 'image')" (Halliwell 2002, 57) simply does not appear in consistent ways between the middle books and book 10.

Finally, it is obvious that the *eidos* of book 10 "does not hang on any particular view of the so-called theory of forms" (Halliwell 2002, 136) derived from this or other dialogues or the intelligible realm described in the analogies of the line and the cave. This is made abundantly clear in Socrates's nonanalogical description of the literal task of education—the elevation of the guardians to the intelligible realm. Their ascent is unequivocally laborious: it requires them to be "hammered at from an early age, until the inevitable consequences of incarnation have been knocked off it—the leaden weights, so to speak, which are grafted on to it as a result of eating and similar pleasures and indulgences and which turn the sight of the mind downwards—if it sheds these weights and is reoriented towards the truth, then . . . it would see the truth just as clearly as it sees the objects it faces at the moment" (519a–b; Waterfield 2008, 246). This is Socrates's literal description of the process of education—the process in which one gains access to the realm of intelligibility, knowledge, and *what is*. In the allegory of the cave, it occurs by "being dragged forcibly away from there up the rough, steep slope . . . without being released until he's been pulled out into the sunlight" (515e; Waterfield 2008, 242). This description of a forcible, arduous process is irreconcilable with the description of the craftsman in book 10, who simply has in mind the *eidos* of the bed or table he wishes to make. This *eidos* beyond *mimêsis* simply cannot be equated with the intelligible realm.

Conclusion

This analysis necessarily calls into question the standard definitions of *mimêsis*, the preponderance of which seek within the term "its attendant distinction between seeming and being" (Nehamas 1982, 56), since such searches problematically conflate the *mimêsis* of book 10 with the inconsistent analogical discussions of goodness in the middle books.[27] This is not to suggest, however, that Plato's concept of *mimêsis* is irrelevant to his quest for a firm the distinction between seeming and being—only that the distinction is made not through the relation of *mimêsis* to the sun, the line, and the cave but through its relation to the *pseudos logos* of the sophists.

Several clues in the text indicate that the ultimate object of Socrates's critique is not poets and painters; rather, he ultimately aims to subordinate the imitators that he considers his greatest foe: the sophists. In the following chapter, I explore the significance of the similarities between Socrates's descriptions of the imitative poet in book 3 and the mirror-holder in book 10 as people who "can do and make anything and everything." These descriptions are strikingly reminiscent not only of each other but also of Plato's descriptions of sophists. In the *Sophist* (233d–4b), the visitor from Elea describes sophists as people who claim to have an expertise by which they not only know how to speak well and win disputes, but also "how to make and do everything . . . including you and me and all the animals and plants" (233d–e; 235a; N. White 1993, 21). But, it turns out, he is nothing more than a "cheat and an imitator" (235a; N. White 1993, 22). As explained above, Plato even drops a hint that we as readers ought to make this connection between the two dialogues: he has Adeimantus exclaim, in response to Socrates's description of a craftsman, "An altogether wonderful sophist!" (596d; my translation), and he has Socrates compare Homer to the sophists Protagoras and Prodicus (600c–d).[28] These parallels foreshadow how Plato's rhetorical theory of *mimêsis* will be used in his final siege on sophistry in his *Sophist* dialogue. It is the purpose of the following chapter to demonstrate how the rhetorical theory of *mimêsis* in the *Republic* is crucial to the development in the *Sophist* of a metaphysical distinction between seeming and being that will overcome sophistry once and for all.

For Gilles Deleuze, Plato's concept of *mimêsis* has dominated precisely because the world has forgotten the embeddedness of Plato's theory of *mimêsis* in the larger search for a method of resistance to sophistic culture. What is left is the brute opposition "between the originary and the derived, the original and the sequel, the ground and the grounded, which animates the hierarchies of a representative theology by extending the complementarity between model and copy" (1995, 265). What's left, in other words, is hierarchy and subordination decontextualized from its role as a form of political resistance to particular sophists and their sophistry. And what is also hidden in the process is the crucial role of Plato's rhetorical theory in the development of this resistance. In its place we find only the brute distinction carved by *mimêsis,* which subordinates the lesser category of any and every pair. Since, as this analysis attempts to demonstrate, Plato's *mimêsis* is derived from rhetorical theory and not from (as it is too often assumed) a doctrinal metaphysics, critiques that extend Socrates's condemnation of *mimêsis* to rhetoric (or vice versa) are likewise in need of significant reevaluation.[29]

More important, we discover that in the *Republic* these two theories of *mimêsis*—*mimêsis* as imitative language and *mimêsis* as false representation—both break with prior meanings of the term, and have not yet been unified with each other into a single account of false language. It is precisely this unification in the *Sophist* dialogue that produces Plato's theory of representational language, his theory of the assertion, and the possibility of true and false discourse.

« 6 »

Imitators of Truth

The Rhetorical Theories of *Onoma* and *Rhêma* in the *Sophist* and the *Cratylus*

Where Socrates has engaged with Protagoras's Heraclitean relativism and *antilogos*, he has struggled in vain to adequately distinguish between truth and appearance and to overcome the inexorability of Protagorean flux and contradiction. In these earlier encounters, Socrates can do little more than temporarily sway the audience in his favor or manipulate the rules of discussion to play to his strengths and exploit his interlocutor's weaknesses. Socrates intuits that a way out may be found through a stable theory of *logos*, which might serve as an external measure by which to judge the truth or falsity of statements. Although he abandons his attempt to define a theory of *logos* in the *Theaetetus*, he gains some ground in the *Cratylus* by defining at the very least some components of *logos*—*onoma* and *rhêma*—if not *logos* as such. In the *Republic*, he gains further ground by casting provisional distrust on appearances through his theory of *mimêsis*, and gestures toward the language of the sophists as the target of this distrust.

The conversation portrayed in the *Sophist* dialogue is in many ways the sequel to the conversations displayed in the *Theaetetus* and the *Cratylus*. It occurs on the following day, on the other side of the same night. Despite the fact that Socrates is absent, Theaetetus is present, just as he was for one of the conversations on the previous day. All three dialogues depict sophistic methods of discussion derived from pre-Socratic ontology along with a pressing need to define a theory of *logos* that can rise above the flux of *phusis*. As Catherine Zuckert has noted, "In the *Sophist* Plato shows the Stranger answering two questions Socrates proved unable to resolve in two of his conversations the day before. In the *Theaetetus* Socrates admitted that he had long been perplexed by the fact of false opinion; he was not able to explain how it was possible. Likewise, in the *Cratylus* Socrates and his interlocutors were not able to determine satisfactorily the relation between names and things to which they refer" (2000, 65–66).

In the *Sophist*, Theodorus and the Stranger from Elea collaboratively construct a theory of language that will defeat the *logos* of the sophist not by swaying the crowd or exploiting a handicap, but by delimiting the category of false speech. The theories of *onoma*, *rhêma*, and *mimêsis* in this dialogue become the building blocks of Plato's false statement (*pseudos logos*), which is itself the ultimate method of resisting and overturning the sophists because it capacitates associating sophistry with seeming, appearance, and falsehood. Whereas, as we've seen in the *Cratylus* and the *Theaetetus*, Protagorean linguistics bars any escape from the interminable flux of *phusis* as defined by Heraclitus's ontology (and vice versa), in the *Sophist*, in Socrates's absence, Plato's theory of the assertion loosens the fetters of both Protagorean contradiction and Heraclitean flux. The purpose of the theory is not only "the rejection of current linguistic theories" (Sprague 1971, 367) supplied by sophists like Protagoras; it is also (and more important) the formalization of the concept of a false or a true statement—a supertheory that would be able to defeat not only particular sophists but falsehood as such. It is Plato's rhetorical theory, begun in the *Republic* and the *Cratylus* and finished in the *Sophist*, that makes it possible for the Stranger from Elea to implicate the sophist in "imitation of the contrary-speech-producing, insincere, and unknowing sort, of the appearance-making kind of copy-making, the word-juggling part of production that's marked off as human and not divine" (268c–d; N. White 1993, 65).

In what follows, I examine how Plato's theories of *logos*, *onoma*, and *rhêma* in the *Sophist* dialogue ensnare the sophist by severing the cords of Protagorean-Heraclitean contradiction and *antilogos*. I explain how Louis Bassett's etymology of *onoma* and *rhêma* in the *Cratylus* illuminates the language theory of the *Sophist*, which is Plato's ultimate resistance to Protagorean linguistics and eristics, grounded in an understanding of language as signification and mimetic representation.

The Stranger's Method of Division and the Sophist's Heracliteanism

At the outset of the conversation that culminates in the definition of sophistry as "imitation of the contrary-speech-producing, insincere, and unknowing sort" (268c; N. White 1993, 65), we are led to believe that Socrates is present, given that his name appears before the second turn in conversation, when someone named Socrates asks Theodorus who his unnamed companion is, indicating that it might be a god in disguise (216a). Theodorus responds—perhaps in a veiled reference to Protagoras and his man-measure doctrine—"That's not our visitor's style, Socrates. He's more measured [*metriôteros*] than the enthusiasts for debating are. And he isn't believed by me to be a god at all. He *is* divine—but then I call all philosophers that" (216b; N. White 1993, 1; translation modified). Plato is playing a subtle joke on his reader in a way that is thematically in line with the theoretical work of the dialogue: he *names* Socrates at the beginning of the dialogue and in doing so leads us to believe that Socrates is there in material form. But then we learn that this is not *the* Socrates but *a* Socrates. Theaetetus tells the visitor he is Socrates's namesake, the young Theaetetus's peer and companion, and not (as we were led to believe) the aged philosopher, who we presume is at that very moment hearing the charges against him that will result in his death.[1] In this case, the *onoma* of Socrates, which denominates the man, cannot be relied on for its signifying function. This subtle joke is symbolic of the aims of the dialogue: to transfer to language as such the signifying function of *onomata* and, by counterstroke, to show how that signifying function produces false discourse.

The conversation that follows is presented as an attempt to define the sophist "by searching for him and giving a clear account of what he is" (218b; N. White 1993, 3). And, in the same way that the *onoma* "Socrates" does not guarantee that they are naming the same person, the visitor remarks that, while they might both use the *onoma* of "sophist," there is no guarantee that both he and Theaetetus are using the word to denominate the same thing in the world. For this reason, they ought to make sure they are "in agreement about the thing itself by means of a verbal explanation, rather than doing without any such explanation and merely agreeing about what to call him" (218c; N. White 1993, 3; translation modified).[2] The visitor proposes they first establish their heuristic and "focus on something trivial and try to use it as a pattern for the more important issue" (218d; N. White 1993, 3).

What follows is a sprawling method of division, which defines one thing (in the first example, an angler) by separating it from what it is not. Ultimately, all these divisions and separations—expert/nonexpert, acquisition/production, combat/hunting, and so on—result in a seemingly endless proliferation of the places where the sophist may be found. It is these proliferations that are ultimately unsatisfactory: because the sophist appears anywhere and everywhere, the Stranger and Theaetetus cannot, by this method of division, come to an agreement about what the term *sophist* denominates. Through this method he appears as a hired hunter of wealthy young men, both a wholesaler and a retailer of learning about the *psychê*, a peddler of his own learning, an athlete in verbal debate, and a cleaner of the *psychê* (summarized at 231d–e). With each new appearance, he evades their attempts at unequivocal denomination. The Stranger from Elea expresses his dissatisfaction and dismay at the inelegance of this procedure, which results in the fact that "the sophist has appeared in lots of different ways" (231b; N. White 1993, 18), some of them even positive (an outcome that unsettles Theaetetus and the visitor alike, 231a). Rose Cherubin has suggested that the visitor's method is at bottom sophistic: "He claims to 'hunt' (218d) for the sophist as hunter, and to 'discriminate' (*diakrinein*, 226–27) to find the sophist as discriminator. . . . Could his enterprise be characterized generally as using sophistry to look for the sophist in general or as such?" (Cherubin 1993, 227).[3]

The Stranger subtly indicates not only that he is using the very tools of the sophist himself, but that those tools are predicated on an implicit Protagoreanism–Heracliteanism. Cherubin describes the resemblance of the visitor's method to Protagoras's widely known doctrine that for each *pragma* there are two opposing sides. Similarly, she writes, "the Stranger winds up describing the sophist variously such that the sophist falls in different cases on *opposite sides* of such supposedly exclusive divisions as productive versus acquisitive arts, exchange versus hunting, and so on" (1993, 228).

Moreover, the Stranger offers a brief, seemingly tangential metacommentary on the method of division as such (which is disguised as a further practice of the method itself). He offers a series of seemingly random *onomata* (226b) of menial household tasks, many of which, it just so happens, relate to the activity of weaving: "to strain" (*diêthein*), "to sift" (*diattan*), "to winnow" (*brattein*), "to separate" (*diakrinein*), "to comb" (*xainein*), "to weigh down" (*katagein*), and "to separate the web" (*kerkizein*). Bearing in mind that this conversation takes place the very next day following the conversation in the *Cratylus*, we are compelled to recall the list of infinitives that Socrates offers there, and to notice not only their grammatical similarity, but also the similarity of their Heraclitean content.[4] There (*Cra.* 426e), Plato lists numerous similar infinitive verbs: "κρούειν (strike), θραύειν (crush), ἐρείκειν (bruise), θρύπτειν (break), κερματίζειν (crumble), ῥυμβεῖν (whirl)" (426e; Jowett 1961, 461; Greek in the original). The infinitives in the *Cratylus* refer to general concepts related to the Heraclitean tension of opposites and the theory of flux; the infinitives in the *Sophist* center around a specific activity, weaving, that proceeds by virtue of the tension of opposing forces of weaving, represented in the activities of separation, winnowing, straining, and so on. One of Heraclitus's fragments even refers to the weaver's comb as an example of the unity of opposites ("the path of the carding-combs is straight and crooked" [DK 22b59; Barnes 1987, 103]). In the *Sophist*, the Stranger suggests that all these activities are different types of dividing (*diaretikos*) or discriminating (*diakritikos*): carding separates fibers from one another, combing filters out other contents or contaminants from the primary fiber, and so on. The very terminology Plato uses to describe this method of division indicates that the Heraclitean ontology underlying Protagorean epistemology and linguistics is still at work, and that their method of division is no different from the antilogical tactics of the sophists.

In other words, the very same process of division, separation, and discrimination that the Stranger ascribes to the sophist's practice of refutation is identical to the method that the Stranger himself uses. This parity explains why the visitor's hunt is destined to fail if it does not exceed these divisional tactics, which themselves expose the inadequacies of sophistry.[5] The method the Stranger will develop at the end of the dialogue must exceed the basic format of contradiction and gainsaying.

Plato's Heraclitean analogy of weaving emphasizes the point: dividing and discriminating on its own, without any synthetic resolution, is nonproductive. Thus the sophists' antilogic, separation, discrimination, and refutation, all of which separate "what's worse from what's better and . . . like from like" (226d; N. White 1993, 13), is a useful tool but an incomplete one. The ultimate purpose of weaving is not merely diaeretic or diacritical—separating fiber from fiber and fiber from nonfiber—but integrational and productive. The art of weaving would be no art at all if it were halted at this stage of oppositional and separating practices. It will be the aim of the rhetorical theory, developed at the end of the dialogue, to complete and correct the tool.

It is due to the inadequacy of this method, which the Stranger has both deployed and defined, that he seeks at the end of the dialogue to develop a more capacious method than the eristics of sophistry. He describes the goal of such a method:

> We should be able to follow what a person says and scrutinize it step by step. When he says that what's different is the same in a certain way or that what's the same is different in a certain way, we should understand just what way he means, and the precise respect in which he's saying that the thing is the same or different. But when someone makes that which is the same appear different in just any old way, or vice versa, or when he makes what's large appear small or something that's similar appear dissimilar—well, if someone enjoys constantly trotting out contraries like that in discussion, that's not true refutation. It's only the obvious newborn brain-child of someone who just came into contact with *those which are*. (259c–d, N. White 1993, 54; translator's emphasis)

This in essence indicates the way out of the sophist's verbal snares: in contrast to entanglements in sophistic contradiction, the Stranger proposes an analysis of the *language* of contradiction as such. The aim, then, is to identify how, in speech, the sophist carries out a contradiction without being ensnared in the contradiction itself (236e–237a, 239d, 243b–d, 244a). Attention to language, as opposed to entrapment in two-*logoi* and antilogic, entails that, as the Stranger puts it, "we won't agree with somebody who says that negation signifies [*sêmainein*] a contrary. We'll only admit this much: when 'not' and 'non–' [*to mê kai to ou*] are prefixed to *onomata* that follow them, they indicate something *other* than the *onomata*, or rather other than the things to which the *onomata* following the negation are applied" (257b–c; N. White 1993, 51; translation modified). It is this attention to language that produces the rhetorical theory of *onoma-rhêma-logos.*

Louis Bassett and the Problem of *Onoma* and *Rhêma*

The question the Stranger from Elea introduces here—what it means to affix a negating prefix to an *onoma*—constitutes an attempt to provide a theory of *logos* that is capable of overcoming the impossibility and inexorabilty of sophistic contradiction. In other words, his aim is to consider contradiction qua the language of contradiction precisely as a means of escape from contradiction. For the full development of this theory, the understanding of *onoma* and *rhêma* Plato develops in the *Cratylus* is essential prereading.

Plato's unconventional uses of *onoma* and *rhêma*, commonly but wrongly translated as "noun" and "verb," are the very building blocks of the concept of *logos*-as-assertion. Inasmuch as this is the case, Plato's "theory of knowledge" and theory of *logos* are the result of his rhetorical theory of *onoma* and *rhêma* and theory of rhetoric.[6] Plato's use of these terms in his *Sophist* and *Cratylus* dialogues differs from the earlier uses in the literature prior to Plato. And, as in other cases where Plato deliberately modifies existing language to give it new meaning, such work is evidence of important theory-building.

The term *onoma*, which in its earliest uses referred exclusively to the proper names of persons, by the fifth century BCE could refer to the general concepts denoted by "term" or "word" as well as "name"; and the term *rhêma* consistently governed a wide range of uses, referring to words, speech, language, and phrases in general.[7] Plato at times uses *rhêma* interchangeably with *onoma* as "words and phrases" (*Cra.* 421e, 425a; *Symp.* 221e), and even to indicate the naming of things (*Plt.* 303c; *Soph.* 237d; *Rep.* 462c; *Leg.* 906c)—the very function he elsewhere assigns exclusively to *onoma*. That these terms governed a wide domain is evident in the preponderance of Plato's own uses of both terms. Both, on the whole, refer to the general concept of words, terms, and phrases.

We witness a radical break with these nontechnical uses of the terms *onoma* and *rhêma* in the *Cratylus* and the *Sophist*. In both cases, Plato uses these terms to build a theory of language that is capable of serving as a theoretical counterweight to sophistic contradiction and Heraclitean flux by affixing a representational function to language. In these dialogues, *onoma* and *rhêma* are reconceived as differentiated components of discourse that are blended together to construct a *logos* (*Cra.* 424e–425a; *Soph.* 262a–d). What, precisely, is the nature of this differentiation?

In an important essay from 2004 titled "Platon et la distinction nom/verbe," Louis Bassett convincingly argues on the basis of Plato's uses in these two texts for an alternate interpretation of *onoma* and *rhêma*, not as "noun" and "verb," but as "word" and "phrase," the combination of which forms the content of a *logos*.[8] Bassett's observations about the critical distinction between *onoma* and *rhêma* offer crucial indications of the relevance of rhetorical theory in Plato's thought. In brief, Plato's use of these two terms, when defined in tandem with the theory of *mimêsis* first introduced in the *Republic* and then reintroduced in the *Sophist*, forms the core of a linguistic vocabulary, or language about language, that can withstand the dizzying antilogos of the sophists.

The focused discussions of *onoma* and *rhêma* in the *Sophist* and the *Cratylus*, where the terms are not merely used in passing but explicitly theorized, suggest a very different sense of these two terms from their traditional translation as "noun" and "verb." *Onoma* is not "noun" but an elementary part of a more complex phrase, or *rhêma*, in the same way that a simple sound is an elementary part of a more complex syllable (Bassett 2004, 302). Bassett points to the painting analogy at *Cra.* 424e, which is offered as an illustration of the point. The *onomata* are the simple colors prior to their mixing and composition in the larger *logos*—*rhêma* is the midway point between the basic, isolated *onoma* and the complete *logos*, equivalent to the mixed colors that have not yet fully composed a complete picture ("qui doivent donc être les équivalents des couleurs composées" [Bassett 2004, 302]). In the same way that the mixed colors are an intermediate step between a single color and a picture, or a syllable is an intermediate step between the basic sound and the word, the *rhêma* is not a "verb" but an intermediate step between the *onoma* and the *logos* (Bassett 2004, 303).

Bassett's central claim is that while *onoma*, even when it is interpreted to mean "name" or "noun," still retains the "dual heritage" of its oldest meanings, "*rhêma* meanwhile lost for centuries its . . . sense outlined by Plato" (2004, 313).[9] This is the case because *onoma*, when translated as "noun," still retains its proper (for Plato) sense of *dénomination*, or an index that denominates a discrete aspect of reality Bassett (2004, 308). While this meaning is not strictly equivalent to "noun," it is not entirely obscured by its translation as "noun." *Rhêma*, on the other hand, translated as "verb," utterly covers over Plato's use of the term to mean "phrase" or "string of *onomata*" (Bassett 2004, 309), and the root of his neologism *rhêtorikê*. However, the significance of Bassett's analysis far exceeds this preliminary observation that the logical content of *rhêma* is obscured by what later developed as a grammatical category.

Why is Bassett's redefinition of Plato's *onoma* and *rhêma* essential for this theory of *logos* and, by extension, the overturning of sophistic thought? By emphasizing the function of the term *onoma* as the linguistic unit that can be most concretely linked up with the material world, and then developing a definition of *rhêma* as a string of *onomata* that ultimately composes a *logos*, Plato is able to construct a theory of language that essentially transfers the denominative properties of *onoma* to *rhêma*, and ultimately, to *logos* as such. Since *onomata* is the term for words that have a certain counterpart in the real world, by defining *rhêma* as a collection of *onomata* that are strung together, and *logos* as a collection of *rhêmata*, Plato is laying the groundwork for transferring the referential function of *onoma* to *logos* as such, wherein *logos* is merely a longer, more complex word and "stating is reduced to naming" (Fine 1977, 290). What will result, in the end, is a concept of the statement that is capable of overcoming sophistic paradoxes, contradictions, and division—in other words, a rhetorical theory that is strong enough to resist sophistry.

The significance of Bassett's hypothesis may be observed in a formal aspect of Socrates's Heraclitean etymologies in the *Cratylus*. In the etymologies, Socrates regularly comments on the form that their investigation of *phusis* via words takes: with each etymology, they transform a single word (*onoma*) into a longer phrase (*rhêma*) or sentence (*logos*). If, over the course of not only the *Cratylus* but also the *Sophist* dialogue, Plato is, through Socrates and the Stranger from Elea, attempting to transfer to *logos* as a whole the function that was assigned to *onoma* in its oldest and most conservative sense, then it is telling that the form of Socrates's etymological investigations of discrete *onomata*—which are both predicated on and revelatory of a Heraclitean ontology of flux—implies that hiding within each *onoma* are, as Socrates points out, *rhêmata* and *logoi*. For example, of his etymology of "man" (ἄνθρωπος), Socrates explains that "the *onoma* ἄνθρωπος . . . was once a *rhêma* and is now an *onoma*. . . . I mean to say that the word *man* implies that other animals never examine, or consider, or look up at (ἀναθρεῖ) what they see, but that man not only sees (ὄπωπε) but considers and looks up at that which he sees, and hence he alone of all animals is rightly called ἄνθρωπος, meaning ἀναθρῶν ἃ ὄπωπεν" (399b–c; Jowett 1961, 436; Greek text in the original, translation modified). All the etymologies that follow demonstrate the same method, to which Socrates calls self-conscious attention. He takes a single term (*onoma*) and expands it into a phrase of cognates (*rhêma*), for which he then offers a full explanation (*logos*).

He drives the point home, not incidentally, in his etymologies of the *onomata* for "the greatest and noblest" (421a; Jowett 1961, 456) things: "truth" (ἀλήθεια), "falsehood" (ψεῦδος), "being" (ὄν), and the name for "name" (ὄνομα). These terms themselves constitute the larger aims of his theory-building in both the *Cratylus* and the *Sophist*: to define a theory of true and false speech. In his etymology of *onoma*, Socrates points out that "the word ὄνομα seems to be a compressed *logos*, signifying ὄν οὗ ζήτημα (being for which there is a search), as is still more obvious in ὀνομαστόν (notable), which states in so many words that real existence is that for which there is a seeking (ὄν οὗ μάσμα)" (421a; Jowett 1961, 456; translation modified). Similar etymologies for *alêtheia*, *pseudos*, and *to on* follow (421b–c). Here, in the apogee of Socrates's etymologies, not only do we learn that within each *onoma* is hiding a Heraclitean ontology of flux, we also learn that within each *onoma* lies a *logos*, which is itself composed of *onomata*, which themselves contain a *logos*, and so on. At the heart of each etymology lies this triple content: an ontology of Heraclitean flux, a *logos* that cannot be fully extracted from that ontology, and a potential promise for that extraction in the form of denominative *logos*.

Plato has Socrates point out this method—the expansion of an *onoma* to a *rhêma* and a *logos*, the compression of a *logos* into an *onoma*—in order to indicate subtly that his aim is the transference of the referential properties of *onomata* to *logos* as such. One word gives way to a phrase that is itself composed of words, each of which will, upon investigation, also give way to a phrase. And so the process continues, ad infinitum (421d–e). Ultimately, he concludes, "one principle is applicable to all *onomata*, primary as well as secondary—when they are regarded simply as *onomata*, there is no difference in them. . . . All the names that we have been explaining were intended to make visible what is / being [*tôn ontôn*]" (422c–d; Jowett 1961, 457; translation modified). In other words, if all *logoi* and *rhêmata* are regarded as *onomata*, then the way in which they reveal *what is* might not be a matter of their embeddedness within *phusis* and *what is*, but a matter of defining how it is that they reference, index, or correspond to *phusis* and *what is* (in the manner that *onomata* do). This is perhaps the most explicit place where Plato is assigning to *logos* as such the function that had otherwise only been given to individual names or terms for something: *logos* makes being / *what is* visible *by naming it.*[10]

Onoma, *Rhêma*, and the *Logos* of *Mimêsis*

It is at this point in the *Cratylus* that Socrates seems to have reminded himself of another discussion that led to a similar conclusion: his concept of *mimêsis*, as it was developed in the *Republic*, which led him to a similar two-part structure of things and their representation. Imagining for a moment that it would be possible to reach the beginning of language—to find the irreducible *onomata* which are not compressed *logoi* but the first names, "which need not be resolved any further" (422b; Jowett 1961, 457)—he questions how it is that these words reveal being. It is clear from the foregoing discussion that the "secondary" terms are able to make being visible by means of the "primary" ones. But when we hit bottom and are forced to consider how it is that the primary *onomata* make being visible (without reference to other *onomata*), what account can we give? In other words, when the sense of a word cannot be explained through an assemblage of other words but is instead, raw, isolated, and irreducible, how does that primary *onoma* reveal *what is*? "How do the primary names, which lie under the others, make manifest/visible *what is* [*phanera . . . poiêsei ta onta*], as far as *what is* can be shown, which is what they must do if they are to be real *onomata*?" (422d; Jowett 1961, 457; translation modified).

To answer this question he returns, analogically at first, to his concept of *mimêsis*. He reasons that language must function in a way that is similar to bodily imitation:

> Suppose that we had no voice or tongue, and wanted to communicate with one another. Should we not, like the deaf and dumb, make signs [*sêmainein*] with the hands and head and the rest of the body? . . . We should *imitate* [*mimoumenoi*] *phusis* by our actions; the elevation of our hands to heaven would mean lightness and upwardness; heaviness and downwardness would be expressed by letting them drop to the ground; . . . for only by imitation can the body make things visible. . . . Then the *onoma* is, as such, a vocal imitation of that which the vocal imitator *names or imitates.* (422e–423a; Jowett 1961, 457–58; translation modified, emphases mine).

The first *onomata*, which are not mere assemblages of other *onomata*, must, he concludes, function in the same way as these raw, alinguistic, imitative gestures.

But this hypothesis proves unsatisfactory, because it entails the conclusion that "the people who imitate sheep, or cocks, or other animals, *name* [*onomazein*] that which they *imitate* [*mimountai*]" (423c; Jowett 1961, 458; emphasis mine), which they clearly do not.[11] Because this doesn't make sense, at Hermogenes's request, Socrates attempts to define more carefully "what sort of an imitation [*mimêsis*] is a name" (423c; Jowett 1961, 458). The imitation that is done by means of language does not imitate the sound of something, as in the case of musical imitation, or the look of something, as in the case of pictorial imitation, but the very being of the thing (423d–e).

How does this imitation of the essence proceed? And "what is the method of division [*diaireseôs*] with which the imitator begins to imitate? Imitation of *what is* is made by compound sounds and single letters. Ought we not, therefore, first to separate the letters?" (424b; Jowett 1961, 459; translation modified). Once this imitator has separated out and defined the most atomistic linguistic unit—the discrete letters—then it can be determined to what they ought to be applied and how they ought to be combined. This, in sum, is the work of the rhetorician: just as a painter knows how to combine discrete colors to create an overall pictorial representation, "so, too, we shall apply letters to the revealing of objects, either single letters when required, or several letters, and so we shall form syllables, as they are called, and from syllables make *onomata* and *rhêmata,* and thus, at last, from the combinations of *onomata* and *rhêmata* arrive [at *logos*], large and fair and complete. And as the painter made a figure, *even so shall we make* logos *by the* technê *of naming, or rhetoric, or some other* technê" (424e–425a; Jowett 1961, 459; translation modified, emphasis mine).

By this explanation, language and the arts of rhetoric can only be another case, like painting and music, of imitation. This hypothesis emerges first and foremost because of the structural similarity between the function of the term *onoma,* the only linguistic term through which a direct relationship is established between words and reality ("un rapport direct étant établi entre les mots et les réalités" [Bassett 2004, 301]), and the two-part structure of *mimêsis,* which likewise creates a copy of real things. In the same way that a name or a picture or a way of speaking can be used to represent a person, so all language—from its smallest *onoma* to *logos* as a whole—refers to *phusis.*

In the *Cratylus,* much is accomplished toward establishing a theory of *logos*—including the agreements that a correct *onoma* reveals or indicates how something is (428e); that this indication works in the same way that painting or building works, by copying something (429a); that this process, like with painting or building, can be done well or badly (431a–432e); and since an *onoma* can be badly or wrongly assigned, then *logos* as such can also wrongly represent *what is* (432e). Nevertheless, Socrates and Hermogenes cannot gain escape velocity from the Heraclitean cosmos. As S. Montgomery Ewegen describes it, they end up instead "radicalizing" the Protagorean position (2014, 74).

If the first name-giver began in error, then "he may have forced the remainder into agreement with the original error and with himself" (436c–d; Jowett 1961, 470). And so they too are driven back to their original consideration that "all things are in motion and progress and flux, and that this idea of motion is expressed by names" (436e; Jowett 1961, 470). Since the names of their earlier investigation all express and reveal the flow of the Heraclitean universe of which they are a piece, there is all the more reason to doubt that the first name-giver ever could have devised an *onoma* that would reveal the being of that which the *onoma* named (particularly when so many *onomata* denote rest and stasis, in direct contradiction to universal flux, 437c).

In this sense, Socrates presents the conversation in the dialogue as fruitless; but in another sense, he indicates how their conversation will ultimately be resolved through a theory of *onoma* and *logos*. He concludes the discussion by dramatically giving up his search for the "greatest and noblest" purpose of the preceding discussion—defining the interrelationship of *alêtheia*, falsehood, being, and *onomata* (421a)—concluding instead that "how what is [*ta onta*] is to be learned or discovered is, I suspect, beyond you and me" (439b; Jowett 1961, 473; translation modified). But he is careful to point out that "it is worthwhile to have reached the conclusion that *what is* is learned and sought through itself, not through *onomata*" (439b; Jowett 1961, 473; translation modified). It is less important, John Sallis notes, that "in his last pronouncement [of the *Cratylus*] he has relinquished the very possibility of true *logos*, of a *logos* which would say things as they are; and more than once he has rejected the possibility of false *logos*" (1986, 311) than that he has made inroads to a *logos* that carries the representational function of *onoma* and bears a contingent relation to *phusis*.[12] In other words, he indicates that although the rhetorical theory which the better part of the conversation was devoted to building fails to facilitate their investigation of *what is*, and likewise fails to overcome the linguistic consequences of a Heraclitean ontology of flux, the rhetorical work begun here is not yet finished. It is completed only in the *Sophist*, when the Eleatic Stranger revisits the same rhetorical theories to complete the work that Socrates began formulating in the *Cratylus*.

Onoma and *Rhêma*, *Logos* and *Mimêsis* in the *Sophist*

By pointing out that sophistic contradiction is at root merely a linguistic matter, it is inevitable that language will be detached from *phusis*. The Stranger from Elea suggests that their method of scrutinizing the sophist's *logos* step-by-step reveals that the terms of contradiction—*mê* and *ou*—are merely something "other than the things to which the *onomata* following the negation are applied" (257b–c; N. White 1993, 51; translation modified). They are not, in other words, indications of nonbeing. He suggests that the self-conscious consideration of language as such—of the actual *onoma* for negation—offers a possible antidote to the dizziness that results from the perpetual turning-round of sophistic contradiction and the Heraclitean flux. It does so by exposing the very medium of that contradiction.[13]

Since "to dissociate each thing from everything else is to destroy totally everything there is to say" (259e; N. White 1993, 54), the Stranger announces that he seeks some synthetic purpose beyond mere negation, separation, and "constantly trotting out contraries." Instead, and in order to allow for the scrutiny and understanding that the sophists' practices obliterate, he proposes that "the weaving together of *eidos* is what makes speech possible for us" (259e; N. White 1993, 54; translation modified).[14] In the above example regarding the negations *mê* and *ou*, the prefixes are to be understood as being interwoven with the *onomata megas* (large) or *kalos* (beautiful) (257d–258c). This is no longer a question of nonbeing in *phusis*, but a verbal indication of linguistic difference—difference in name, not difference in nature, and difference from that which is assigned the *onoma* of "large," "beautiful," and so on, rather than the "not large" or "not beautiful" as such.

This example of weaving together of the *onomata* of negation, of largeness, of beauty, and so forth, is a further instantiation of the theory of *onoma* and *rhêma* from the *Cratylus*. The Stranger initiates the final phase of the conversation by announcing that their purpose has shifted from finding what is denominated by the *onoma* "sophist" to what is denominated by the *onoma* "logos." He observes that coming to an agreement about what *logos* is is a complex task; while "*logos* is one kind among *those that are*," nevertheless "we'd be able to say nothing if speech were taken away from us and weren't anything at all. And it would be taken away if we admitted that there's no blending of anything with anything else" (260a–b; N. White 1993, 55; translation modified).

It is for this reason that the Stranger returns to the subject of *onomata*: "Come on, then. Let's think about *onomata* again, the same way as we spoke about forms and letters of the alphabet. What we're looking for seems to lie in that direction" (261d; N. White 1993, 56; translation modified). *Onoma*, as a smaller, discrete portion of a larger *logos*, indisputably populates its content. His question, then, is how they are blended together, and "whether they all fit with each other, or none of them do, or some of them will and some of them won't" (261d; N. White 1993, 56). To make this determination, he invokes the same set of concepts from the *Cratylus*: that a *logos* is not and cannot be a random string of *onomata*; *onomata* must be mixed as *rhêmata* in order for the sounds to gain sense and in so doing compose a *logos* (262b–c). And when one speaks, one "doesn't just give *onomata* to things, but one completes something by weaving *rhêmata* with *onomata*. That is why we say 'he speaks' [*legein*] and not just 'he names' [*onomazein*]. In fact, this weaving is what we use the word *logos* for" (262d; N. White 1993, 58; translation modified). Because he has defined speech as an expanded *onoma*—*onomata* interwoven as *rhêmata*—he is able, again, to reinforce the view that *logos* fundamentally functions in the same way as an *onoma* "Whenever there's speech it has to be about something. It's impossible for it not to be about something" (262e; N. White 1993, 58). In the same way that one cannot name without naming *something* or *someone*, by tying *logos* to *onoma*, one cannot speak without speaking *about something*. The Stranger has introduced the idea of the statement.

The sophist is finally ensnared once the Stranger fuses the two-level model of *logos* (*onoma* and *rhêma* that speak about something) with the two-level model of *mimêsis* (an image that copies something). Finally the sophist's *logos* can be defined, once and for all, as false.[15]

The topic of *mimêsis* is introduced once at the very beginning of the dialogue (219a–b), then quickly abandoned, and then reintroduced at the end of the dialogue. The two discussions of *mimêsis* that bookend the *Sophist* hint at the importance *mimêsis* has for the theory of language that Plato is building in this dialogue. By weaving together the two different senses of the term that were developed in the *Republic* and binding these to his concepts of *onoma*, *rhêma*, and *logos*, Plato not only completes the rhetorical theory of *mimêsis*, he also initiates the understanding that language, truth, and falsity function by means of reference and correspondence, thus introducing for the first time, via the rhetorical theories of *onoma*, *rhêma*, and *mimêsis*, the sovereignty of the signifier and the correspondence theory of truth.

Toward the end of the dialogue, when the topic of *mimêsis* is revisited, deliberately evoking the descriptions of the all-powerful imitator from the *Republic*, it is concluded that the sophist himself must be some sort of imitator, since he too seems to be able to know, make, and do everything (232e–233d). The sophist, the Stranger explains, engages in controversies about anything and everything, and in so doing comes off as an expert in anything and everything—that's what makes the sophist's abilities so marvelous and magical (233a).

> *Str.* If someone claimed that by a single kind of expertise he could know, not just how to say things or to engage in controversies with people, but how to make and do everything, then . . .
>
> *Tht.* What do you mean *everything*? [. . .]
>
> *Str.* Well, I mean *everything* to include you and me and also the other animals and plants . . .
>
> *Tht.* What are you talking about?
>
> *Str.* If someone claimed that he'd make you and me and all the other living things . . .
>
> *Tht.* What kind of making are you talking about? You're not talking about some kind of gardener—after all, you did say he made animals.
>
> *Str.* Yes, and also I mean the sea and earth and heaven and gods and everything else. And furthermore he makes them each quickly and sells them at a low price.[16]
>
> *Tht.* You're talking about some kind of game for schoolchildren.
>
> *Str.* Well, if someone says he knows everything and would teach it to someone else cheaply and quickly, shouldn't we think it's a game?
>
> *Tht.* Of course.

In an explicit cross reference to the *Republic*'s description of a poet who can imitate any sound in language and an artist who can imitate any appearance in painting, the Stranger defines the sophist as the consummate master imitator. As Catherine Zuckert describes, "Although no human being can actually know everything, the sophist's ability to refute anyone, even a person who actually knows about the particular matter in question, makes the sophist appear to know all—especially to the young" (2000, 77). Precisely because this kind of comprehensive power-knowledge is impossible (233a–c), it can only be a species of imitation, not unlike the imitation that is done by artists.

But where the critique of imitation in the *Republic* stalls without clearly defining the relationship between the different mimetic strands, leaving Glaucon only to marvel at the endless powers of the sophist, this conversation continues, closing in on the illusive sophist:

Str. Do you know of any game that involves more expertise than the imitative [*mimêtikon*] kind, and is more engaging?

Tht. No, not at all, since you've collected everything together and designated a very broad, extremely diverse type.

Str. So think about a man who promises he can make everything by means of a single kind of expertise. Suppose that by the art of making marks he produces imitations that have the same names as real things.[17] Then we know that when he shows his etchings from far away he'll be able to fool the more mindless young children into thinking that he can actually produce anything he wants to.

Tht. Of course.

Str. Well then, won't we expect that there's another kind of expertise—this time having to do with speech [*logous*]—and that someone can use it to trick young people when they stand even farther away from the truth about things? Wouldn't he do it by putting words in their ears, and by showing them spoken images of everything, so as to make them believe that the words are true and that the person who's speaking to them is the wisest person there is?

Tht. Yes, why shouldn't there be that kind of expertise too?

Str. So, Theaetetus, suppose enough time has passed and the sophist's hearers have gotten older, and that they approach closer to real things and are forced by their experiences to touch up palpably against them. Won't most of them inevitably change their earlier beliefs, which made large things appear [*phainesthai*] small and easy things appear hard? And won't the facts they've encountered in the course of their actions completely overturn all the appearances [*phantasmata*] that had come to them in the form of words [*logois*]? (233d–234e; N. White 1993, 20–22; translation modified)

In this as yet unresolved discussion, the Stranger has blended the two definitions of *mimêsis* developed in the *Republic.* By the first definition, the sophist is one who does a convincing impression of a person who has actual knowledge and expertise (the traditional meaning of *mimêsis*); by the second, the sophist's *logos* might just be a copy as opposed to the thing itself (the new meanings of the term developed in books 3 and 10).

The six definitions of the sophist, which the Stranger and Theaetetus have just composed, make it possible for the Stranger to propose that it is no wonder that people take the sophist to be an expert at so many things (232a)—even to Theaetetus and the Stranger he seems to be a shape-shifting sorcerer. The very fact that he appears in so many places—indeed, in every place the Stranger and Theaetetus look for him—mirrors the sophist's own claim that by a single *technê* he could create and do anything and everything (233d). His arts of language, which persuade people by "putting words in their ears," words that "create spoken images of everything" and are the ultimate manifestation of mimetic *logos* and mimetic appearances. With such powers of linguistic *mimêsis* at hand, the "marvelous sophist" (*Rep.* 596d) can "persuade the jurors in the courts, the members of the Council, the citizens attending the Assembly—in short, to win over any and every form of public meeting of the citizen body. Armed with this ability, in fact, the doctor would be your slave, the trainer would be yours to command, and that businessman would turn out to be making money not for himself, but for someone else—for *you* with your ability to speak and to persuade the masses" (*Grg.* 452e; Waterfield 1994, 13).

What is only passing and implicit in the *Republic* is here made firm and explicit: by this bricolage definition, it is now obvious that the sophist is ensnared, and "we have to regard him as a cheat and a *mimêtic*" (235a; N. White 1993, 22; translation modified). The sophist is able to do with words—both written and spoken—what painters can do with pictures and what *onomata* can do with things: make people believe that what they are hearing is true, that what they are naming exists, and that what they have spoken must be. Representational language—language that does not speak but speaks about—exposes the sophist as a creator not of actual likenesses but false appearances, *phantasmatic* rather than *eikastic* imitation.[18] Through this theory, the Stranger is able to hem in the sophist "with one of those net-like devices that words provide for things like this" (235b; N. White 1993, 22) and, as a result, evade the web of Protagorean paradox and contradiction. Precisely by applying his two-level model of *mimêsis* to the *onomata* and *mimêsis* of the sophist, the Stranger can define, in language, false speech for itself—as a misnomer, a bad imitation, and a lack of correspondence.

In the examples at the end of the dialogue, the Stranger demonstrates how this works in practice. He weaves together the *onomata* "Theatetus" and "sits" and "Theaetetus" and "flies" to create the two *logoi* of "Theaetetus sits" and "Theaetetus flies" (263a). Properly conceived as woven *onomata*, these terms, when blended together, indicate something about how the things they denominate in the world are blended together. While both Theaetetus and the Stranger would have agreed from the outset of the dialogue that the first statement was true and the latter false, they would not have been able either to define the statement's falseness or to negate it without ultimately being ensnared in the web of Protagorean contradiction. Now, however, they are able to articulate a theory of false speech outside the frame of contradiction, and within the frame of correspondence and representation, and seeming and being.

A *logos* is nothing more nor less than the blending of discrete *onomata* that denominate discrete designata. When blended, *logos* denominates complex designata. The *logos* of the sophist—who by definition can only be an imitator because no one can do, make, and know everything—succeeds precisely through creating a *phantasmatic* imitation not of things as they are, but of things as they are believed to be. Falseness then is not a matter of speaking *what is not,* but a matter of improperly weaving together *onomata* and *rhêmata*: "If someone says things about you, but says different things as the same or not beings as beings, then it definitely seems that false speech really and truly arises from that kind of putting together of *rhêmata* and *onomata*" (263c; N. White 1993, 59; translation modified). Their definition of the sophist is complete: "Imitation of the contrary-speech-producing, insincere and unknowing sort, of the appearance-making kind of copy-making, the word-juggling part of production that's marked off as human and not divine. Anyone who says the sophist is of this 'blood and family' will be saying, it seems, the complete truth" (268c–d; N. White 1993, 65).[19]

Conclusion

While this pronouncement of victory suggests that they have succeeded in defining the sophist, which was their professed goal at the outset of the dialogue, they have in fact accomplished much more than this. A declaration of victory in 1945 probably carries less cultural and historical significance than the numerous technological developments and the birth of the American military-industrial complex that enabled it; similarly the development—through a self-conscious analysis of language *as* language and a metalinguistic vocabulary—of a correspondence theory of language and truth has more profound consequences in the history of ideas than the momentary, political expedience of defeating the sophists. The full flowering of Plato's rhetorical theory of *mimêsis,* when applied to his rhetorical theory of *onoma* and *rhêma*, fundamentally detaches *logos* from the flux of Heraclitean *phusis* by redefining it as "*logos* about": one no longer speaks; one speaks about something. The initial disjunction of *logos* from *phusis* coincided with the beginning of linguistic self-consciousness in the pre-Socratics, but this first rupture is drastically accelerated by Plato, whose rhetorical theory weaponized *logos* to become "the assertion" and "the locus of truth in the sense of correctness." As Heidegger puts it, "We arrive at Aristotle's proposition according to which logos as assertion is what can be true or false. Truth . . . now becomes a property of logos. . . . Logos is now *legein ti kata tinos*, saying something about something" (2000, 142; original pagination 199).[20] Out of Plato's rhetorical theory, in other words, is born the *logos* as assertion, truth as correspondence, and the monolithic "sovereignty of the signifier" that would lay the template for the distinction between seeming and being, truth and appearance, and for metaphysics and representational thinking in the future history of thought in the West.

« EPILOGUE »

The Past and Future of Plato's Rhetorical Theory

I have attempted to present an alternate view of rhetorical theory in Plato's dialogues. This view aims not to presuppose a condemnation of rhetoric—or any form of linguistic falseness, for that matter—that is predicated on a full-fledged metaphysical system of thought, but to interrogate how the literate and metadiscursive theoretical investigations of language portrayed throughout these dialogues, which themselves constitute Plato's rhetorical theory, are essential to the process of the restriction of being from seeming and early developments in Platonist metaphysics. By this rereading, the condemnation in the *Gorgias* points away from a fixed notion of falseness as such and toward historical exigencies that cannot be universalized as a critique of rhetoric. The clashes with both Protagoras and Gorgias are inconclusive precisely because Plato has yet to provide his interlocutors access to a theory of language *as* language, detached from *phusis*; and so the sophists' *logos* cannot be fully differentiated from or subordinated to the *logos* of the philosopher. In such a state, the language of the cleverer contestant need only tap into the visceral, erotic verbal power once wielded by the archaic poet. Our very bodies will be carried away in his river of song and his sonorous Orphic voice. Yet, through a metadiscursive consideration of written eloquence itself (the written speech in the *Phaedrus*, Homer in the *Republic*) and the development of a theoretical taxonomy to define how that language functions as language (from *onoma* to *rhêma*, from *rhêma* to *logos*), interlocutors develop a critical self-awareness of what in the language causes its profound effects. This awareness is the foothold needed for a more robust rhetorical theory that will hamper the force of *logos*. The rhetorical taxonomy that develops from these investigations—the theories of *mimêsis*, *onoma*, and *rhêma*—ultimately make it possible for Plato to redefine *logos*, not as a force of *phusis* that sweeps the hearer up in its corporeal tide, but as a detached method of imitation, signification, and representation. The sophist no longer speaks what is; he merely imitates it.

As I explain in the introduction, one need not swallow Heidegger's prioritization of Greek thought when taking as a guide his interpretation of the radical changes that took place between Parmenides and Heraclitus on the one hand and Plato and Aristotle on the other. Of particular interest here is his explanation of how in Heraclitus and Parmenides *logos* is at once fused with the material world (*phusis*) and at the same time in the process of being extracted from it, eventually to become *logos*-as-assertion and assertion-as-truth. In the same way that the strife of opposing forces that is the very architecture of *phusis* inheres in *logos* itself for Heraclitus, the monistic *phusis* of Parmenides absorbs language into that totality. Although we can observe the nascent separation of *logos* and *phusis* in these thinkers, this is not yet the deterioration of *logos* to a mere sign, to "speaking about" (Heidegger 2000, 190; original pagination 136). That only happens with Plato.

It is at the "end" of Greek philosophy, in Plato and Aristotle, that *logos* becomes assertion, and "logos as assertion becomes the locus of truth in the sense of correctness. . . . Truth . . . now becomes a property of logos. . . . Logos is now *legein ti kata tinos*, saying something about something" (Heidegger 2000, 199; original pagination 142). What results, ultimately, is the assertion, the statement, which—fully formulated particularly in the rhetorical tradition—would forever alter how the West would conceive of what language is and can be. In this way, the rhetorical theories of *onoma*, *rhêma*, and *mimêsis* are much more than a taxonomy of language about language: they are the intellectual raw material for a representational theory of language, which, according to Heidegger, was the foundational structure par excellence in Greek philosophy for the development of metaphysics in the West that would wrest language from the grip of *phusis* once and for all.

In the West we have long since abandoned any naive belief that, because things developed historically and sequentially in this way, such a development vis-à-vis language was inexorable or indicative of some form of scientific progress. Indeed, any number of linguistic investigations and metaphysical overturnings of the twentieth century—from Saussure's structuralist linguistics and the post-structuralist critique, to Wittgenstein's language games, to Austin's theory of performativity and Chomsky's universal grammar—might be marshaled to indicate, to the contrary, that signification simply cannot account for language. At every turn, language defies reference. And while Derrida may teach us to "defer," to "differ," and to "play" with signification, he has not taught us to unthink it, and such Derridean play is in no way consequence-free. Nearly a century and a half of battling to think outside the strictures of Platonist metaphysics and the subsequent political resurrection of sophistic nihilism in the so-called "post-truth" era is anything but a promise fulfilled. At the same time, it is no more reasonable to assume that language-as-signification was necessarily a step in the direction of a "correct" theory of language than it is to assume that because things were once a different way the originary state is to be preferred. I'm seeking in this work to promote neither the naive wish to return to an originary *logos*, nor the dangers of uncritically embracing Plato's metaphysical solution to the epistemic crisis of sophistic thought, nor a contemporary return of sophistic nihilism that comes in the wake of the *de-struktion* of metaphysics. It is on this point that I wish to allow myself room to speculate about some of the less obvious effects of Plato's reduction of *logos* to mediation, presuming neither an intellectual purity or rawness about what was "originary," nor an intellectual superiority or advancement about what replaced it, nor a groundless optimism about what seems to have replaced the replacement in our own time.

Michel Foucault famously claimed in his 1970 lecture *L'ordre du discours* (*The Discourse on Language*) that what is most powerful in the selection, control, organization, and ordering of discourse is what seems to be most essential to it: namely, "the opposition between true and false" (1972, 217). Despite the fact that he does not mention Heidegger on this point, it is doubtful that Heidegger was far from his mind. This basic opposition between true and false would seem to be an inherent and therefore neutral property of language as such, and neither based on nor productive of a "system of exclusion" (Foucault 1972, 217). He gives voice to the obvious objection: "How could one reasonably compare the constraints of truth with those other divisions, arbitrary in origin if not developing out of historical contingency—not merely modifiable but in a state of continual flux, supported by a system of institutions imposing and manipulating them, acting not without constraint nor without an element, at least, of violence? Certainly, as a proposition, the division between true and false is neither arbitrary, nor modifiable, nor institutional, nor violent" (Foucault 1972, 217–18). Perhaps, he goes on to claim, anticipating the study I offer here, it was in fact developed historically, modifiably, and (eventually) institutionally.

The *Sophist* is our best window into the culmination of this historical development, the very template for the language ideology that would undercut all implicit and explicit theories of language in the West, from the late classical to the contemporary era. The end result of this split of *logos* from *phusis*—which makes it possible for the sophists' *logos* to be evacuated of its power—does not entail that *logos* is in fact representational, or (and here is my speculation) that it was ever detached from *phusis* in the first place. The full flowering of the rhetorical arts, which would elaborately "technologize the word," in Ong's terms, may simply mask, rather than evacuate, the physical, material power of speech.

This is, at heart, Heidegger's own observation: he writes that "the persuasive sway [i.e., *phusis*] becomes no less overwhelming because humans take up this sway itself directly into their violence and use this violence as such"—in other words, the physical, material power of language becomes no less physical, no less powerful, no less *violent*, once humans make out of it a tool by recasting it as "statement," "assertion," or "proposition." On the contrary, its powers far outstrip its paltry truth-value. Heidegger continues: "This merely conceals the uncanniness of language, of passions, as that into which human beings as historical are disposed <*gefügt*>, while it seems to them that it is *they* who have them at their disposal <*verfügt*>. The uncanniness of these powers lies in their seeming familiarity and ordinariness" (2000, 166; original pagination 120). In other words, our sense that we *use* language, that we are its masters, that we order and control it, hides from us its most essential power. Its correspondence-truth value is banal, petty by comparison to what it is able to accomplish; in fact, the understanding that reduces its archaic force to an assertive truth value is precisely what makes it all the more powerful. Because we delimit and restrict its truth value to its correspondence function, we miss entirely how it is really functioning in all its material, visceral, physical potency to force beliefs on us that are in no way true. Once "the word sinks down to become a mere sign" (2000, 183; original pagination 131), its actual function to dictate everything we think about *what is* is still operational, and made all the more dangerous, because we think all along that we can wrangle it by seeking in it its *signifié*. Far from disarming the dangerous power of the sophists' *logos*, Plato weaponized it by tricking us into thinking that it is "mere language," and in so doing, he concealed from us its greatest strength.

The apparatus of rhetorical theories designed by Plato as prophylactic against the dangerous force of the sophists' language, when mistaken for language as such in its most basic and essential function, leaves the hearer exposed and vulnerable, unarmed against the overwhelming, archaic power of speech. This, in essence, is the past and future of Plato's rhetorical theory.

Notes

Introduction

1. The full-fledged understanding that language indexes or symbolizes referents in the real world is commonly identified in Arist., *Int.* 1.1–6. The work begins: "First we must settle what a name [*onoma*] is and what a verb [*rhêma*] is, and then what a negation, an affirmation, a statement and a sentence [*logos*] are. Now spoken sounds are symbols of the affections of the soul, and written marks symbols of spoken sounds. . . . Just as some thoughts in the soul are neither true nor false while some are necessarily one or the other, so also with spoken sounds" (1.1–18; Ackrill 1984, 25). Aristotle's formulation—the first clear example of the *logos* as a propositional statement, leading to the full-fledged development of logic, grammar, and rhetoric that would dominate the West's notion of language up to the present day—is commonly regarded as derivative of Plato's language theory. See, for example, Francis M. Cornford (1935, 300n2, 303n1, 305, 307). Cornford suggests that Aristotle's formulation of *onoma* and *rhêma*, which was "necessary and sufficient for the minimum statement that can be true or false" (1935, 307), is nothing more than a repetition of Plato's discussion of the terms at *Soph.* 262aff. and *Cra.* 425aff., that even Plato's formulation "is taken as familiar without explanation" (1935, 307).

2. For studies that investigate Plato's theory of falsehood and false statements, see Denyer 1991; and Crivelli 2012.

3. Havelock 1963 is a fine example of Plato scholarship that has absorbed the understanding of the effects of literacy during the period in which Plato was writing, but

nevertheless remained insulated from the literary-dramatic interpretive movement that was contemporaneous with his own scholarship.

4. These criticisms may be found in Street 1984; and Finnegan 1988.

5. For the most prominent articulations of this critique, see Farias 1991 and Faye 2009.

6. See, for example, the critique of Heidegger's etymology in Barnes 1990. For critiques of Heidegger's reading of Plato, see Gonzalez 2002, 2006, 2008, and 2009. For the influence of Heidegger's ethnocentrism on his interpretation of the Greeks, see Most 2004.

7. See, for example, the essays collected in Hyland and Manoussakis 2006. The authors represented therein supply a voluminous literature on this topic.

8. This is a related but nevertheless different question from the question of Heidegger's treatment of rhetoric. While there are references to rhetoric scattered across his published works and lecture courses, Heidegger's most extended treatment of rhetoric (in particular, Aristotle's *Rhetoric*) appears in his 1924 lecture course on Aristotle, *Grundbegriffe der aristotelischen Philosophie*, published in English as *Basic Concepts of Aristotelian Philosophy* (2009). See also the essays collected in Gross and Kemmann 2005. The current study considers how Heidegger's analysis of the "restriction" or "limitation of being" in the development of metaphysics in the West might inform our understanding of the development of rhetorical theory within Plato, rather than Heidegger's understanding of ancient rhetoric or Aristotelian rhetoric as such.

9. In parentheses in the 1953 edition.

10. The influence of this way of reading Plato may be found in numerous philosophical works following Heidegger. See, for example, Gilles Deleuze's rich reading of Plato's metaphysics in *Difference and Repetition* (1995, 126–38 and 264–69), Jacques Derrida's analysis of Plato's distrust of *mimêsis* and the development of a transcendent truth (1981b, 186n14), and Foucault's description of the Greek development of true discourse out of Plato's conflict with the sophists in *L'ordre du discours*, published in English as "The Discourse on Language" (1972, 217–18). The influence of Heidegger's *de-strukting* of the Platonist tradition on these and other later thinkers makes this particular aspect of Heidegger's philosophy relatively less controversial.

11. An exhaustive list of citations on this point might easily include the whole of the *Gesamtausgabe*. Nevertheless, prominent examples where Heidegger attempts to address historically the philosophical development of truth and metaphysics include his 1926 lecture course published in English as *Basic Concepts of Ancient Philosophy* (2008); the 1927 lecture course *Basic Problems of Phenomenology* (1982); the 1933 lecture course *The Fundamental Question of Philosophy* (2010); the 1937–38 lecture course *Basic Questions of Philosophy* (1994); the 1942–43 lecture course on Parmenides (1992); and numerous essays from the 1940s: "The Anaximander Fragment" (1975), "Metaphysics as History of Being," "Sketches for a History of Being as Metaphysics," and "Overcoming Metaphysics" (1973).

12. This view is traced to Hermann (1839) 1976, 352–71. Tigerstedt 1977 offers a historical summary of the developmental perspective (see 25–51). See also Crombie 1962;

Cross and Woozley 1964; Raven 1965; Vlastos 1970, 1991; J. Gould 1972; N. White 1976; Irwin 1977b; R. Robinson 1984; Prior 1985; Klosko 1986; and Kraut 1992.

13. This perspective was spearheaded by the Tübingen School, which suggested on the basis of the explicit suspicion of writing expressed in both the *Phaedrus* dialogue as well as the *Seventh Letter* that Plato could not have committed his true beliefs to writing but must have preserved them for oral instruction. The contradiction between, on the one hand, claiming that Plato did not commit his own views to writing and, on the other hand, basing this claim on the fact that Plato expressed *in writing* his suspicion of writing does not seem to have troubled this interpretation. For proponents of this view, see Gaiser 1959; Reale 1987; Krämer 1990; and Szlezák 1996.

14. For different articulations of this observation, see Strauss 1964; Mulhern 1971; Klagge and Smith 1992; Cohen and Keyt 1992; and the essays in Press 2000.

15. For the difficulties of dating the compositions, see Thesleff 1989; J. Howland 1991; and Nails 1995 and 2002. For the difficulties of looking for Plato outside of his dialogues, see Sayre 1993; and Corey 2015, 11.

16. By promoting this particular strand of Plato scholarship, I do not wish to suggest that the doctrinal readings of Plato have been entirely superseded by literary-dramatic ones. In fact, in his commentary on the *Protagoras*, C. C. W. Taylor writes in direct response to Michael C. Stokes (1986), one of the editors of the volume that contains the article by Schofield (1992) quoted above, that "no one would deny . . . that Plato, in writing these words, intended them to express Socrates's (and therefore Plato's) understanding of what the argument was supposed (by Socrates, and therefore by Plato) to establish. It would hardly be necessary to labour what is thus obvious, had not Michael Stokes expended so much energy and ingenuity on the attempt to present Socrates's arguments as largely *ad hominem*, and in passing criticized me, together with others, for excessive readiness to interpret Socratic utterances as assertions or as rhetorical questions instead of as genuine questions designed to elicit the views of the interlocutor" (C. C. W. Taylor [1976] 1991, xiv). He continues: "I sometimes assume, and sometimes argue . . . that a view ascribed to Socrates was held by Plato at the time of writing" (xvi). As Taylor's response to Stokes indicates, the doctrinal view persists alongside the literary-dramatic one.

17. Two exceptions particularly worthy of note are McCoy 2008 and Corey 2015. McCoy's book is devoted to showing precisely how Plato "presents Socrates' philosophical practice as rhetorical" (2008, 3), whereas Corey's book is devoted to dispensing with "the 'mouthpiece' assumption" (2015, 11) where the sophists are concerned. This study is deeply sympathetic to the contributions of McCoy and Corey, but nevertheless departs from them in two ways. One has to do with the understanding of the term *rhetoric*, the other with the term *sophist*.

McCoy explicitly defines rhetoric according to "its broad, contemporary sense of 'the means used to persuade through words.' [McCoy's] definition of *rhetoric* here is deliberately general, for Socrates does not limit his use of rhetoric to one or two devices; his rhetoric is guided by the particular needs of the soul of the person with whom he is speaking. Socrates is interested in persuading his audience and not always or exclusively through affecting the intellects of his interlocutors" (2008, 3–4). As I explain, there are important reasons to separate persuasion and eloquence generally from rhetoric, given the methods of rhetorical theorizing that were contemporaneous with Plato, and which Plato himself contributed to formulating. In the final two chapters of the book, I show how Plato has Socrates and the Eleatic Stranger develop a theoretical taxonomy about language and discourse, and this activity is given the chronologically appropriate denomination *rhetorical theory*. So while I agree wholeheartedly with McCoy's overall thesis that rhetoric is an important tool for Plato's differentiation between the sophist and the philosopher, I believe his use of this tool is highly technical and more specific than the concept of persuasion generally. As I explain, he invents the very metadiscursive terminology that makes the differentiation possible.

Secondly, although I agree with Corey's assertion that Plato goes to great lengths to differentiate between "rhetoric" and "sophistry," I am unconvinced that he similarly differentiates between "sophists" and "rhetoricians." While rhetoric is detachable from sophists for Plato, sophistry is, by definition, what they practice (which is sometimes but not always rhetoric). I depart from Corey in that I see Plato's treatment of "sophists" as almost exclusively negative.

18. A number of studies attempt to revise the dominant understanding of sophistic thought that has prevailed since Plato. Schiappa (2003) provides a very useful summary of the different ways the term has been defined over time (see 3–10). One can point back as far as Nietzsche and Hegel to identify the origin of the revisionist movement, which is carried out by, among others, Grote (1851–56); Untersteiner (1954); Segal (1962); Guthrie (1971); Kerferd (1981); Jarratt (1991); de Romilly (1992); Poulakos (1995); Brisson (1997); Marback (1999); Tell (2011); and Enos (2012). Nevertheless, the general revision has not yet given way to the kinds of serious analysis that, for example, Schiappa and Hoffman (1994) called for, in which sophistic thought would be studied as a serious engagement with and response to pre-Socratic ontology (156–59).

19. The extant fragments are collected in Sprague 1972.

20. See, for example, *Prt.* 155a–56a and *Ap.* 33e.

Chapter 1

1. The harshness of the criticism is identified by numerous scholars. For example, Alessandra Fussi points out that Plato must have been "enraged" (2000, 39) when he wrote the dialogue. James Doyle notes that the tone of the dialogue is more acrimonious than any other, that it even degenerates to "naked hostility" (2006, 89). As these and other examples indicate, the "developmentalist" approach has been influential in explaining the differences between the *Gorgias* and *Phaedrus* dialogues (see the introduction).

2. This translation differs from the traditional translations, which render the analogy as a Platonic distinction between the soul and the body, a difference that turns on Plato's use of the term *psychê*. Plato writes: *tên men epi tê psychê politikên kalô, tên de epi sômati* (τὴν μὲν ἐπὶ τῇ ψυχῇ πολιτικὴν καλῶ, τὴν δὲ ἐπὶ σώματι). Here I believe Plato is eliding the *psychê* in the second phrase, which amounts to a distinction between what we would call the *life* of the *polis* and the *life* of the *body*, and not a distinction between soul and

body. This translation is far more plausible, given that *politikên* is in the accusative, modifying *psychê* in the first phrase. The dative *sômati* in the second phrase implies "that *of the body.*" Amending the translation in this way solves the seeming imbalance in the analogy, pointed out by E. R. Dodds, that one set of practices deals with the individual and the other the group (1959, 227).

3. This analogy is an elaboration of the one offered originally by Gorgias in his *Encomium of Helen,* where he states: "The effect of speech upon the condition of the *psychê* is comparable to the power of drugs over the nature of bodies. For just as different drugs dispel different secretions from the body, and some bring an end to disease and others to life, so also in the case of speeches, some distress, others delight, some cause fear, others make the hearers bold, and some drug and bewitch the soul with a kind of evil persuasion" (DK 82b11.14; Kennedy 1972, 53). Dodds suggests that this analogy predates even the historical Gorgias, since its antecedent occurs in Aeschylus, who has Oceanus say, "Do you not know then, Prometheus, that words are the physicians of a disordered temper?" (Dodds 1959, 379–80). Plato repeats the analogy between medicine and rhetoric in *Phaedrus* 270b.

4. Similarly, Ilham Dilman writes, "The counterfeit varieties of these arts aim only at the *appearance* of what their genuine counterparts aim at—apparent beauty, apparent well-being, apparent knowledge" (1979, 24). See also Stauffer 2006, 49; Plochmann and Robinson 1988, 65–67; and Benardete 1991, 33.

5. I am grateful to an anonymous reader who suggested to me the possibility that the historical Gorgias himself may very well have played with this distinction between seeming and being in his work *On Nature, or On Non-being.* This impression comes from Sextus Empiricus's commentary on the text, the primary testimony for the fragment, particularly in sections 83–86 of *Against the Schoolmasters* (in Sprague 1972, 42–46). There, Sextus claims that Gorgias distinguishes between *logos,* perception, and being. This is nevertheless Sextus's commentary on Gorgias's thought, an explanation that aims to make Gorgias's puzzling text more transparent. While Sextus was relying on a Platonic distinction between seeming and being to elucidate Gorgias's *On Non-being,* the testimony does not suggest that Gorgias made such a distinction himself.

6. There are a handful of commentators and translators who link *kommôtikê* to other terms with the stem *komm–*, but the majority relate it to *komaô.*

7. Diogenes Laertius records the second titles of most works in the Platonic corpus, and indicates that Thrasylus also used the second titles. R. G. Hoeder suggests, however, that the second titles for the works came much earlier, since such inclusion was common practice as early as the fourth century BCE, perhaps even originating with Plato himself (see especially 1957, 19–20).

8. See, for example, Waterfield 1994, x; and Lamb 1925, 255.

9. See, for example, T. Griffith 2010, viii. Again, the developmentalist approach has been highly influential in the interpretations of the *Gorgias.*

10. While I agree with Doyle that there are too few accounts of how the themes may be united, he perhaps overstates the situation. For example, Robert Wardy has offered an excellent account of the "problematic . . . relation between rhetoric and democracy" (1996, 86). Similarly, David McNeill notes how Gorgias's claim that he can teach rheto-

ric to anyone is fundamentally an argument that runs against "the traditional aristocratic distinction between 'the many' (οἱ πολλοί) and 'the few' (οἱ ὀλίγοι)" (2001, 134). Brian Vickers identifies a unity in the dialogue in the form of "Plato's hatred of Athenian democracy, and especially its use of oratory as the main visible means of influencing opinion" (1988, 88).

11. Tom Griffith points out that this term refers to members of the Athenian polis who had no legitimate trade of their own, but made their living by bringing lawsuits against other citizens. In this way, the term refers to a dubious practice of exploiting the Athenian legal and political structures for self-gain (2010, 28n26).

12. The influence of the distinction between *seeming* and *being* is also on display in the translations of the dialogue. For example, in his analysis of the analogy (464c–d), Socrates says, "The art of flattery[,] which . . . divides itself into four, plunges itself into each of the subdivisions, and makes itself out to be the very thing it has crept into" (my translation). Tom Griffith (2010) and Waterfield (1994) translate "attaches" or "plunges" (ὑποδῦσα) as "impersonates." Tom Griffith (2010) and Lamb (1925) translate "makes out to be" (προσποιεῖται εἶναι) as "pretends." Similarly, at the end of the dialogue (527b), Socrates presents the famous maxim that "we have to take greater care to avoid doing wrong than we do to avoid suffering wrong, and that above all else we must concentrate not on leading people to expect [δοκεῖν] that we're good, but on being good" (Waterfield 1994, 134). Lamb (1925) translates this as a distinction between "seeming good" and "being good." While these translations may seem very close to the essential meaning, they nevertheless reflect a firm distinction between seeming and being that is arguably not present in the text.

13. Marina McCoy (2009) has identified contemporary uses of the term *rhêtorikê* in Alcidamas and Isocrates, which, due to the necessarily circular nature of dating Plato's texts, makes definitive attribution of the term to Plato somewhat difficult.

14. As Schiappa notes, "Plato coined nearly dozens of terms ending in *–ikê*" (2003, 44). On this point he provides thirty examples, including *kommôtikê* (see 60n18). Schiappa also points to Pierre Chantraine's (1956) astute observation that of more than 350 words with the *–ikos* stem used by Plato, 250 are not found in any earlier texts.

15. See Thompson (1871) 1973, 147. Dodds mentions that, among many scholars toward the beginning of the twentieth century, it was a common practice to strike the phrase that included *kommôtike* from 465c (1959, 231).

16. As far as I can tell, Dodds's commentary marks the end of the practice; he defends the strangeness of the word, since it is "intelligible in light of what has preceded it" (1959, 231). Nevertheless, "what has preceded it" is simply the same strange, possibly indecipherable word, and not an explanation of the word's meaning.

17. See, for example, Plutarch, *Fragmenta* (Sandbach 1969), frag. 147; and Galen, *De compositione medicamentorum secundum locos libri* (v. 12, 439–512).

18. In the many editions of Lamb's translation published between 1925 and 1983, the term is rendered as either "self-adornment" or "personal adornment." Tom Griffith uses the term "fashion" (2010, 30). Waterfield uses "ornamentation" (1994, 32). Kennedy uses "cosmetics" in his summaries of the analogy (1994, 37; 1999, 62).

19. Although Thucydides does not use the particular term *komaô*, he nevertheless

describes the same activities that are elsewhere captured by this term. The phrase Thucydides uses is ἀναδούμενοι τῶν ἐν τῇ κεφαλῇ τριχῶν.

20. The scholiast who derived the term from *kommi* was referring not to the *Gorgias* but to *Republic* 373c, recorded in both the Greene (1938) and the more recent Cufalo (2007) editions. The scholiast cited by Thompson ([1871] 1973, 147) defines *kommôtikê* by claiming it is related to the contemporaneous term *kommôtriôn*, a ladies' maid or dressing woman. Both of these terms, the scholiast suggests, come from the term *kommi*.

21. This derivation arises originally as a result of the fact that *kommi*, a gum that oozes out of a tree, was used as a hairstyling product in order to make one's hair seem more effeminate, and, it seems, it was most valuable when used unmixed and pure, straight from its source. The etymology is as follows: κομμωτριῶν. κόμμι λέγεται τὸ ἐκ τῶν δένδρων ἅτε δὴ δάκρυον ἀπορρέον ὑγρόν, ᾧ χρῶνται πρὸς τὰς τρίχας τῶν γυναικῶν ὥστε μὴ διαχεῖσθαι ἀλλὰ μένειν ὡς ἄγαν συνημμένας ἐφ' οὗ βεβούληνται σχήματος αἱ κομμώτριαι, παρ' ὃ καὶ ἀπὸ τοῦδε τοῦ κόμμεος λέγονται, καὶ ἡ τέχνη κομμωτική.

22. For the full speech, see Lysias 2000, 342–46. Elsewhere, Athenaeus quotes Antiphanes, the playwright of the late fifth/early fourth century BCE, who points to Egyptian perfume as the particularly expensive type (15.690a; Gulick 1941, 195). Insofar as perfume was controversial for its cost, the Egyptian kind was likely to have been the most expensive.

23. Indeed, this may account for the controversial place perfume held in Athenian society. Athenaeus recounts how Solon's laws in early sixth century forbade the perfumer's trade: "The Lacedaemonians expel[led] from Sparta the manufacturers of perfumes, on the ground that they spoil the olive oil; so, too, those who dye raw wool, because they destroy the whiteness of the wool. And the wise Solon in his laws forbade the selling of perfume by men" (15.687a; Gulick 1941, 178–79). And he cites a false etymology for the word for perfume: "Chrysippus, too, declares that perfumes (*mura*) took their name from the great toil and foolish labour [*moros*] with which they are obtained" (15.686; 177).

24. The link between the use of costly goods and corruption of the polis serves as a bridge to a later point in the conversation, when Socrates insults his host by similarly demeaning sophistry. In the same way that he defines perfume use as a kind of corruption, he defines self-adornment as a kind of sophistry, wedding the two activities together by likening both to the work of a pimp. He says, "It is the function of a good pimp to render the man or the woman he is serving attractive to his or her associate. . . . Now, one thing that contributes to rendering a person attractive is a comely arrangement of hair and clothing"; and another, he claims, is for the pimp "to teach only the *words* that tend to make one attractive" (4.57–62; Todd 2006, 593–97).

25. The Greek of this passage is as follows: ὥστε ποιεῖν ἀλλότριον κάλλος ἐφελκομένους τοῦ οἰκείου.

26. I am grateful to Professor Manfred Kraus for drawing my attention to the potential relevance of these terms. It may be the case that κομμοῦν and κομμώτρια both are derived from κομμώ, as speculated by both Immanuel Bekker (1814, 273) and Felix Solmsen (1901, 501). Bekker defines κομμώ as "ἡ κοσμοῦσα τὸ ἕδος τῆς Ἀθηνᾶς," or the

name for a priestess who adorned the statue of Athena in the Acropolis. Nevertheless, this attribution still does not explain the geminated μμ. Solmsen speculates that the μμ in these terms may result from an "affectionate" lengthening of the sound (Felix Solmsen 1901, 504), but this explanation is unlikely, since it would be unusual to speak with affection of such self-indulgent activities. In any case, Solmson's attempt to account for the gemination only reinforces its strangeness. Similarly, the verb κομμόομαι ("to be clean; to decorate or embellish") also begins appearing in the fifth century. Frisk's etymology suggests that its origin is unknown, and he notes that it may have been a "fashionable new creation or a borrowed term" ("eine modische Neuschöpfung oder Entlehnung zu sein," 1954–72, 1:109). Frisk's attribution of this verb to improvisation and borrowing further supports the possibility that the root is borrowed from another language, perhaps Egyptian (κόμμι). All these examples indicate neologisms that date to the fifth century, whose μμ gemination has been unaccounted for.

27. Regarding the latter interpretation of the *Gorgias*, the main conversation seems to concern the extent to which Plato and Socrates were pro-democratic and pro-authoritarian, or the reverse. See, for example, Saxonhouse 1983, 139–69, especially 165–67; Rutherford 1995, 151–2; Monoson 2000, 11n23, 12n24; and Tarnopolsky 2010, 13n54–5.

28. Aristotle's *Politics* 1256b–1266b; Solon's fragments 13.71, 4c, 34.7–9, in M. L. West 1992.

29. Arlene Saxonhouse (1983, 1992) rightly insists that Thucydides is essential background reading for the *Gorgias*.

Chapter 2

1. Aristotle describes this portion of the text in the following way: "It is excusable that an angry person calls a wrong 'heaven-high' or 'monstrous.' And [this can be done] when a speaker holds the audience in his control and causes them to be stirred either by praise or blame or hate or love. Those who are impassioned [*enthousiasai*] mouth such utterances, and audiences accept them because they are in a similar mood. That is why [this emotional style] is suited to poetry, too, for poetry is inspired. It should be used as described—or ironically [*eirôneia*], as Gorgias did and as in the *Phaedrus*" (1408b; Kennedy 2007, 236–37; translation modified). There can be no doubt which speech from the *Phaedrus* Aristotle has in mind here; Aristotle's terminology is a direct reference to Plato's terminology of "enthusiasm" and "divine inspiration" used to describe the palinode.

2. It is likely that the true object of critique here was not Lysias, but Plato's rival Isocrates, who used written speeches for instruction in his school, and whom Plato mentions by name at 278e. R. L. Howland views the *Phaedrus* "as a direct and comprehensive attack on the educational system of Isocrates" (1937, 152); and Gerrit de Vries interprets Isocrates's *Antidosis* as a self-defense against Plato's attack in the *Phaedrus* (1953). See also Coulter 1967; de Vries 1971; Voliotis 1977; and McAdon 2004 for further affirmations of the that the *Phaedrus* is an outright attack on or ironic praise of Isocrates.

3. On the overall importance of the theme of *eros* throughout Plato's works, see Gordon 2012.

4. For accounts of this view, see Hunt 1962; Brownstein 1965; E. E. Ryan 1979; and McAdon 2004.

5. For accounts of this view, see Black 1958; Quimby 1974; and Schiappa 1999, 10.

6. T. Gould 1964, 72; Chroust 1973, 116.

7. See E. E. Ryan 1979.

8. I would add that the bitterness of tone in the *Gorgias* is dramatically appropriate for a confrontation with a notorious sophist who brought Athens to her knees, while the friendliness of the *Phaedrus* is dramatically appropriate for a private tryst outside the city walls. Plato's own feelings and tone may simply be irrelevant to the action of the dialogues. See Ingram 2007, 294.

9. This problem has been discussed at length. I will not reproduce those arguments here; they may be found in Helmbold and Holther 1950–52; Plass 1968; Heath 1989a, 1989b; Rowe 1989; and Kastely 2002. The apparent disunity of the dialogue is a major reason that the ancient writers—in particular, Olympiodorus—believed it to be one of Plato's early works, since the use of hiatus is assumed to be the certain mark of an inexperienced writer (Hackforth 1952, 3); as Derrida notes, the *Phaedrus* "was obliged to wait almost twenty-five centuries before anyone gave up the idea that it was a badly composed dialogue" (1981a, 66). De Vries has suggested that it is not only the hiatus between the palinode and rhetoric that lends a sense of disunity, but the proliferation of themes that lack a clear cohesion. These themes include love, rhetoric, *psychê*, the good, the beautiful, dialectic, mania, divine possession, and anamnesis (de Vries 1969, 22).

10. Charles Griswold has pointed out that "one might thus argue that the unity of the *Phaedrus* is that of an example and the rules it exemplifies. . . . This argument (which most interpreters reject anyhow, since it does not explain the length and complexity of the palinode) is not a sound one" (1986, 138). He goes on to explain the unity of the dialogue by claiming that the myth of the palinode provides a reflection on self-knowledge—the same self-knowledge that motivates Socrates's remarks on rhetoric and the technical understanding of "the logos appropriate to self-knowledge" (1986, 137). Nevertheless, Griswold does not account for the palinode's flagrant abuses of the technical rules laid out at the end of the dialogue; see 1986, 136–201.

The same problem confronts David White's study of the dialogue. However, he claims the dialogue is unified, despite its apparent disjointedness, because it "shows Socrates leading Phaedrus to the philosophical life and, on a more general level, describes the nature of the philosophical life to anyone who, resembling Phaedrus in character, would care to be informed about that life" (1993, 178). Again, this proposed confluence between the demonstration of the myth and the descriptions of rhetoric overlooks the glaring disparity between the rhetorical form of the myth and the prescriptions regarding rhetoric. See D. White 1993, 175–202 and 229–250.

11. De Vries notes that this vocabulary marks a "purely mechanical connection between the parts of the discourse" (1969, 59), and Paul Ryan emphasizes that it is "a connective empty of logical force" (2012, 109). Whether or not this and other terms forge strong logical connections may be less significant than the fact that the speech is, in fact, using the scientific language of apodeixis (or "mechanical," "connective" terms, as de Vries and Ryan call them) rather than the poetic language of the epic.

12. For more on these linguistic developments, see Aly 1929, 40–41, 56–58, 94; van Groningen 1958, 48, 238–45; and de Vries 1969, 72. For a detailed explanation of the demonstrative and argumentative uses of these terms and their introduction into the Greek tongue, see Denniston (1934) 1959, 162–89, 555–64, and 568–80. Denniston notes Lysias's frequent use of τοίνυν ([1934] 1959, 568).

13. In other words, Lysias's speech is mimetic discourse, while in Socrates's first speech, the mimetic discourse is contextualized by diegetic narration. And Phaedrus is imitating Lysias in the sense that he is giving a speech as though he were Lysias himself, while the author Plato is imitating Isocrates in the name of Lysias.

14. Paul Ryan has suggested that these references to possession by nymphs would have been a known superstition during Socrates's and perhaps also Plato's time: "Nymphs could bring about madness. In the fifth century—perhaps during Plato's childhood—a metic named Archedemus from the island of Thera took over a cave on Mount Hymettus, decorated it, planted a garden, and had inscriptions that referred to him as νυμφόληπτος. . . . This was a genuine psychological phenomenon and not merely a metaphorical manner of speaking" (2012, 143–44).

15. For evidence that dithyrambic vocabulary was considered old-fashioned and laughable, de Vries (1969, 88–89) cites Ar., *Pax* 829, with scholia, and the scholiast on Ar., *Av.* 1393. Elsewhere Plato also scorns the dithyramnb: "Plato's judgment is the same: a long and irrelevant answer is characterized by διθύραμβον τοσουτονί (*Hp. mai.* 292c); a word built in such a way that it is striking even in the *Cratylus* is called διθύραμβῶδες (409c)" (de Vries 1969, 88–89).

16. It is Phaedrus who notes the abruptness of the speech's ending: "But I thought you were only halfway through. . . . You seem to have stopped, Socrates. Why?" (241d; Waterfield 2002, 22). It is the verse form itself that would reveal to Phaedrus the imbalance and rupture of Socrates's discourse, since, as Paul Ryan explains, the break is more apparent in dithyrambic meter and dactylic hexameter that Socrates has been using: "Ancient verse forms were stricter than ours, so that both Greeks and Romans were much more sensitive to sequences of metrical feet occurring in prose, even if they fell short of a whole line" (2012, 159).

17. Proclus continues: "Perhaps we shall act properly in invoking the gods, that they will enkindle the light of truth in our soul, and in supplicating the attendants and ministers of better natures to direct our intellect and lead it to the all-perfect, divine, and elevated, end of the Platonic theory" (1.1; T. Taylor 1985, 2–3).

18. The divine choir following the gods to their elevated end described here by Proclus is almost an exact mirror to the train of the gods described in Socrates's myth. Buckley emphasizes why this should be a source of interpretive suspicion: "As the myth is read literally in the *Platonic Theology,* and the philosopher's way is taken as truth, the conclusion must be drawn that Proclus saw himself and his predecessors not just as readers of the myth, but also actors in its drama. If one identifies oneself and one's predecessors as true philosophers and initiates, as Proclus does (6.7. 9–19, 69.6–15; 1.6.24), the myth must speak to one almost as an *ad hominem* argument" (2006, 129).

19. Although Lysias was not technically counted as one of the "older sophists," his representation here is linked to the sophistic movement through his writing of

speeches, a primary method of sophistic activity. As many have argued, the speech may be an imitation of not of Lysias, but of the methods Isocrates used in his school. See sources cited in note 2, above.

20. The sophists' practice of reversing common wisdom as a means of diversion is explicitly acknowledged, for example, at the end of Gorgias's "Encomium of Helen," where he writes, "I wished to write a speech which would be a praise of Helen and a diversion [*paignion*] to myself" (DK82b11.21; Kennedy 1972, 54). As discussed in the previous chapter, the danger arises when the diversions and "playthings" of the sophists are used in statecraft. The same theme is echoed here. The skill that thrills hearers by "eulogizing some miserable donkey as if it were a horse" may also cause catastrophic political harm when issues of state are handled "by making bad seem good" (260c; Waterfield 2002, 47). This is not to suggest that all Gorgias's works should be read as "playthings." As Schiappa (1999, 130–32) has argued, the significance of the closing line of Gorgias's *Helen* has been overemphasized in the history of scholarship on Gorgias's thought, and as Carol Poster (2017) has argued, it is unreasonable to assume that Gorgias could have worked in one genre and one genre only. Indeed, it may have been necessary for Gorgias to point out that *Helen* was intended as a "diversion" precisely because it could have been mistaken for sincerity, indicating that he was known to produce the latter.

21. As Michael Wiitala (2010, 61) claims, in the final speech Socrates identifies completely with the poetic tradition. Once the myth of the charioteer takes flight, "his language loosens up, and seems positively florid compared with the rigor and economy of the previous passage" (Bett 1986, 3). In other words, the voice of the living Socrates is drowned out by the voice of the divine surging up within him.

22. In the speech that is meant to offer an encomium of madness, Socrates describes the dark horse who is most like the implied mad lover of the previous two speeches as though it were the "bad" part of the *psychê*, while the part most like the nonlover (and least like love)—the part that exhibits self-control and restraint—is most like the "good" horse. This description undermines the promise that this third speech would offer a correction to the previous two speeches, which erroneously praise the love of the non-lover, by providing "proof" that the madness of love should be considered alongside the madness of divine possession and poetic inspiration. In fact, this is proof against his own rhetorical purpose as he defined it: that in certain cases like love, prophecy, and poetry, unrestrained madness is good and temperate restraint is inferior.

23. Again, de Vries identifies here "a playful reminiscence of Hom. *Il.* 5, 368f" (247e4–6; 1969, 138). Paul Ryan points out that this paragraph closes with "a string of three gnomic aorists. One of the principle uses of the gnomic aorist is to render vivid scenes that originate in imagination rather than experience. Consequently, the myth is replete with them" (2012, 193). This supports the idea that the myth syntactically mimics epic storytelling. De Vries notes Plato's use of a divided subject at 248a and 255c, which he attributes to a "Homeric syntactical pattern" (de Vries 1969, 138).

24. De Vries also has identified that the horse is "a conscious allusion to Hom. *Il.* 1, 423f" (247a8; 1969, 133).

25. See also Linforth 1946, 135 and 151.

26. Anne Lebeck points out that, in this passage, "many of the words have multiple associations and some of them are onomatopoeic. As a result they tease both mind and ear, and the passage produces that tickling irritation which it so well describes. Thus the delineation of sexual excitement stimulates intellectual excitement" (1972, 273).

27. Eric Havelock's description of the "paideuctic spell" cast by poetry seems a fitting explanation in the context. He describes how, in the poetic performance, the bodies of poets and listeners would be joined in rhythmic sympathy, and "the regularity of the performance had a certain effect of hypnosis which relaxed the body's physical tensions and so also relaxed mental tensions. . . . Fatigue was temporarily forgotten and perhaps the erotic impulses, no longer blocked by anxiety, were stimulated. . . . The Muse, the voice of instruction, was also the voice of pleasure" ([1963] 1998, 152).

28. Although the scope of some of Havelock's claims has been critiqued, his overall picture of the intensity of the audience's response to the poetic performance is generally accepted. See, for example, Friedrich Solmsen, who offers a strong criticism of Havelock, but nevertheless assents to the view that "the Greeks responded to a performance . . . with an intense involvement of their emotions" (1966, 100).

29. De Vries notes that the phrase used to describe pinning the horse, ὀδύναις ἔδωκεν, is yet another Homericism, found in *Il.* 5, 397, and *Od.* 17, 567 (1969, 171). As Paul Ryan puts it, "Their struggle is epic" (2012, 224).

30. Rutherford claims that Plato is borrowing from Alcidamas's "On Those Who Write Written Speeches" (1995, 244), which was written as an attack on Isocrates, who used written speeches in his rhetorical instruction. Nevertheless, Rutherford notes, Isocrates also discusses the superiority of improvised speeches (5.f27–5, *Ep. Dionys.* 2–3), and is representative of a larger "long-standing prejudice against . . . those who wrote speeches for others to deliver in court. . . . The orators themselves exploit this prejudice" (1995, 267). Here Rutherford cites Antiphon fr. 1a col. 2; Aeschines 1.94, 170; and Demosthenes 35.38–43. This argument has an earlier precedent in Diés 1927.

31. I am grateful to an anonymous reader who pointed out this parallel to me.

Chapter 3

1. In addition to the extended treatments of Protagoras and his thought in the *Theaetetus* and the *Protagoras,* Plato makes numerous other references to him, including in the *Phaedrus* (267c), the *Euthydemus* (286c), the *Meno* (91d), the *Cratylus* (386a–391c), and the *Sophist* (232e).

2. The phrase *dissoi logoi* also refers to a treatise on twofold arguments by an anonymous author (see Sprague 1972, 279–93). Although that text is widely understood to be Protagorean in nature, its authorship is not attributed to Protagoras. My use of the phrase two-*logoi* refers to the fragment "On every thing there are two arguments opposed to each other" (*kai prôtos ephê logous einai peri pantos pragmatos antikeimenous allêlois*) and not to the anonymous text *Dissoi logoi.*

3. Due to the lack of surviving literature, little can be established conclusively about the influence of pre-Socratic thought on the fifth-century sophists. Nevertheless, several connections have been noted, such as the following: parallels between Gorgias's *On Nonbeing, or Peri phusis* and the fragments of Parmenides's *Peri phusis* (Kerferd 1955;

Mansfeld 1990, 98, 112–18, 123n48; Schiappa and Hoffman 1994); parallels between Gorgias's *On Nonbeing*, Protagoras's advocacy of contradictory arguments, and Zeno's thought (Kirk, Raven, and Schofield 1983, 279); all "controversialists" (ἀντιλογικοί) were considered Heracliteans (Peck 1962, 159; McCabe 2000, 94); Gorgias as an opponent to pre-Socratic thought (Guthrie 1971, 15, 180, and 194) and yet influenced by his teacher Empedocles (Untersteiner 1954, 92); Protagoras's doctrine of the impossibility of contradiction being derived from Parmenides's doctrinal denial of speaking of nonbeing (Levinson 1971, 260); his man-measure doctrine as "a logical extension of Heraclitus's doctrines" (Schiappa 2003, 95; see also M. Lee 2005, 77–117); Parmenides, like the sophists, being concerned with *onomata* (Woodbury 1971).

4. On the latter point, see Irwin 1977a, 5; Cherubin 1993, 216–28; Allred 2009, 14; and Crotty 2009, xiv.

5. In addition to Plato, Diogenes Laertius (9.51) and Sextus Empiricus (*Adv. Math.* 7.60) attest to these being the precise words of the opening lines of the book. See Gagarin 1968, 125.

6. Ugo Zilioli points out that since Sextus's testimony is not dependent on Plato, it is "essential reading" for adding to our understanding of the relation between Protagoras's and Heraclitus's thought (2007, 37). Although the link between Protagoras's thought and Heraclitus's ontology is not explicitly dealt with in the *Cratylus* dialogue, we are not able to forget that Plato elsewhere links the two explicitly; see *Tht.* 152b–161e. Edward Schiappa's view that "Protagoras provided a logical extension of Heraclitus's doctrines" (2003, 95) is uncontested in contemporary scholarship, and may even have been common knowledge among Plato's contemporaneous readership.

7. Elsewhere I have argued that this is a fundamental component of the riddle of Heraclitus's "first fragment," often interpreted as his "doctrine of the *logos*." I have suggested (Reames 2013, 2017) that the double meaning of *logos* in the fragment works as a subtle clue that Heraclitus conceived of *logos* as bearing the same tension of opposites and power of opposing forces that he ascribed to the material universe (or *phusis*).

8. In these questions, Socrates is moving the conversation explicitly in the direction of sophistic and Eleatic discourse: the question of speaking of nonbeing. This part of the discussion serves as a brief detour, since we're brought right back to the question of convention; but Plato does not want us to forget, I think, that what he is ultimately after is a way of defining *true and false logos*, which will be the product of the *Sophist* dialogue (discussed in chapter 6, below).

9. This question is typically, and wrongly, interpreted as a question of whether the correctness of names is determined by *nomos* or *phusis*, which itself is viewed as the common sophistic debate about the subordination of law to nature or vice versa, as disputed, for example, in *Grg.* 482c–486d and *Rep.* 1.338cff. and 2.359aff. As Kerferd has documented, in such disputes, "the first step is to set up an antithesis: that which is required by law is contrary to that which is required by nature" (1981, 116). The term *nomos* does appear at *Cra.* 384d—on this point, see R. Robinson 1969, 112; Williams 1982, 90n6; and Sedley 2003, 5–6. Nevertheless, it is clear that there is no essential opposition between *phusis* and the limitations of *phusis* that are imposed by law. Rather, the question is simply whether the correctness of names is derived from habits

established by agreement and custom or from *phusis*. The standard phrase is *sunthêkê kai ethos*, meaning "agreement and custom," but not necessarily with the overtones of *nomos*, which are, according to G. B. Kerferd, "always prescriptive and normative, and never merely descriptive" (1981, 112). The inapplicability of the *nomos*/*phusis* opposition is more obvious when directly compared to the discussions in the *Gorgias* and the *Republic*, where *nomos* functions as an artificial mechanism to limit and regulate the domination of the strong over the weak—the basic structure of the strife of *phusis*. For the influence of the *nomos*/*phusis* interpretation of this question in the *Cratylus*, see Nehring 1945. For the sophistic theme of *nomos* versus *phusis*, see Kerferd 1981, 111–30.

10. It is worth noting that this interpretation may iron out some of the wrinkles in the so-called "problem of Cratylus," pointed out by Geoffrey Kirk and others (see Kirk 1951; Allan 1954; Mondolfo 1954; Cherniss 1955). This problem, such as it is, is that the portrait we receive of Cratylus in the dialogue that shares his name, where he professes to believe in the natural rightness of names, seems to be at odds with Aristotle's testimony that Cratylus was an extreme Heraclitean (*Meta.* Γ 1010a7ff.). This is a contradiction, critics argue, because one who believes that names have a correctness that is determined once and for all by nature cannot also believe in a radically unstable natural world.

11. In the argument that precedes this pronouncement, Socrates reasons that (1) things are not entirely relative to the individual but have their own proper essence [*ousia*], which is a property not of the individual's measure but according to what the thing is in itself as a process and product of *phusis* (386d, 387a); (2) this applies not only to things but also to actions (387b); (3) speaking (*legein*) is also a kind of action (387b); and (4) naming (*onomazein*) is a kind of speaking. In other words, since things and actions not only are relative to us but are processes of *phusis*, and since speech is a kind of action, speech too is a process of *phusis*.

12. As I discuss in chapter 6, this is the same pattern of discussion—*diakritikê*—that is displayed in the Sophist dialogue's "method of division." The term Plato uses here and in the *Sophist* dialogue, *diakritikê*, refers to dividing things by kind as opposed to merely verbal contradictions, or *antilogikê*.

13. Socrates goes on to reinforce the idea that the investigation of names, according to Cratylus's view, uncovers the flux of Heraclitus's ontology. See the discussion that spans from 411d–422c.

14. In this analysis, I refer to *onoma*, or "name," as the smallest unit of language, which collectively composes a larger discourse, or *logos*. This interpretation of the relation between *onoma* and *logos* is established in Bassett 2004, and explained in greater detail in chapter 6, below.

15. Protagoras's radical view would dictate, for instance, that there can be "no such thing as a bad man" (386b; Jowett 1961, 424), which does not square with either Socrates's or Hermogenes's experience that there are indeed very many bad men and very few good ones (386b).

16. There is clearly a connection between the dizziness produced by Heraclitean flux and the dizziness produced by its linguistic offspring in sophistic thought. For

the idea that the "controversialists," or *antilogikoi*, like Gorgias and Protagoras were Heracilteans, and for the similar effects these thought systems produced, see Allan 1954, 271; Michaelides 1975, 19; Kahn 1986, 257; Cherubin 1993, 216–28; McCabe 2000, 94; and Adomenas 2002, 423–44.

17. Plato's interpretation of Protagoras's doctrine betrays significant redaction when it is compared to the exact words he quotes at *Tht.*152a. For examples of the tendency to confuse Plato's Protagoras doctrine with the one articulated by Protagoras, see Bailey 1997, 71, 75; Hestir 2000, 11; and Jolley 2006.

18. This is the same paraphrase as *Cra.* 385e–386a, discussed above: "But would you say, Hermogenes, that things differ as the names differ? And are they relative to individuals as Protagoras tells us? For he says that man is the measure of all things, and that things are to me as they appear [*phainetai*] to me, and that they are to you as they appear to you" (Jowett 1961, 424).

19. The dubiousness of Socrates's equivocation on this point has not escaped scholarly notice. In his 1968 doctoral dissertation, for example, Michael Gagarin observes how this difference between Protagoras's exact words and Plato's extrapolation clearly indicates an intentional shift in meaning. "The basic division," he writes, "is between the form of the statement with φαίνεται (αἰσθάνεται is clearly Plato's own substitution for φαίνεται in 152a–c), and that with δοκέω" (1968, 127), and this "substitution" must not be mistaken for Protagoras's own idea. The shift in meaning, in other words, entails an equation between Protagoras's man-measure doctrine, perception, appearance, and belief that does not exist in Protagoras's original formulation. This moves Joseph Maguire (1973, 117) to suggest that Socrates's paraphrastic synthesis of Protagoras's doctrine is a dubious manipulation, precisely insofar as it makes belief, perception, and appearance synonymous with one another, when in fact they are not. In fact, according to at least one critic, they are even logically incongruent (Zilioli 2007, 43).

However, in his deliberations over the problem of Protagoras's thought, Socrates displays a sincere effort at parsing the obscure doctrine, an exercise that requires additional vocabulary to define nontautologically the ambiguous terms. Despite the fact that "the sum of our evidence, in Plato and our other sources, points to the conclusion that this restriction [of knowledge to perception and sensation], and the *Theaetetus*' theory of sense perception are un-Protagorean" (Versenyi 1962, 179), Socrates's version of the doctrine may simply be an effort at interpretation, not manipulation nor "purely a fiction to be discredited" (Schiappa 2003, 127). And moreover, Socrates's admission of dissatisfaction with his own methods, leading to the famous "apology of Protagoras," moves us to consider the purpose of this interpretation as something other than naked manipulation. See also M. Lee 2005, 12–21.

20. This is the same method in reverse that we witness Socrates use in the interpretation of Simonides's poem in the *Protagoras*, where he makes synonymous terms mean different things. See chapter 4, below.

21. On the question of this method of argument and the (possible) self-refutation of Protagoras's doctrine, see E. N. Lee 1973; Burnyeat 1976; Waterlow 1977; Matthen 1985; Bostock 1988; Denyer 1991; and Chappell 1995.

22. Bostock claims that Protagoras did not intend for the man-measure doctrine to apply to the doctrine itself (1988, 89–95). For a refutation of this view, see Chappell 1995, 337–38.

23. He quotes the same fragment (DK 28b7) again at *Soph.* 258d.

24. It will be made clearer that the problem is partially a problem of the denominative function of language that Plato is in the process of inventing. If "nonbeing" is an *onoma*, to what does that *onoma* refer? By merely using it *as* an *onoma*, "nonbeing" implies "being," which raises the question "What should the *onoma*, *that which is not*, be applied to?" (*Soph.* 237c; N. White 1993, 25; translation modified). See chapter 6, below.

25. Of central importance to the question of nonbeing as it is explored in the *Sophist* dialogue is Charles Kahn's landmark work *The Verb "Be" in Ancient Greek* (1973). Although in the second edition (2003) he disavows the linguistic relativism that informed the original thesis, there is no denying that the verb does not correspond directly of our *to be* in English, and that its range of uses in the Greek tongue which obscures the riddle that saying "nonbeing" would have had for them. The fact that the concept is more regularly and easily contrasted with becoming and seeming should bear testimony to its dissimilarity of the range of concepts associated with our *to be* (see Kahn 1981, 111). Kahn's is the most important of a lengthy literature on the relevance of the verb *to be* for Plato's concept of false statements and the problem of nonbeing in the *Sophist*; see also Ackrill 1957; Kahn 1966, 1976, 1981; Phillip 1968; Owen 1971; Flower 1980; McDowell 1982; Bostock 1984; and L. Brown 2012.

Grammatical implications have been a dominant feature of Plato's concept of nonbeing and have taken precedence over the question of how Plato was attempting to engage with sophistic (particularly Protagorean) negation. For more on Plato's association of the saying that "contradiction is impossible" with sophistic thought, see the discussion in Cornford 1935, 310. Despite clear indicators in the text that Plato is not interacting directly with Parmenides but with Protagoras's Parmenidean sophistry in the *Sophist*, the Stranger is read as a"kind of stand-in for his master Parmenides" (Kahn 2007, 49) and the dialogue as a "rejection of Eleaticism" (Curd 1988, 318). See also E. N. Lee 1972 and Pelletier 1990.

26. Kirk, Raven, and Schofield (1983, 182) posit that some of Parmenides's fragments were indirect references to Heraclitus, in opposition to his dyadic structure of being.

27. Socrates proposes they define what they mean by "logos": in other words, that they devise a *logos* of *logos*. It cannot be merely "making one's thought apparent vocally by means of words and verbal expressions" (206d; Levett 1990, 345), since that is something "everyone is able to do more or less readily . . . if he is not deaf or dumb to begin with" (206d; Levett 1990, 345–46). Neither can it be "to give an answer by reference to [a thing's] elements" (207a; Levett 1990, 346), since one can have correct judgment about a thing and give a *logos* of its elements, but still lack a grasp of how the individual elements comprise the whole. Neither can it be an ability "to tell some mark by which the object you are asked about differs from all other things" (208c; Levett 1990, 348), since that notion is already embedded in the concept of a correct judgment, and therefore cannot truly be a property of *logos* as such. They cannot define knowledge in a way

that overcomes Protagoras's Heraclitean instability precisely because they cannot devise a theory of *logos* proper.

Chapter 4

1. See, for example, Plato's descriptions at *Phdr.* 261; *Tht.* 167e; and *Euthyd.* 272a.

2. See, for example, *Rep.* 537e–539a, 454a; and *Tht.* 164c–d.

3. Timmerman and Schiappa suggest that this term is used far more frequently than *elenchus* to refer to Socrates's preferred method (2010, 20n3). Kahn notes that Plato uses *elenchus* in a less technical sense than *dialegesthai* (1996, 302).

4. For a long time, the only scholarly attention the poem received were attempts at interpreting or reconstructing the poem's meaning and structure on the basis of the fragments quoted by Plato. This trend followed the influential work of Wilamowitz-Moellendorff (1898; see also Woodbury 1953; Parry 1965; and Rohdich 1979), and betrayed an implicit belief that it held no other real philosophical value for the dialogue in which it was transported. See, for example, A. E. Taylor 1926; Vlastos 1956, xxiv; C. C. W. Taylor [1976] 1991, 141–48; Beresford 2005, 150n60; and Denyer 2008, 160–61.

5. This point has been made in Frede 1986; Scodel 1986; Pappas 1989; Carson 1992; McCoy 1999; and Beresford 2009.

6. Interestingly, the poem technically is not present in the dialogue as a written copy. Unlike the text of Lysias's speech and the *Phaedrus* or Homer in the *Republic*, both of which are described with terminology that unambiguously refers to a written text, Protagoras and Socrates are clearly recalling the poem from memory. This works as a further confirmation of Cole's hypothesis, since it is the analysis of the written texts that produces a theoretical metalanguage.

7. The depiction of Socrates in the *Protagoras* provokes no small amount of angst among Plato's readers, who resist surrendering the belief that the fundamental correctness of Socrates's motives could never lie too far below the surface of any perceived error. This resistance leads to dense and complicated attempts to "rescue Socrates from a charge of wilful inconsistency" (Woolf 1999, 24). The desire to exonerate Socrates is evident in nearly every study of the interpretive portion of the dialogue. It is evident, for example, in the efforts to prove, in solidarity with Socrates, that in fact his interpretation of Simonides's poem is legitimate (see Parry 1965, 315; C. C. W. Taylor [1976] 1991,143; Beresford 2005, 150n60; and Denyer 2008, 161).

It is equally evident in the more common tendency to simply define this portion of the text as a parody of sophistic methods of argumentation and, on those grounds, to set this portion of the dialogue aside, firm in the belief that Socrates cannot be held accountable for words spoken in satirical imitation. Despite Socrates's straightforward account of his own wayward motives, he is readily viewed as though he were "ridiculing the pedantic devices" (Clapp 1950, 493) of the sophists, such that any similarity between his methods and theirs serve as "clear indications that he is parodying the critical techniques of such sophists as Hippias and Prodicus" (Parry 1965, 299), and not what Socrates himself admits they are: the available means at his disposal to persuade the audience of the superiority of his interpretation over Protagoras's. Socrates's admission of guilt is set aside—since "Socrates was, no doubt, less staggered by all this than he pretended" (Woodbury 1953, 141). Even where the incoherence and bad reasoning is acknowledged, scholars tend to explain it through recourse to a higher purpose—the philosophical nobility of his ends justifies the dubiousness of his means, in other words (see McCoy 1999; Beresford 2009, 215; and Trivigno 2013, 539).

Where the poem has received serious consideration, this has likewise taken place by turning a blind eye to Socrates's blatant confession that he was not offering a sincere interpretation of the poem but simply was trying to recover from Protagoras's stunning blow. Such studies propose as an alternative to outright insincerity the idea that Socrates was sincerely using Simonides's poem as a mirror for his own views (Scodel 1986, 34; Pappas 1989; Woolf 1999, 25), and doing so constitutes "a coherent and deliberate method" (Pappas 1989, 249) that aims to erase the views he seems to put forward simply by handling them badly (Beresford 2009, 215). In short, "A common assumption of both positions seems to be that if Socrates's interpretation is a parody, then it can be safely ignored as philosophically insignificant; this implies that if it has philosophical significance, it is not a parody" (Trivigno 2013, 511). One exception may be found in Marian Demos (1999), who suggests that we are not meant to and should not attempt to exonerate Socrates (or Plato, for that matter). Since "Socrates must adopt the sophistry of Protagoras in order to take up the latter's challenge" (1999, 19), Demos claims that we should not attempt to make his argument coherent and sound—it is intended to be unpersuasive and erroneous.

8. For observations about the intellectual validity of Protagoras's thought as it is portrayed in his "great speech," its consistency with (and perhaps even influence on) Plato's and Aristotle's positions, and the implicit respect with which Plato treats Protagoras, see Kerferd 1953; Gagarin 1968; Schiappa 2003, 190–94; Zilioli 2007, 144; and Corey 2015, 39–67.

9. Note that in the first scenes of the dialogue, Socrates has assumed the three postures—sitting, lying, and pacing—that, in Callias's house, will be assumed by the three sophists, Hippias, Prodicus, and Protagoras. See note 13, below.

10. Pind., *Isthm.* 5.28; Aesch., *PV* 62, 944; DK 64a4; Hdt. 2.49.1; Diog. Laert., *Lives* 1.12. On the neutral and pejorative uses of the term, see Kerferd 1981, 1–14; Schiappa 2003, 3–12; Denyer 2008, 73; and Tell 2011, 21–37.

11. Here, Socrates alludes again to the comparison between medicine and gymnastic, education and the consumption of foreign goods. See chapter 1; and *Grg.* 464b–466a.

12. The fact that Socrates indicates that the servant who opened the door was a eunuch is another mark of Callias's ostentatious wealth. And the servant mistaking Socrates and Hippocrates for sophists is a comedic predictor of the sophistic methods Socrates will soon resort to. Indeed, "Socrates is publicly received into the circle of sophists" (Woodbury 1953, 149), and even from the very beginning of the dialogue, he is indistinguishable from them.

13. Upon his arrival at Callias's house, Socrates witnesses the three sophists in each of the three postures he himself had inhabited earlier in the dialogue: seated like Hippias with his unnamed friend, reclining like Prodicus when Hippocrates arrives at his house,

and walking like Protagoras to pass the time before dawn. See note 9, above. On the comic device of portraying sophists in bed, see Sidwell 2005.

14. This is an obvious and explicit reference to *Phdr.* 275d–e, where Socrates levies the same criticism against writing.

15. The nature and teachability of virtue, and the apparently hedonist position Socrates assumes at 353b–356e, dominate the philosophical investigations of the *Protagoras.* It is precisely this domination that has led to the neglect of the Simonides interpretation. For useful summaries of this focus in scholarship on the *Protagoras,* see Balaban 1987, 371; and Richardson 1990, 7–8. For the question of Socrates's hedonism, see Sullivan 1961; Irwin 1977b; Zeyl 1980; and Nussbaum 1984 and 1986; on the *Protagoras* as an anticipation of pragmatism, see Moysan-Lapointe 2010. These interpretations render the dialogue as a prototype of later moral philosophy, and, accordingly, are (problematically) reliant on anachronistic vocabulary: hedonistic calculus, consequentialism, utilitarianism, the commensurability or incommensurability of goods are all applied backward onto a dialogue that does not contain these or synonymous terms. This would have us treat the discussion of virtue as though it were straightforward, thus neglecting the economic role of the sophists who plied virtue for a fee, and causing us to overlook Socrates's many admissions of his very *unvirtuous* desire to undermine Protagoras using whatever means necessary.

The chronologically more appropriate sophistic "two sides" (or *dissoi logoi*) for understanding Socrates's discourse of pleasure and pain, greater and lesser, near and distant is obscured by this focus on later moral philosophy. The relevance of the rhetorical *dissoi logoi* for this aspect of the *Protagoras* dialogue has received scant investigation. Arist., *Top.* and *Rh.*, catalog both exhaustively and partially statements of comparison and difference such as these discussed in *Prt.* 355e–357b. In fact, it is perhaps telling that, in suggesting that what's needed is a science of measurement to decide between relative excesses, deficits, or equilibrium of these comparative pairs, Socrates says he will explain at a later time what skill or branch of knowledge this might be (357b). As Arist., *Rh.* and *Top.*, demonstrate, this branch is at least in part the science of rhetoric. His investigation of the commonplaces is meant to be a science that can reach conclusions based on these value-laden comparative dyads with such a rigorous methodology that it would "satisfy the criteria of dialectic" (Moss 1996, 119) but on topics that are "about the class of things that can be proved in words" (Bloomer 2001), if not only in words. Whereas Aristotle's catalog will formulate a procedure for handling rigorously these comparative dyads, Socrates and Protagoras's discussion at this portion of the dialogue merely points to the lack and the need of such a procedure.

16. The phrase Socrates's friend uses upon encountering him in the street—*pothen . . . phainê*, or "where did you appear from?"—conveys the sense of a surprise encounter. Thus Socrates was not planning to meet with this friend and indeed had nowhere he had to be.

17. The division between Protagoras and Socrates at this point is possibly symbolic of Athenian politics in the late fifth century BCE. When Socrates stands up to leave, the Athenians Callias and Alcibiades take sides against one another in the conflict (Callias

with Protagoras, Alcibiades with Socrates), and the foreign sophists argue in favor of compromise and unity. Hippias's speech at this point is of particular interest (337c–e)—he offers what might be construed symbolically as an argument for pan-Hellenism, similar to those offered by the likes of Isocrates (Papillon 2017), or those we might imagine Gorgias using to persuade Athens for the Sicilian campaign. It is unlikely that this similarity is incidental. As Nicholas Denyer points out, this view finds its natural opposite in Athenian isolationism: "Greeks did not always find it easy to accept that one might be concerned for people beyond one's own πόλις. An extreme instance is a fifth-century Athenian epitaph, which describes its subject first as 'having slain seven men, and having broken off seven spears in their bodies', and then as 'having harmed no man upon the earth; the seven were not Athenians, and so did not count'" (2008, 142; 337c7).

18. This reference to "looking at" the poem implies the act of reading it, or of going over more carefully and critically a written version of the text. There is no explicit indication that the poem was there with them, available for Socrates's rereading. But Socrates's refusal at this point is an obvious point of contrast to his activity in the *Phaedrus*, where he goes over the text of Lysias's speech several times and, upon each rereading, the quality of the speech diminishes in his estimation. The poem by Simonides, by contrast, maintains its excellence in Socrates's view in part because of his refusal to reread it critically. In the same way that the palinode of the *Phaedrus* was immune to criticism because it could not be studied, the fact that the poem is remembered and not read contributes to his inability to diagnose its errors. The fact that the discussion is not tethered to a stable, written text contributes to the further problem that both Socrates and Protagoras can extract whatever meaning they wish from the poem (Clapp 1950, 496; Woolf 1999, 28), and trample over the poet's own meaning (Carson 1992, 122).

19. On the dubiousness of Plato's wordplay here, see Beresford 2005, 150n60; and Denyer 2008, 161.

20. These so-called "violent transgressions" are also, by another definition, a demonstration of sophistic *orthoepeia*, or correctness of words and names. According to Charles Segal, this portion of the dialogue is an imitation of this method of sophistic discourse "in which Protagoras interpreted and 'destroyed' celebrated poets with the weapon of his ὀρθοέπεια" (1970, 161).

21. We are largely (though not exclusively) reliant on Plato for this testimony. Aristotle also attributes to Prodicus an art of distinguishing between synonyms, or *orthoepeia*. He describes Prodicus's method as though it were a matter of absurd hairsplitting and groundless terminological distinctions: "There is the case where someone has claimed that an accidental characteristic of a thing is different from itself, just because its name is different, as Prodicus did, distinguishing three forms of pleasure: 'joy' [*chara*], 'delight' [*terpsis*], and 'good cheer' [*euphrosyne*]; but all of these are just different names for the same thing, 'pleasure'. . . . Prodicus attempted to assign to every term its own peculiar significance. . . . But this is the sort of thing said by men who love to lay down trivial laws but have no care to say anything sensible" (DK 84a19; Stewart 1972, 78). That Prodicus emphasized the defining of words and the correctness of names is also attested to at DK 84a9 (Marcellin., *Life of Thucydides* 36), DK 84a11 (Pl., *Cra.* 384b), DK 84a16 (Pl., *Euthyd.* 277e), DK 84a17 (Pl., *Lach.* 197d), DK 84a18 (Pl., *Char.* 163d).

22. For the various interpretations of this fragment, see Schiappa 2003, 103–16.

23. Marian Demos (1999) is the only scholar I've encountered who also concludes that Socrates is indifferent to his own interpretation, since his true purpose is simply to claim victory over Protagoras.

24. I demonstrate in chapter 2 how Socrates's investigation of Phaedrus's written speech stands in stark contrast to this analysis of Simonides: as he studies the written text, its meanings narrow and shrink with each rereading precisely because rhetorical theory serves as an external measure for evaluating the *logos*.

25. See Scodel 1986, 27; and Most 1989, 249, 271.

26. See Beresford 2005, 154n85.

27. On the former point, it is Protagoras, not Socrates, who is arguing against the standard view that one will be done to as they have done: "Traditional Greek thought works with the simple principle of 'be done by as you did': e.g., Pind., *N*[*em.*]. 4.32 'when one does a thing, then it is seemly to suffer it too [ῥέζοντά τι καὶ παθεῖν ἔοικεν]; Aesch., *Choephori* 312–14 'let him repay bloody blow for bloody blow. Thrice-old is the tale that says this: suffer upon doing' [ἀντὶ δὲ πληγῆς φονίας φονίαν | πληγὴν τινέτω. δράσαντι παθεῖν, | τριγέρων μῦθος τάδε φωνεῖ]; and *Laws* 872d–873a relays an old story that the cosmos arranges, by reincarnation if need be, for the application of this to matricides and patricides" (324b3; Denyer 2008, 112).

28. See Griswold 1999, 302; and Gonzalez 2014, 46.

29. The theory of *logos* developed in the *Sophist* and the *Cratylus*, discussed in chapter 6, is anticipated numerous times at the end of the *Theaetetus*. See, for example, Socrates's account of his dream at 201e–206b, which prefigures both the etymologies of the *Cratylus* and the discussion of the "weaving together" of *onomata* in the *Sophist*.

Chapter 5

1. Notable exceptions that treat the rhetoric of the *Republic* include Yunis 2007; McCoy 2008, 85–110; and Kastely 2015. In contrast to these studies, which examine the rhetorical or dialectical techniques and structures of the *Republic*, I examine how the concept of *mimêsis* developed therein functions as a theory of rhetoric.

2. Although the sophist Thrasymachus plays a role in this dialogue and articulates the standard sophistic theme of *phusis* versus *nomos*—according to which "morality is nothing other than the advantage of the stronger party" (338c)—the role of the sophists in Athenian education, and the role of that education in buttressing the sophistic view, is strangely neglected in the dialogue. For summaries of the role of the sophists in Athenian education, see Jaeger 1945, 286–331; Marrou 1956, 46–60; Guthrie 1971, 27–54; Kerferd 1981, 4–23; de Romilly 1992; Woodruff 1999; Gagarin and Woodruff 2008; and Tell 2011.

3. In his Marburg lecture "Plato and the Poets," published originally in essay form in 1934, Hans-Georg Gadamer noted for what I believe is the first time the peculiarity of Plato's focus on poetry in the *Republic* and attendant neglect of the sophists. Because the dialogue is about the proper relation between the human and the state, Gadamer argues, the emphasis on education qua poetry cannot be taken as straightforward. Gadamer's crucial point is that the "critical motive" behind the criticism of poets and

poetry is ulterior and not at all the direct attack it seems to be. Rather, it was an attack on "the sophism that had come to define the spirit of education" (Gadamer 1980, 50).

4. Jeff Mitscherling (2009) provides a useful summary of the primary ways that Plato's attack on poets and poetry has been interpreted, and offers more nuanced categories than Havelock's division between those who favor a "face value" interpretation and those who do not; see Havelock [1963] 1998, 15n12, 16n13, 17n36, and 33n37. Mitscherling's sixth category suggests that Plato's actual target in his attack on the poets and poetry was in fact the sophists. Mitscherling argues that "below the target of Plato's criticism of poetry was in fact the imitative character not only, or even primarily, of poetry itself, but of the Sophist's activity and teaching, which Plato recognized as already beginning to bring about this 'decline of Greek thought' whereby philosophy was destined to be reduced to mere imitation" (2009, 58). He claims, rightly, that Plato's criticism of the poets and sophists are interanimating—that one cannot be understood without the other (Mitscherling 2009, 66).

5. Derrida and Deleuze both follow Heidegger in their critiques of metaphysics in the West, but the implication of *mimêsis* in this critique belongs to those working after Heidegger and not Heidegger himself. It is a rarely discussed topic in Heidegger, and where it is discussed, Heidegger has a surprisingly traditional reading of it, aligning *mimêsis* with a correspondence theory of truth. See his Nietzsche lectures, Heidegger 1991, original pagination 198–217; and *Introduction to Metaphysics*, Heidegger 2000, original pagination 141. In addition to Deleuze and Derrida, Walter Benjamin, Theodor Adorno, Helmuth Plessner, and Paul Ricoeur all have interrogated the monolithic influence of *mimêsis.* See Benjamin and Tarnowski 1979; Benjamin 1999; Adorno 1984; Plessner 1970, 61–63; and Ricoeur 1990.

6. On the different meanings of *mimêsis*, and whether those meanings are coherent or inconsistent, the primary sources are Koller 1954, Else 1958, and Sörbom 1966, as well as Verdenius 1949 and McKeon 1951. See also Phillip 1961, 457, 468; Golden 1969, 148; 1975, 118; Griswold 1981, 141; Nehamas 1982, 47–51; Urmson 1982, 127–28; 1997, 266; Belfiore 1984; Dyson 1988; Rabel 1996, 366–68; Pappas 1999, 61; Treanor 2001; Lear 2011; Marušič 2011, 219; Cain 2012, 189; and Risser 2013.

7. Nevertheless, it is apparent that the dangers of poetry are defined precisely as things that are not read but *heard*, thereby putting the auditors at risk. In other words, poetry is not dangerous *as such*; it is only dangerous when it is spoken and performed by a particularly good poet, and heard by a susceptible and vulnerable audience. It is, he suggests, the enchanting *sound* of the poetry in real-time performance—its rhythm and music—that threatens to enslave the hearer. This danger is manifest only in and through the actual moment of poetic performance, when the hearer is enslaved by the aural charm of the poet's voice.

8. Although the novelty of this distinction between *mimêsis* and *diêgêsis* is widely attested (see Dyson 1988, 43), it is not generally recognized that Plato's emphasis on ways of using language is what makes this distinction novel.

9. Alexander Nehamas has suggested that "the little we know about the early history of *mimeisthai* ('to imitate') and its cognates suggests that these terms were originally connected with speech and poetry rather than with painting, with hearing rather

than with seeing" (1982, 55–56).To a large extent, Nehamas is correct, but not without significant qualification. The most common senses of the term in texts that predate Plato or are contemporaneous with him, *mimêsis* refers to following an example, emulating a model, or speaking, behaving, and acting in a manner that is similar to someone else. While it is true that Xen., *Mem.* 3.10; Hdt. 3.37.2; and Isoc., *To Demonicus* 11, all relate *mimêsis* to painting, these are nevertheless unusual uses of the term. Isocrates draws an explicit analogy between the act of *imitating* the example set by one's father in the same way that a painter represents (*apeikazein*) beautiful things. Despite this use of the term in a discussion of painting, this example describes one activity (imitation) in terms of a different activity (painting).

Even with more "visually" inflected uses of the term, such as when Aristophanes uses it to refer to adopting the look or visual appearance of another person (*Thesm.* 850; *Ran.* 109), those senses are appropriate to poetic or dramatic performance. In contrast to this understanding, Stephen Halliwell claims that the term *was* used in relation to visual phenomena prior to Plato: he claims that, in addition to musicopoetic arts, "mimesis had by the first half of the fifth century become associated with visual art too" (2002, 19). However, the example he gives to substantiate this claim is from Aeschylus's satyr play *Theôria*, "in which a chorus of satyrs admires votive images of themselves for their remarkable degree of likeness, speaking of a particular 'image' (*eidôlon*)—which is so like their form that it 'only lacks a voice'—as 'the mimetic work [*mimêma*] of Daedalus,' a phrase in which the noun *mimêma* must refer to an object that is taken (however comically, in context) to be mimetic in the sense of rendering appearances in a lifelike or convincing manner" (Halliwell 2002, 19, 19n45; Aesch. fr. 78a.1–12). I read this example differently, however. It seems to me that this is an example of *spoken mimêsis*, despite the obvious invocation of visual imagery. In the example from Aeschylus, the visual is incidentally coincident with the mimetic—the images would be mimetic if and only if they had a voice. And although Halliwell discusses an old tradition of comparing poetry and painting (perhaps the very tradition Plato is referencing at *Rep.* 378e), this does not necessarily link *mimêsis* to painting (or, for that matter, *mimêsis* to poetry as such).

10. This sense of *mimêsis* as emulation is consistent throughout the bulk of the ancient literature, appearing in the compositions Isoc., *Paneg.* 36, *Phillip* 114, *Archidamus* 81–83, *Areopagiticus* 84, *On Peace* 142, *Bus.* 20, 40, *Panath.* 78, 100, 137, 153, *C. soph.* 18, *Plataicus* 22; Ar., *Vesp.* 1019, *Thesm.* 156, 850, *Plut.* 306; Andoc., *Mysteries* 141, *Against Alcibiades* 6; and Xen., *Lac.* I.2, *Oec.* 4.4. The preponderance of the evidence suggests that, while the term could be used to refer to sound or sight, these uses were less common than uses that refer more to the act of following an example or emulating a model. In other words, the most common senses of the term do not evoke concepts of representation at all, either seen or heard.

11. Note that Plato here has Socrates imitate Homer's *diêgêsis* and narrate his *mimesis*.

12. Socrates's rhetorical analysis of Homer's written eloquence and, on the back of it, development of the theoretical metalanguage of *mimêsis* are hiding in plain view in the discussion that spans from 379d to 393b, immediately preceding the first discourse on *mimêsis*, explicitly introduced as a discussion of a *written* text. Socrates prefaces what

is to come as a critique "using the written word to give a distorted image of the nature of the gods and heroes, just as a painter might produce a portrait which completely fails to capture the likeness of the original" (377e; Waterfield 2008, 72). It might be objected that this passage does not contain terminology that explicitly refers to written discourse, but given the numerous other references to writing, Waterfield's translation is appropriate. Plato explicitly calls attention to the visual nature of the written text by comparing it to visual arts—both are accomplished by making visual marks: "ὅταν εἰκάζῃ τις κακῶς οὐσίαν τῷ λόγῳ . . . ὥστερ γραφεὺς μηδὲν ἐοικότα γράφων οἷς ἂν ὅμοια βουληθῇ γράψαι" (377e). The same term he uses for "painter"—*grapheus*—could also mean "writer." Plato makes it clear that they are being identified in a written text and not simply being recalled from aural memory. Socrates refers to "plastering over" (*exaleipsomen*, 386c) and "marking out by lines" (*diagraphômen*, 387b) passages that he considers to be objectionable.

13. This observation of Plato's method helps to explain why the understanding of poetry in the *Republic* differs so profoundly from the view of poetic craft in the rest of Plato's work and in Greek culture as a whole, a point that has puzzled numerous scholars. In a recent article, Nicholas Pappas explains why Plato's theory of poetry-as-*mimêsis* stands at odds not only with what Plato wrote of poetry elsewhere, such as in the *Ion* and *Phaedrus* dialogues, but also with the standard view of poetry in the classical world; in short, according to the traditional view "imitation and inspiration should not go together" (2012, 670). The incompatibility of these two concepts is obvious: a poets' skill was supposed to have been so remarkable and profound, so remarkably impactful and intensely present, that the muses themselves must be appealed to in order to explain what has been made manifest in the poet's words. Griswold rightly points out the deliberate avoidance of the question of divine inspiration, to such an extent that his quote of the "first lines" of the *Iliad* conspicuously skips past the actual first lines that make a direct appeal to divine inspiration ("Sing in me, O Goddess . . . ," *mêmin aeide thea . . .*) (1981, 150). The incompatibility of these two concepts and the inconsistent uses of the term in other of Plato's texts have also been noted by numerous scholars, including Golden 1969, 148; 1975; Gadamer 1980, 42; P. Murray 1992, 27–29, 39; Halliwell 2002, 39; and Collobert 2011, 41–45.

14. For example, James Urmson writes: "The book 3 distinction is simply irrelevant to book 10. . . . We can represent the argument of book 10 as resuming that of book 3 only by doing gross violence to one or the other or both" (1997, 226). Similarly, Julia Annas claims *mimêsis* in book 10 is "impossible to reconcile with Book 3" (1981, 336).

15. This shift of applications for the term *mimêsis* has likewise been noted by numerous scholars; see, for example, Phillip 1961, 468; Hwang 1981, 36–37; Cain 2012, 189n3; and Risser 2013. Several authors have disputed the claim that the meaning of the term changes, and insist instead that the meaning remains the same and only the term's application broadens; see Belfiore 1984; Treanor 2001, 164; Lear 2011; and Marušič 2011, 219.

16. See Annas 1981, 353.

17. The word *poiêsis* on its own, without accompanying terms, to reference the work of the bards and poets is relatively rare prior to Plato. Typically, additional terms are needed to explain *what "poetic" thing* has been made. Even throughout the majority

of Plato's work, in the context of verbal arts, one does not "make poetry" but "songs," "hymns," "lyrics," and "epics" (*elegos, hymnos, melos, epos* [*Rep.* 10.607a]), and *poiêsis* is used in conjunction with these other terms in order to specify what has been made. See also *Symp.* 223d; and *Phd.* 60d–61b.

18. Indeed, the interlocutor has been swapped—Plato's eldest brother, Adeimantus, has been replaced by a younger brother, Glaucon, not unlike how one sense of *mimêsis* is about to be replaced by another.

19. Although this analogy is often referred to as one of the places that Plato develops his theory of the Forms, this interpretation is problematic, as I explain below.

20. This connection has also been noted by Rebecca Cain (2012, 187–90).

21. The analogies are another place where there seems to be a firm distinction between seeming and being. However, it is essential to recognize that the concepts of seeing, sight, and appearance remain necessary both for those who know the truth of what is and for those who do not (476d–480a, 500b–c). Those who do not are distracted by ephemeral manifestations; but philosophers are "sightseers of truth" (*tês alêtheias . . . philotheamonas*; 475e; Waterfield 2008, 196), and as such, their access to truth is dependent on seeing, sight, and the appearance of what's seen no less than the "theater-goers and sightseers are devoted to beautiful sounds and colours and shapes, and to works of art which consist of these elements" (476b; Waterfield 2008, 196). The difference is not between appearance and truth, but between people whose "minds are constitutionally incapable of seeing and devoting themselves to beauty itself" (476b; Waterfield 2008, 196) and people who are constitutionally endowed "with the ability to approach beauty itself and see beauty as it actually is" (476b; Waterfield 2008, 196). A person who knows what is remains reliant on seeming, appearance, and sight; indeed, "his eyes are occupied with the sight of things which are organized, permanent, and unchanging" (500c; Waterfield 2008, 223). On the importance of vision in this concept of truth, see Nightingale 2004.

22. Socrates equates not knowing with becoming—"something which is subject to generation and decay." It is worth stressing the point here that he does not define knowledge as things that are intelligible and nonknowledge as things that are visible. Rather, he *compares* knowledge with intelligibility and nonknowledge with visibility as the four terms of an analogy The crucial distinction for defining *what is* is the distinction between *being* and *becoming.* Thus the visible is not subordinated to the intelligible; it is used to explain the intelligible.

23. This method of placing an analogy within an analogy mimics Socrates's descriptions of the divided line itself, in which the originals of the visible realm supply the likenesses of the intelligible realm. His example is geometry, not unlike the geometric figure of the divided line.

24. It's almost surprising that Socrates doesn't mention mirrors here. This seems to be an intentional avoidance.

25. This lack of clarity is nowhere more apparent than in the speculations over what might be contained in segment C. Nicholas Smith describes how, in answer to the question, "What, then, are the images of Forms we should now expect to find in the next subsection down?" scholars have responded with "a chaos of possibilities" (1996,

32). See Smith's extensive source citation; options include "mental images of Forms," "mathematical objects," "only Forms," "mathematical intermediates, between visibles and Forms," "they are propositional, like the axioms of geometry," "figures," and "visible originals" (1996, 32). The influence of the *mimêsis* of book 10 on these interpretations is apparent.

26. Appearance and visibility permeates both the visible (cave) and intelligible (surface) domains. The cave corresponds to the visible realm, and the likenesses of the visible realm correspond to the shadows on the wall of the cave, cast by the artificial light of the fire which burns behind several objects on a wall ("artefacts, human statuettes, and animal models carved in stone and wood and all kinds of materials"; 514b–c; Waterfield 2008, 241), which are the originals of this visible realm. Outside the cave, which represents the intelligible realm, the likenesses correspond to the "things up on the surface of the earth" (516a; Waterfield 2008, 242), which are themselves the likenesses of *what is*—"the light of the stars and the moon. . . . And at last, I imagine, he'd be able to discern and feast his eyes on the sun—not the displaced image of the sun in water or elsewhere, but the sun on its own, in its proper place" (516b; Waterfield 2008, 242).

27. See, for example, Else 1958, 78, 87; Golden 1975, 130; and Urmson 1997, 228.

28. See Cain 2012, 187–90.

29. For arguments that tend to conflate the critique of *mimêsis*, rhetoric, poetry, and writing, see Partee 1974: "Poets, in common with sophists and rhapsodes, use their stylistic powers to call attention to their discourse. . . . The spoken word of poetry shares the subordinate status of writing" (203–07); and Stern-Gillet 2004: "Socrates extends to poetry his condemnation of rhetoric. Poets, like rhetoric, he argues, use language to gratify their audience, without giving thought to the moral effects of their words. No more than rhetoric, Socratus [*sic*] thus implies in the *Gorgias*, is poetry a *technê*" (186).

Chapter 6

1. Debra Nails notes that there were roughly eighteen Athenians named Socrates "apparently of the right age to be the younger Socrates" (2002, 269).

2. This must be an intentional and obvious reference, not only to the fact that Socrates is named at the outset of the dialogue and yet Plato does not use the *onoma* to refer to the person we naturally expect him to refer to, but also to the discussion in the *Cratylus* of whether *onomata* are a product of agreement or determined by *phusis.*

3. That the method of division is a display of sophistic practice is not a commonly held view. I discuss what I feel is the strongest support of this view, offered by Rose Cherubin, below (n5). More often it is taken to be an important tool offered only in the later dialogues for Plato's development of his theory of the Forms; see, for example, Cohen 1973; and Moravcsik 1973.

4. The list of infinitives in the *Cratylus* is what leads translators to interpret *rhêma* as verb. Here, Plato offers these terms as examples of *onomata.*

5. Cherubin writes, "Using sophistry to look for the sophist as such reveals a challenge to sophistry's most fundamental claims and assumptions. Just as the one hunting hunters cannot through his/her own hunting catch him/herself, and the discriminator seeking to isolate discriminators does not in doing so capture him/herself, so the

practitioner of sophistry will fail to find at least one person who is being a sophist. The art of discriminating, e.g., finds discriminators as they appear for purposes, or from the standpoint, of discriminating. But the art of discriminating cannot by its practice provide a complete, noncircular, nonregressive account of itself. The same will be true of any art, including sophistry, if it is an art" (1993, 228).

6. This is not entirely a new observation. It was made in part by Martin Heidegger in 1935, who recognized that "the terms *onoma* and *rhêma* were already known before Plato, of course. But at that time, and still in Plato, they were understood as terms denoting the use of words as a whole. . . . Both terms originally governed an equally wide domain. . . . The two terms *onoma* and *rhêma,* which at first indicated all speaking, narrowed their meaning and became terms for the two main classes of words. In the dialogue cited (261e ff.), Plato provides the first interpretation and foundation of this distinction. Plato here proceeds from a general characterization of the function of words" (Heidegger 2000, 60–61; original pagination 43–44).

7. The exclusively personal-appellative function of *onoma* is captured in Homer's and Aeschylus's uses (see, for example, *Od.* 9.16, 364–66; 19.183; Aesch., *Pers.* l 284; *Sept.* l 577; and *Supp.* l 320), and this restriction of the term's meaning, I would argue, designates a peculiar domain of meaning in the archaic tongue. It is not the purpose of this chapter or the current study to fully develop this speculation, but I believe the literature that has come down to us demonstrates that the early Greek language had a very limited range of linguistic terminology, or language that refers to language. The naming of a person—the father's performative act of naming at the birth of his child—is a unique linguistic function in an oral world, given that the linguistic culture did not carry a nascent belief that all language functions in this indexical manner. Thus *onoma* designates a particular linguistic function that is not applied generally to words as such. But by the time we reach the fifth century BCE, we see with Thucydides, for example, an expanded use of this term to refer to names of other things—systems of government are called democracy, oligarchy, and so on (Thuc. 2.37.1); people are called Athenian, Macedonian, and so on (Thuc. 2.64.3); towns, cities, and places have names (Thuc. 3.102.1, 4.701, 6.4.1–5, 6.64.2, 7.64.2). By the end of the fifth and beginning of the fourth century, the term is used much more broadly. According to a more extreme view, "*Onoma* never has the sense of just 'word'" (de Rijk 1986, 219). This interpretation is debatable, since some texts contemporaneous to Plato seem to use *onoma* as a term for words in general. See, for example, Isoc., *Areopagiticus* 20.2; Isae., *De Menecle* 20.9; Xen., *Mem.* 2.2.1, 4.2.23; *Hell.* 6.12.3; *Oec.* 6.4.2, 6.12.3, 6.14.2, 7.3.4; and *Cyn.* 13.5.4. It is interesting, given this trend toward generalization, that it is the earlier senses of *onoma* as proper names or terms for things that Plato explicitly uses and, in the *Sophist* and *Cratylus* dialogues, theorizes to apply to language as such.

8. Although aspects of Bassett's basic hypothesis appear here and there in prior scholarship, his essay is the first place where the argument is worked out fully and explicitly. Similar observations were made in passing in Pfeiffer 1972, 101, and Sallis 1986, 264n33. Following Bassett, see Hoekstra and Scheppers 2003. All translations from Bassett 2004 are my own. Bassett explains that the infinitives Plato lists at *Cra.* 426e have wrongly led his interpreters to translate *rhêma* as verb (298–300). As the

discussion above illustrates, Plato also uses the term *onoma* to refer to a list of infinitives (*Soph.* 226b). Furthermore, in the passage immediately preceding *Cra.* 426e, Plato uses *onoma* as a synonym for *rhêma*. See 426d.

9. "*Onoma* a gardé le double héritage de son origine à valeur large et de sa spécialisation plus nettement référentielle. . . . *Rhêma*, quant à lui, après avoir perdu pendant des siècles un sens proprement logique ébauché par Platon, au profit d'un sens grammatical, renaît aujourd'hui dans un sens non grammatical, mais pas pour autant logique" (Bassett 2004, 312–13).

10. This issue has been discussed by R. Robinson (1969) and Fine (1977), who address how, in the *Cratylus*, "stating is reduced to naming" and names are thought of as "little sentences" (Fine 1977, 290). Although Fine believes this is a point of failure and oversight on Plato's part, I suggest it is actually an intentional move to transfer the denominative properties of *onomata* to the act of speaking.

11. Here Socrates is using the term *mimêsis* in its traditional sense and not in the sense he develops in books 2, 3, and 10 of the *Republic.* See the discussion in chapter 5.

12. On the "incomplete" ending of the *Cratylus*, which is completed in the *Sophist*, see also Thornton 1970, 582; and Fine 1977, 291.

13. On this point, see Adomenas 2002, 422–44.

14. What is meant by the above statement is uncertain and has been the subject of longstanding dispute, particularly whether or not this is one of the places where Plato is developing his theory of the Forms. For example, Cornford points out that this section "explains how there can be Falsity in speech and thought. In the *Theaetetus* all attempts to explain this failed because the discussion was deliberately confined to an apparatus which excluded the Forms. These have now been brought into account, and we shall find that, when Forms are recognized as the meanings of common names and therefore as entering into the meaning of all statements, it will be possible to give false statements a meaning without invoking non-existent things or facts for them to refer to" (1935, 298). Hackforth offers a precise explanation for this interpretation of the passage: "*Meaning* is not the same thing as correspondence to objective fact. What is *meant* by the verb in the proposition 'Theaetetus flies' is the Form 'Flying'; that there is no objective fact to which 'flies' corresponds is immaterial: since 'flies' has a meaning, the proposition 'Theaetetus flies' also has a meaning, and the Sophist's problem, or poser, is disposed of" (1945, 57).

Setting aside for the time being the fact that, as Hackforth's explanation of Cornford's interpretation makes clear, the latter's interpretation requires the presumption that both the distinction between noun and verb as well as a correspondence theory of language had already been adequately theorized by the time of Plato's writing, Hackforth suggests that Plato's attention to the *onoma* and *rhêma* of a *logos* indicates that he was less interested in developing a theory of the Forms than he was in investigating how the components of a *logos*—*onoma* and *rhêma*—when they were broken down, could be shown to be uniting things together that really are different from one another or differentiating between things that actually belong together. The consequences of this hypothesis would suggest that the Stranger is proposing to replace sophistic refutation, contradiction, differentiation, and contrariety with a metadiscursive analysis not only of differentiation as such, but also its inverse—blending and uniting.

If, however, a theory of the Forms is not presumed, a simpler interpretation might be proposed: since speech is part of material *phusis*, to speak of *what is not* is to materialize in *phusis* what is not and cannot, will not, and should not be materialized. (Cornford even admits that "*eidos* is a vague word, sometimes meaning no more than 'entity,' 'thing'" [1935, 302]; we might add to this list "image," "shape," "idea," or "concept.") In this case, Plato is simply reaching for a vocabulary that is not so immediately and inextricably bound to *phusis* as speech and *logos* are. Nevertheless, Cornford's view has gained general acceptance. See, for example, Thornton 1970, 582. See also Bluck 1957.

15. A similar observation has been made by Paul Kalligas, who observes how sophistic refutation and eristic opposition proliferate horizontal differences, while *onoma* and *rhêma*, which rely on a two-level structure of thought predicated on Plato's idiosyncratic understanding of *mimêsis*, develop a vertical difference (2012, 398).

16. This description of the sophist/imitator parallels those in *Rep.* 397a and 596b–d, discussed in chapter 5.

17. I translate as "making marks" Plato's term γραφικῇ, which is commonly translated as "painting." The term is ambiguous, since it was used to refer both to drawing and to writing. Because I believe Plato intentionally preserves and plays on this ambiguity in both the *Republic* and the *Sophist*, I prefer the phrase "making marks."

18. In the absence of the theory of language supplied in the later discussion of the dialogue, even the discussion of *mimêsis* is caught in the sophist's web of contradictions: "So if we say he has some expertise in appearance-making, it will be easy for him to grab hold of our use of words in return and twist our words in the contrary direction. Whenever we call him a copy-maker, he'll ask us what in the world we mean by a 'copy.' . . . He'll laugh at what you say when you answer him in that way, with talk about things in mirrors or sculptures, and when you speak to him as if he could see. He'll pretend he doesn't know about mirrors or water or even sight, and he'll put his question to you only in terms of words" (*Soph.* 239d–240a; N. White 1993, 28–29). He gives an example to show how this "only in terms of words" strategy works: the sophist will get you to define what a copy is ("what runs through all those things which you call . . . by the one name, *copy*," and then he'll focus on the language to force nonbeing into being. If the copy is "something that's made similar to a true thing and is another thing that's like it,", the sophist will get you to admit that "it really is a likeness," thereby "using this interweaving [of nonbeing with being] to force us to agree unwillingly that *that which is not* in a way is" (240a–c; N. White 1993, 29.).

19. I hope that this provides an answer to the question raised by Malcolm Schofield (1982, 80) of how the *Sophist* completes the theory of language-as-imitation that is first approached in the *Cratylus* but finally abandoned. On this point, see also Annas 1982, 109.

20. Although Heidegger may be a somewhat controversial source in support of the argument that this marks the first entrance in the history of ideas of a correspondence theory of truth and *logos*-as-assertion, he certainly is not the only advocate of this view.

See also W. M. Pfeiffer, who writes that the *Cratylus* and the *Sophist* dialogues offer "a formulation—probably the first articulate one in the history of Western thought—of a correspondence theory of truth for discourse generally, and it establishes that names can be spoken as true or false within the context of discourse" (1972, 88). And Pfeiffer rightly indicates the impact of this development: "Truth is no longer something the attainment of which is physically outside the sphere of human competence, and dependent on the disclosure of things in regions thought of as being elsewhere in space and time; but rather it is present in the things that are, to be discovered by the powers of the intellect operating here and now, and to be expressed in utterances which can be evaluated in terms of their correspondence with the things that are available to all thinking men. From step one of this argument in the *Cratylus,* Plato seems to be trying to dissociate truth and falsity from the act of speaking in the sense of the old act of revelation, and, more importantly, from the speaker, the agent whose usage it is, whether god or man. He proposes instead a view of truth and falsity as characteristics of what is uttered, to be assessed in terms of objective criteria, independently of the utterer" (1972, 96–97).

Bibliography

Ackrill, J. L. 1957. "Plato and the Copula. *Sophist* 251–59." *Journal of Hellenic Studies* 77:1–6.

———, trans. 1984. *Aristotle: De Interpretatione*. In *The Complete Works of Aristotle*, edited by Jonathan Barnes, 1:25–38. Princeton, NJ: Princeton University Press.

Adomenas, Mantas. 2002. "The Fluctuating Fortunes of Heraclitus in Plato." In *Qu'est-ce que la philosophie présocratique?*, edited by André Laks and Claire Louguet, 419–47. Pas-de-Calais: Presses Universitaires du Septentiron.

Adorno, Theodor W. 1984. *Aesthetic Theory*. Translated by C. Lenhardt. London: Routledge.

Alexandrakis, A. 1980. "A Differing View: Plato's Books III and X of the *Republic*." *Diotima: Review of Philosophical Research* 8:196–97.

Allan, D. J. 1954. "The Problem of Craylus." *American Journal of Philology* 75 (3): 271–87.

Aly, Wolfgang. 1929. *Formprobleme der frühgriechischen Prosa. Philologus* Supplementband 21 (3). Leipzig: Dietrich.

Allred, Ammon. 2009. "The Divine 'Logos': Plato, Heraclitus, and Heidegger in the Sophist." *Epoché* 14 (1): 1–18.

Annas, Julia. 1981. *Introduction to Plato's "Republic."* Oxford: Clarendon Press.

———. 1982. "Knowledge and Language: the *Theaetetus* and the *Cratylus*." In *Language and Logos*, edited by M. Schofield and M. Nussbaum, 95–114. Cambridge: Cambridge University Press.

Archie, J. P. 1984. "Callicles' Redoubtable Critique of the Polus Argument in Plato's *Gorgias*." *Hermes* 112:167–76.

Athanassakis, Apostolos N., trans. 1983. *Hesiod: Theogony, Works and Days, Shield.* Baltimore: Johns Hopkins University Press.

Avgousti, Andreas. 2012. "By Uniting It Stands: Poetry and Myth in Plato's Republic." *Polis: The Journal of the Society for the Study of Greek Political Thought* 29 (1): 21–41.

Bailey, A. R. 1997. "Is Man the Measure?" *Philosophical Inquiry* 19 (1–2): 71–84.

Balaban, Oded. 1987. "The Myth of Protagoras and Plato's Theory of Measurement." *North American Philosophical Publications* 4 (4): 371–84.

Balot, Ryan. 2001. *Greed and Injustice in Classical Athens.* Princeton, NJ: Princeton University Press.

Barnes, Jonathan. 1987. *Early Greek Philosophy.* London: Penguin.

———. 1990. "Heidegger spéléologue." *Revue de métaphysique et de morale* 95 (2): 173–95.

Bassett, Louis. 2004. "Platon et la distinction nom/verbe." In *L'imaginer et le dire: Scripta minora,* edited by I. Boehm, 295–314. Lyon: Maison de l'Orient et de la Méditerranée.

Bekker, Immanuel, ed. 1814. *Anecdota graeca.* Vol. 1. Berlin: Nauck.

Belfiore, Elizabeth. 1981. "The Role of the Visual Arts in Plato's Ideal State." *Journal of the Theory and Criticism of the Visual Arts* 1 (1): 115–27.

———. 1984. "A Theory of Imitation in Plato's *Republic.*" *Transactions of the American Philological Association.* 114: 121–46.

———. 2006. "Dancing with the Gods." *American Journal of Philology* 127 (2): 185–217.

Benardete, Seth. 1991. *The Rhetoric of Morality and Philosophy: Plato's "Gorgias" and "Phaedrus."* Chicago: University of Chicago Press.

Benjamin, Walter. 1999. "On the Mimetic Faculty." In *Walter Benjamin: Selected Writings Volume 2, 1927–1934,* 720–22. Cambridge, MA: Belknap.

Benjamin, Walter, and Knut Tarnowski. 1979. "Doctrine of the Similar (1933)." *New German Critique* 17: 65–69.

Beresford, Adam, trans. 2005. *"Protagoras" and "Meno" by Plato.* London: Penguin.

———. 2009. "Erasing Simonides." *Apeiron* 42 (3): 185–220.

Bett, Richard. 1986. "Immortality and the Nature of the Soul in the *Phaedrus.*" *Phronesis* 31(1): 1–26.

———. 2001. "Immortality and Nature of the Soul." In *Essays on Plato's Psychology,* edited by Ellen Margaret Wagner, 335–62. Lanham, MD: Lexington Books.

Black, Edwin. 1958. "Plato's View of Rhetoric" *Quarterly Journal of Speech* 44 (4): 361–74.

Blanco, Walter, trans. 1998. *Thucydides: The Peloponnesian War.* New York: Norton.

Bloomer, W. Martin. 2001. "Topics." In *Encyclopedia of Rhetoric,* edited by Thomas O. Sloane, 779–82. Oxford: Oxford University Press.

Bluck, R. 1957. "False Statement in the *Sophist.*" *Journal of Hellenic Studies* 77:181–87.

Bostock, D. J. 1984. "Plato on 'Is Not' (*Sophist* 254–9)." *Oxford Studies in Ancient Philosophy* 2:89–119.

———. 1988. *Plato's "Theaetetus."* Oxford: Oxford University Press.

Brisson, Luc. 1997. "Les sophistes." *Philosophie grecque,* edited by M. Canto Sperber, 89–102. Paris: Presses Universitaires de France.

Brogan, Walter. 1997. "Plato's Dialectical Soul: Heidegger on Plato's Ambiguous Relationship to Rhetoric." *Research in Phenomenology* 27:3–15.

Brown, Lesley. 2012. "Negation and Not-Being: Dark Matter in the *Sophist*." In *Presocratics and Plato: Festschrift at Delphi in Honor of Charles Kahn*, edited by Richard Patterson, Vassilis Karasmanis, and Arnold Hermann, 233–54. Las Vegas: Parmenides Publishing.

Brown, M., and J. Coulter. 1971. "The Middle Speech of Plato's *Phaedrus*." *Journal of the History of Philosophy* 9:405–23.

Brownstein, Oscar L. 1965. "Plato's *Phaedrus*: Dialectic as the Genuine Art of Speaking." *Quarterly Journal of Speech* 51 (4): 392–98.

Brun, Jean-Pierre. 2000. "The Production of Perfumes in Antiquity: The Cases of Delos and Paestum." *American Journal of Archaeology* 104 (2): 277–308.

Buckley, Tim. 2006. "Historical Cycle of Hermeneutics in Proclus' *Platonic Theology*." In *Reading Plato in Antiquity*, edited by Harold Tarrant, 125–34. London: Duckworth.

Burke, Seán. 1996. "The Textual Estate: Plato and the Ethics of Signature." *History of the Human Sciences* 9 (1): 59–72.

Burnyeat, Myles F. 1976. "Protagoras and Self-Refutation in Later Greek Philosophy." *Philosophical Review* 85 (1): 44–69.

———. 1990. *The "Theaetetus" of Plato*. Indianapolis: Hackett.

———. 2013. "Dramatic Aspects of Plato's *Protagoras*." *Classical Quarterly* 63 (1): 419–22.

Cain, Rebecca Bensen. 2012. "Plato on Mimesis and Mirrors." *Philosophy and Literature* 36 (1): 187–95.

Carson, Anne. 1992. "How Not to Read a Poem: Unmixing Simonides from *Protagoras*." *Classical Philology* 87 (2): 110–30.

Cavarnos, C. 1952. "Plato's Teaching on Fine Art." *Philosophical and Phenomenological Research* 13:487–98.

Chantraine, Pierre. 1956. *Études sur le vocbulaire grec*. Paris: Klincksieck.

Chappell, T. D. J. 1995. "Does Protagoras Refute Himself?" *Classical Quarterly* 45 (2): 333–38.

Cherniss, Harold. 1955. "Aristotle, *Metaphysics* 987 A 32–B 7." *American Journal of Philology* 76 (2): 184–86.

Cherubin, Rose. 1993. "What Is Eleatic about the Eleatic Stranger?" In *Plato's Dialogues: New Studies and Interpretations*, edited by Gerald A. Press, 215–36. Lanham, MD: Rowman and Littlefield.

Chroust, Anton-Hermann. 1973. *Aristotle: New Light on His Life and Some of His Lost Works*. Vol. 1. London: Routledge.

Clapp, James Gordon. 1950. "Some Notes on Plato's Protagoras." *Philosophy and Phenomenological Research* 10 (4): 486–99.

Clegg, J. S. 1976. "Plato's Vision of Chaos." *Classical Quarterly* 26:52–61.

Coby, Patrick. 1987. *Socrates and the Sophistic Enlightenment: A Commentary on Plato's* Protagoras. Lewisburg, PA: Bucknell University Press.

Cohen, S. Marc. 1973. "Plato's Method of Division." In *Patterns in Plato's Thought*, edited by J. M. E. Moravcsik, 181–91. Dordrecht, Netherlands: Reidel.

Cohen, S. Marc, and David Keyt. 1992. "Analysing Plato's Arguments: Plato and Platonism." In *Methods of Interpreting Plato and His Dialogues*, Oxford Studies in Ancient Philosophy, supplementary volume, edited by James C. Klagge, Nicholas D. Smith, and Julia Annas. Oxford: Clarendon Press. 173–200.

Cole, Thomas. 1991. *The Origins of Rhetoric in Ancient Greece*. Baltimore: Johns Hopkins University Press.

Collobert, Catherine. 2011. "Poetry as Flawed Reproduction: Possession and Mimesis." In *Plato and the Poets*, edited by Pierre Destrée and Fritz-Gregor Herrmann, 41–61. Leiden, Netherlands: Brill.

Collobert, Catherine, Pierre Destrée, and Francisco J. Gonzalez, eds. 2012. *Plato and Myth: Studies on the Use and Status of Platonic Myths*. Leiden, Netherlands: Brill.

Connors, R. J. 1986. "Greek Rhetoric and the Transition from Orality." *Philosophy and Rhetoric* 19:38–65.

Consigny, Scott. 1994. "Nietzsche's Reading of the Sophists." *Rhetoric Review* 13 (1): 5–26.

Cook, Albert. 1985. "Dialectic, Irony, and Myth in Plato's *Phaedrus*." *American Journal of Philology* 106:427–44.

Corcoran, Marlena. 1989. "The Last Judgment of Plato's *Gorgias: Mythos* to You, *Logos* to Me." *Iowa Law Review* 74:827–35.

Corey, David D. 2015. *The Sophists in Plato's Dialogues*. Albany: State University of New York Press.

Cornford, Francis M. 1935. *Plato's Theory of Knowledge: The* Theaetetus *and the* Sophist *of Plato*. London: Routledge.

———. 1941. *The Republic of Plato*. Oxford: Oxford University Press.

Coulter, James A. 1967. "*Phaedrus* 279a: The Praise of Isocrates." *Greek, Roman, and Byzantine Studies* 9:225–36.

Crick, Nathan, and John Poulakos. 2008. "Go Tell Alcibiades: Tragedy, Comedy, and Rhetoric in Plato's *Symposium*." *Quarterly Journal of Speech* 94 (1): 1–22.

Crivelli, Paolo. 2012. *Plato's Account of Falsehood: A Study of the Sophist*. Cambridge: Cambridge University Press.

Crombie, I. M. 1962. *An Examination of Plato's Doctrines*. London: Routledge.

Cross, R. C., and A. D. Woozley. 1964. *Plato's "Republic": A Philosophical Commentary*. London: Macmillan.

Crotty, Kevin. 2009. *The Philosopher's Song: The Poet's Influence on Plato*. Lanham, MD: Lexington Books.

Cufalo, Domenico. 2007. *Scholia Graeca in Platonem*. Vol. 1. Roma: Edizioni di Storia e Letteratura.

Curd, Patricia Kenig. 1988. "Parmenidean Clues in the Search for the Sophist." *History of Philosophy Quarterly* 5 (4): 307–20.

Curran, Jane. 1986. "The Rhetorical Technique of Plato's *Phaedrus*." *Philosophy and Rhetoric* 19 (1): 66–72.

De Rijk, L. M. 1986. *Plato's "Sophist": A Philosophical Commentary*. Amsterdam: North-Holland Publishing.

De Romilly, Jacqueline. 1975. *Magic and Rhetoric in Ancient Greece*. Cambridge, MA: Harvard University Press.

——. 1992. *The Great Sophists in Periclean Athens*. Oxford: Clarendon Press.

De Vries, Gerrit J. 1953. "Isocrates' Reaction to the *Phaedrus*." *Mnemosyne* 6 (1): 39–45.

——. 1969. *A Commentary on the "Phaedrus" of Plato*. Amsterdam: Hakkert.

——. 1971. "Isocrates in the *Phaedrus*: A Reply." *Mnemosyne* 24 (4): 387–90.

Deleuze, Gilles. 1995. *Difference and Repetition*. Translated by Paul Patton. New York: Columbia University Press.

Demos, Marian. 1999. *Lyric Quotation in Plato*. Greek Studies: Interdisciplinary Approaches Series, edited by Gregory Nagy. Lanham, MD: Rowman and Littlefield.

Denniston, J. D. (1934) 1959. *The Greek Particles*. 2nd ed. Oxford: Clarendon Press.

Denyer, Nicholas. 1991. *Language, Thought, and Falsehood in Ancient Greek Philosophy*. London: Routledge.

——, ed. 2008. *Protagoras*. Cambridge: Cambridge University Press.

Derrida, Jacques. 1981a. "Plato's Pharmacy." In *Dissemination*, translated by Barbara Johnson, 51–172. Chicago: University of Chicago Press.

——. 1981b. "The Double Session." In *Dissemination*, translated by Barbara Johnson, 173–286. Chicago: University of Chicago Press.

Detienne, Marcel. 1996. *The Masters of Truth in Archaic Greece*. New York: Zone Books.

Diès, A. 1927. *Autour de Platon: Essais de Critique et d'Histoire*. Vol. 2 of *Les dialogues: Esquisses doctrinales*. Paris: Gabriel Beauchesne.

Dilman, Ilham. 1979. *Morality and the Inner Life: A Study in Plato's "Gorgias."* New York: Macmillan.

Dodds, E. R. 1959. *Plato: Gorgias: A Revised Text with Introduction and Commentary*. Oxford: Clarendon Press.

Doyle, James. 2006. "The Fundamental Conflict in Plato's *Gorgias*." *Oxford Studies in Ancient Philosophy* 30:87–100.

Duncan, Roger. 1978. "Courage in Plato's *Protagoras*." *Phronesis* 23 (3): 216–28.

Dyson, M. 1982. "Zeus and Philosophy in the Myth of Plato's *Phaedrus*." *Classical Quarterly* 32:307–11.

——. 1988. "Poetic Imitation in Plato *Republic* III." *Anitchthon* 22:42–53.

Else, Gerald. 1958. "'Imitation' in the Fifth Century." *Classical Philology* 53:73–90.

Enos, Richard Leo. 2012. *Greek Rhetoric before Aristotle*. 2nd ed. Anderson, SC: Parlor Press.

Evelyn-White, Hugh G., trans. 1914. *Hesiod: The Homeric Hymns and Homerica*. Loeb Classical Library. Cambridge, MA: Harvard University Press.

Ewegen, S. Montgomery. 2014. *Plato's "Cratylus": The Comedy of Language*. Bloomington: Indiana University Press.

Farias, Victor. 1991. *Heidegger and Nazism*. Translated by Tom Rockmore and Joseph Margolis. Philadelphia: Temple University Press.

Faye, Emmanuel. 2009. *Heidegger: The Introduction of Nazism into Philosophy in Light of the Unpublished Seminars of 1933–1935*. Translated by Michael B. Smith. New Haven, CT: Yale University Press.

Ferrari, G. R. F. 1987. *Listening to the Cicadas: A Study of Plato's* Phaedrus. New York: Cambridge University Press.

Fine, Gail. 1977. "Plato on Naming." *Philosophical Quarterly* 27 (109): 289–301.

Finnegan, Ruth. 1988. *Orality and Literacy: Studies in the Technology of Communication.* Oxford: Blackwell.

Flower, Robert J. 1980. "G. E. L. Owen, Plato, and the Verb 'To Be.'" *Apeiron* 14 (2): 87–95.

Forbes, R. J. 1955. *Studies in Ancient Technology.* Vol. 5. Leiden, Netherlands: Brill.

Foucault, Michel. 1972. "The Discourse on Language." In *Archaeology of Knowledge,* translated by A. M. Sheridan Smith, 215–37. New York: Pantheon.

Frede, Dorothea. 1986. "The Impossibility of Perfection: Socrates' Criticism of Simonides' Poem in the *Protagoras.*" *Review of Metaphysics* 39 (4): 729–53.

Frentz, Thomas. 2006. "Memory, Myth, and Rhetoric in Plato's *Phaedrus.*" *Rhetoric Society Quarterly* 36 (3): 243–62.

Frisk, Hjalmar. 1954–72. *Griechisches etymologisches Wörterbuch.* 3 vols. Heidelberg.

Frutiger, Perceval. (1930) 1976. *Les mythes de Platon.* Paris: Librairie Félix Alcan.

Fussi, Alessandra. 2000. "Why Is the *Gorgias* So Bitter?" *Philosophy and Rhetoric* 33:39–58.

Gadamer, Hans-Georg. 1980. "Plato and the Poets." In *Dialogue and Dialectic: Eight Hermeneutical Studies on Plato,* translated by P. Christopher Smith, 39–72. New Haven, CT: Yale University Press.

Gagarin, Michael. 1968. "Plato and Protagoras." PhD diss., Yale University.

———. 1969. "The Purpose of Plato's *Protagoras.*" *Transactions and Proceedings of the American Philological Association* 100:133–64.

———. 2001. "Did the Sophists Aim to Persuade?" *Rhetorica: A Journal of the History of Rhetoric* 19 (3): 275–91.

Gagarin, Michael, and Paul Woodruff. 2008. "The Sophists." In *The Oxford Handbook of Presocratic Philosophy,* edited by Patricia Curd and D. W. Graham, 365–82. Oxford: Oxford University Press.

Gaiser, Konrad. 1959. *Platons ungeschriebene Lehre.* Stuttgart: Klett.

Gallop, David, trans. 1972. "Hippias." In *The Older Sophists,* edited by Rosamond Kent Sprague, 94–105. Columbia: University of South Carolina Press.

Gilbert, Allan H. 1968. "Did Plato Banish the Poets?" *Medieval and Renaissance Studies* 2:35–55.

Glazebrook, Allison Mary Jane. 2009. "Cosmetics and Sophrosune: Isomachos' Wife in Xenophon's *Oikonomikos.*" *Classical World* 102 (3): 233–48.

Golden, Leon. 1969. "*Mimesis* and *Katharsis.*" *Classical Philology* 64 (3): 145–53.

———. 1975. "Plato's Concept of *Mimesis.*" *British Journal of Aesthetics* 15:118–31.

Gonzalez, Francisco J., ed. 1995. *The Third Way: New Directions in Platonic Studies.* Lanham, MD: Rowman & Littlefield.

———. 2002. "Dialectic as 'Philosophical Embarrassment': Heidegger's Critique of Plato's Method." *Journal of the History of Philosophy* 40 (2): 361–89.

———. 2006. "Whose Metaphysics of Presence? Heidegger's Interpretation of *Energeia* and *Dunamis* in Aristotle." *Southern Journal of Philosophy* 44 (4): 533–68.

———. 2008. "Plato's Question of Truth (versus Heidegger's Doctrines)." *Boston Area Colloquium in Ancient Philosophy* 23:83–119.

——. 2009. *Plato and Heidegger: A Question of Dialogue*. University Park: Pennsylvania State University Press.

——. 2014. "The Virtue of Dialogue, Dialogue as Virtue in Plato's *Protagoras*." *Philosophical Papers* 43 (1): 33–66.

Gordon, Jill. 2012. *Plato's Erotic World: From Cosmic Origins to Human Death*. Cambridge: Cambridge University Press.

Gould, John. 1972. *The Development of Plato's Ethics*. New York: Russell and Russell.

Gould, Thomas. 1964. "Plato's Hostility to Art." *Arion* 3 (1): 70–91.

Gower, Barry, and Michael C. Stokes, eds. 1992. *Socratic Questions: New Essays on the Philosophy of Socrates and Its Significance*. New York: Routledge.

Greene, W. C. 1938. *Scholia Platonica*. Haverford, PA: Philological Monographs.

Gregory, M. J. 1968. "Myth and Transcendence in Plato." *Thought* 43:273–96.

Grey, D. R. 1952. "Art in the *Republic*." *Philosophy: The Journal of the Royal Institute of Philosophy* 27:291–310.

Griffith, Mark. 2006. "Horsepower and Donkeywork" *Classical Philology* 101 (4): 307–58.

Griffith, Tom, trans. 2010. *Plato: Gorgias, Menexenus, Protagoras*. Cambridge: Cambridge University Press.

Griswold, Charles L., Jr. 1981. "The Ideas and the Criticism of Poetry in Plato's *Republic* Book X." *Journal of the History of Philosophy* 19:135–50.

——. 1986. *Self-Knowledge in Plato's "Phaedrus."* New Haven, CT: Yale University Press.

——. 1999. "Relying on Your Own Voice: An Unsettled Rivalry of Moral Ideals in Plato's *Protagoras*." *Review of Metaphysics* 53 (2): 283–307.

Gross, Daniel M., and Ansgar Kemmann, eds. 2005. *Heidegger and Rhetoric*. Albany: State University of New York Press.

Grote, George. 1851–56. *History of Greece from the Time of Solon to 403 B.C.* 8 vols. London: J. Murray.

Grube, M. A. 1933. "The Structural Unity of the *Protagoras*." *Classical Quarterly* 27:203–7.

Gulley, N. 1977. "Plato on Poetry." *Greece and Rome* 24:154–69.

Gulick, Charles Burton. 1941. *Athenaeus: The Deipnosophists*. Vol. 7. Cambridge, MA: Harvard University Press.

Guthrie, W. K. C. 1971. *The Sophists.* Cambridge: Cambridge University Press.

——, trans. 1985. *Protagoras*. In *Plato: The Collected Dialogues*, edited by Edith Hamilton and Huntington Cairns, 308–52. Princeton, NJ: Princeton University Press.

Hackforth, Reginald. 1945. "False Statement in Plato's *Sophist*." *Classical Quarterly* 39 (1/2): 56–58.

——. 1952. *Plato: Phaedrus*. Cambridge: Cambridge University Press.

Halliwell, Stephen F. 1988. *Plato: Republic 10*. Wiltshire: Aris & Phillips.

——. 2000. "Plato and Painting: Word and Image in Ancient Greece." In *Word and Image in Ancient Greece*, edited by N. Keith Rutter and Brian A. Sparkes, 99–116. Edinburgh: Edinburgh University Press.

——. 2002. *The Aesthetics of Mimesis: Ancient Texts and Modern Problems*. Princeton, NJ: Princeton University Press.

Haskins, Ekaterina Valeri Chugaeva. "Mimesis between Poetics and Rhetoric: Performance Culture and Civic Education in Plato, Isocrates, and Aristotle." *Rhetoric Society Quarterly* 30 (3): 7–34.

Hatab, Lawrence J. 2007. "Writing Knowledge in the Soul: Orality, Literacy, and Plato's Critique of Poetry." *Epoché: A Journal For The History Of Philosophy* 11 (2): 319–32.

Havelock, Eric. 1957. *The Liberal Temper in Greek Politics*. New Haven, CT: Yale University Press.

———. (1963) 1998. *Preface to Plato*. Cambridge, MA: Harvard University Press.

———. 1984. "The Orality of Socrates and the Literacy of Plato." In *New Essays on Socrates*, edited by Eugene Kelly, 67–93. New York: University Press of America.

Heath, Malcolm. 1989a. "The Unity of Plato's *Phaedrus*." *Oxford Studies in Ancient Philosophy* 7:151–73.

———. 1989b. "The Unity of the *Phaedrus*: A Postscript." *Oxford Studies in Ancient Philosophy* 7:189–91.

Heidegger, Martin. 1973. *The End of Philosophy*. Translated by Joan Stambaugh. New York: Harper and Row.

———. 1975. "The Anaximander Fragment." In *Early Greek Thinking*, translated by David F. Krell and Frank A. Capuzzi, 13–58. New York: Harper and Row.

———. 1982. *Basic Problems of Phenomenology*. Translated by Albert Hofstadter. Bloomington: Indiana University Press.

———. 1991. *Nietzsche*. Vols. 1–2. Translated by David F. Krell. San Francisco: Harper.

———. 1992. *Parmenides*. Translated by André Schuwer and Richard Rojcewicz. Bloomington: Indiana University Press.

———. 1994. *Basic Questions of Philosophy: Selected "Problems" of Logic*. Translated by Richard Rojcewicz and André Schuwer. Bloomington: Indiana University Press.

———. 2000. *Introduction to Metaphysics*. Translated by Gregory Fried and Richard Polt. New Haven, CT: Yale University Press.

———. 2008. *Basic Concepts of Ancient Philosophy*. Translated by Richard Rojcewicz. Bloomington: University of Indiana Press.

———. 2009. *Basic Concepts in Aristotelian Philosophy*. Translated by Robert D. Metcalf and Mark B. Tanzer. Bloomington: Indiana University Press.

———. 2010. *The Fundamental Question of Philosophy*. In *Being and Truth*, translated by Gregory Fried and Richard Polt, 3–62. Bloomington: Indiana University Press.

Helmbold, W. C., and W. B. Holther. 1950–52. "The Unity of the *Phaedrus*." *University of California Publications in Classical Philology* 14:387–417.

Hermann, Karl Friedrich. (1839) 1976. *Geschichte und System der Platonischen Philosophie*. Heidelberg. Reprint, New York: Arno Press.

Hershbell, Jackson P. 1995. "Reflections on the Orality and Literacy of Plato's Dialogues." In *The Third Way: New Directions in Platonic Studies*, edited by Francisco J. Gonzalez, 25–39. Lanham, MD: Rowman & Littlefield.

Hestir, Blake E. 2000. "Plato's Beard: Protagoras' Not-So-Secret Doctrine." *Southwest Philosophy Review* 15 (2): 11–22.

Hoeder, R. G. 1957. "Thrasylus' Platonic Canon and the Double Titles." *Phronesis* 1:1–20.

Hoekstra, Marieke, and Frank Scheppers. 2003. "Ὄνομα, ῥῆμα, et λόγος dans le

Cratyle et le Sophiste de Platon: Analyse du lexique et analyse du discours." *L'antiquité classique* 72:55–73.

Howland, Jacob. 1991. "Re-reading Plato: The Problem of Platonic Chronology." *Phoenix* 45:189–214.

———. 1998. *The Paradox of Political Philosophy: Socrates' Philosophic Trial.* Lanham, MD: Rowman & Littlefield.

Howland, R. L. 1937. "The Attack on Isocrates in the *Phaedrus*." *The Classical Quarterly* 31 (3/4): 151–59.

Hunt, Everett Lee. 1962. "Plato and Aristotle on Rhetoric and Rhetoricians." In *Studies in Rhetoric and Public Speaking: In Honor of James Albert Winans*, edited by A. M. Drummond and Everett Lee Hunt, 3–60. New York: Russell and Russell.

Hussey, Edward. 1982. "Epistemology and Meaning in Heraclitus." In *Language and Logos: Studies in Ancient Greek Philosophy*, edited by Malcolm Schofield and Martha Nussbaum, 33–60. Cambridge: Cambridge University Press.

Hwang, P. H. 1981. "Poetry in Plato's *Republic*." *Apeiron* 15:29–37.

Hyland, Drew. 1968. "Why Plato Wrote Dialogues." *Philosophy and Rhetoric* 1 (1): 38–50.

Hyland, Drew, and John Panteleimon Manoussakis, eds. 2006. *Heidegger and the Greeks: Interpretive Essays.* Bloomington: Indiana University Press.

IJsseling, Samuel. 1997. *Mimesis: On Appearing and Being.* Translated by Hester IJsseling and Jeffrey Bloechl. Kampen: Pharos Publishing.

Ingram, Jason. 2007. "Plato's Rhetoric of Indirection: Paradox as Site and Agency of Transformation." *Philosophy and Rhetoric* 40 (3): 293–310.

Irwin, Terence. 1977a. "Plato's Heracliteanism." *Philosophical Quarterly* 27:1–13.

———. 1977b. *Plato's Moral Theory: The Early and Middle Dialogues.* Oxford: Clarendon Press.

Jaeger, Werner. 1945. *Paideia: The Ideals of Greek Culture.* Translated by Gilbert Highet. New York: Oxford University Press.

Jarratt, Susan C. 1991. *Rereading the Sophists: Classical Rhetoric Refigured.* Carbondale: Southern Illinois University Press.

Johnson, Curtis. 1989. "Socrates Encounter with Polus in Plato's Gorgias." *Phoenix* 63:196–216.

Jolley, Kelly Dean. 2006. "Made to Measure. Socrates' 'Exquisite Argument' against Protagoras." *Hermathena* 180:45–63.

Jowett, Benjamin. (1894) 1973. "On the Text of Greek Authors and Especially of Plato." In *Plato's Republic: The Greek Text*, 2:iii–xxix. Edited by Benjamin Jowett and Lewis Campbell. Oxford: Clarendon Press.

———, trans. 1961. *Cratylus.* In *Plato: The Collected Dialogues*, edited by Edith Hamilton and Huntington Cairns, 421–74. Princeton, NJ: Princeton University Press.

Kahn, Charles H. 1966. "Linguistic Relativism and the Greek Project of Ontology." *Aktualitat der Antike* 2:20–33.

———. 1973. *The Verb "Be" in Ancient Greek.* Dordrecht, Netherlands: Reidel.

———. 1976. "Why Existence Does Not Emerge as a Distinct Concept in Greek Philosophy." *Archiv fur Geschichte der Philosophie* 58:323–34.

———. 1981. "Some Philosophical Uses of 'To Be' in Plato. *Phronesis* 26 (2): 105–34.

———. 1986. "Plato and Heraclitus." *Proceedings of the Boston Area Colloquium in Ancient Philosophy* 1:241–58.

———. 1996. *Plato and the Socratic Dialogue.* Cambridge: Cambridge University Press.

———. 2003. *The Verb "Be" in Ancient Greek*, 2nd ed. Indianapolis: Hackett.

———. 2007. "Why Is the *Sophist* a Sequel to the *Theaetetus*?" *Phronesis* 52:33–57.

Kalligas, Paul. 2012. "From Being an Image to Being What-Is-Not." *Presocratics and Plato: Festschrift at Delphi in Honor of Charles Kahn*, edited by Richeard Patterson, Vassilis Karasmanis, and Arnold Hermann, 391–410. Las Vegas: Parmenides Publishing.

Karelis, Charles. 1976. "Plato on Art and Reality." *Journal of Aesthetics and Art Criticism* 34:315–21.

Kastely, James L. 2002. "Respecting the Rupture: Not Solving the Problem of Unity in Plato's *Phaedrus*." *Philosophy and Rhetoric* 35 (2): 138–52.

———. 2015. *The Rhetoric of Plato's "Republic."* Chicago: University of Chicago Press.

Kelley, W. G. 1973. "Rhetoric as Seduction." *Philosophy and Rhetoric* 6:69–80.

Kennedy, George, trans. 1972. "Encomium of Helen." In *The Older Sophists*, edited by Rosamond Kent Sprague, 50–54. Columbia: University of South Carolina Press.

———. 1994. *A New History of Classical Rhetoric.* Princeton, NJ: Princeton University Press.

———. 1999. *Classical Rhetoric and Its Christian and Secular Tradition: From Ancient to Modern Times*, 2nd ed. Chapel Hill: University of North Carolina Press.

———, trans. 2007. *Aristotle: On Rhetoric.* Oxford: Oxford University Press.

Kerferd, G. B. 1953. "Protagoras' Doctrine of Justice and Virtue in the *Protagoras* of Plato." *Journal of Hellenic Studies* 73:42–45.

———. 1954. "The 'Relativism' of Prodicus." *Bulletin of the John Rylands Library* 37:249–56.

———. 1955. "Gorgias on Nature or That Which Is Not." *Phronesis* 1 (1): 3–25.

———. 1981. *The Sophistic Movement.* Cambridge: Cambridge University Press.

Kirk, Geoffrey S. 1951. "The Problem of Cratylus." *American Journal of Philology* 72 (3): 225–53.

Kirk, Geoffrey S., John E. Raven, and Malcolm Schofield. 1983. *The Presocratic Philosophers: A Critical History with a Selection of Texts*, 2nd ed. Cambridge: Cambridge University Press.

Kirkland, Sean D. 2004. "Socrates 'contra scientium, pro fabula.'" *Epoché: A Journal for the History of Philosophy* 8 (2): 313–22.

Klagge, James C., and Nicholas D. Smith. 1992. Introduction to *Methods of Interpreting Plato and His Dialogues.* Oxford Studies in Ancient Philosophy, suppl. vol. Oxford: Clarendon Press.

Klosko, George. 1986. *The Development of Plato's Political Theory.* New York: Methuen.

Knudsen, Rachel. 2013. "Poetic Speakers, Sophistic Words." *American Journal of Philology* 133 (1): 31–60.

Koller, Hermann. 1954. *Die Mimesis in der Antike: Nachahmung, Darstelllung, Ausdruck.* Bern: Francke.

Kostman, J. 1973. "False Logos and Not-Being in Plato's *Sophist.*" In *Patterns in Plato's*

Thought, edited by Julius M. E. Moravcsik, 192–212. Dordrecht, Netherlands: Reidel.

Krämer, Hans Joachim. 1990. *Plato and the Foundation of Metaphysics*, edited and translated by John R. Catan. Albany: State University of New York Press.

Kraut, Richard, ed. 1992. *The Cambridge Companion to Plato*. Cambridge: Cambridge University Press.

Lamb, W. R. M., trans. 1925. *Plato: Gorgias*. Harvard, MA: Harvard University Press.

Lear, Gabriel Richardson. 2011. "Mimesis and Psychological Change in *Republic* III." In *Plato and the Poets*, edited by Pierre Destrée and Fritz-Gregor Herrmann, 195–216. Leiden, Netherlands: Brill.

Lebeck, Anne. 1972. "The Central Myth of Plato's *Phaedrus*." *Greek, Roman, and Byzantine Studies* 13:267–90.

Lee, Edward N. 1972. "Plato on Negation and Not-Being in the *Sophist*." *Philosophical Review* 81: 267–304.

———. 1973. "'Hoist with His Own Petard': Ironic and Comic Elements in Plato's Critique of Protagoras (*Tht.* 161–171)." In *Exegesis and Argument: Studies in Greek Philosophy Presented to Gregory Vlastos*, edited by Edward N. Lee, A. P. D. Mourelatos, and Richard M. Rorty, 225–61. Assen, Netherlands: Van Gorcum.

Lee, Mi-Kyoung. 2005. *Epistemology after Protagoras: Responses to Relativism in Plato, Aristotle, and Democritus*. Oxford: Oxford University Press.

Legowicz, Jan. 1986. "The State of Reason and Measure by Plato." *Danish Yearbook of Philosophy* 23:135–47.

Levett, Mary Jane, trans. 1990. *The Theaetetus of Plato*. Indianapolis: Hackett.

Levinson, Ronald B. 1971. "Language, Plato, and Logic." *Essays in Ancient Greek Philosophy*, edited by John P. Anton with George L. Kustas, 259–84. Albany: State University of New York Press.

Linforth, Ivan M. 1946. "The Corybantic Rites in Plato." *University of California Publications in Classical Philology* 13 (5): 121–62.

Lodge, Gonzales. 1890. *Plato: Gorgias*. Boston: Ginn and Company.

Lord, Albert. (1960) 2000. *The Singer of Tales*, 2nd ed. Cambridge, MA: Harvard University Press.

Maguire, Joseph P. 1964. "The Differentiation of Art in Plato's Aesthetics." *Harvard Studies in Classical Philology* 68:389–410.

———. 1973. "Protagoras—or Plato?" *Phronesis* 18 (2): 115–38.

———. 1977. "Protagoras . . . or Plato? II. The *Protagoras*." *Phronesis* 22 (2): 103–22.

Mansfeld, Jaap. 1990. "Historical and Philosophical Aspects of Gorgias' 'On What Is Not.'" In *Studies in the Historiography of Greek Philosophy*, 97–125. Assen, Netherlands: Van Gorcum.

Marback, Richard. 1999. *Plato's Dream of Sophistry*. Columbia: University of South Carolina Press.

Marrou, Henri I. 1956. *A History of Education in Antiquity*. Translated by George Lamb. New York: Sheed and Ward.

Marušič, Jera. 2011. "Poets and Mimesis in the *Republic*." In *Plato and the Poets*, edited by Pierre Destrée and Fritz-Gregor Herrmann, 218–40. Leiden, Netherlands: Brill.

Matthen, Mohan. 1985. “Perception, Relativism, and Truth: Reflections on Plato’s *Theaetetus* 152–160.” *Dialogue* 24:33–58.

McAdon, Brad. 2004. “Plato’s Denunciation of Rhetoric in the *Phaedrus.*” *Rhetoric Review* 23 (1): 21–39.

McCabe, M. M. 2000. *Plato and His Predecessors: The Dramatisation of Reason.* Cambridge: Cambridge University Press.

McCoy, Marina Berzins. 1999. “Socrates on Simonides: The Use of Poetry in Socratic and Platonic Rhetoric.” *Philosophy and Rhetoric* 32 (4): 349–67.

———. 2005. “Reason and Dialectic in the Argument against Protagoras in the *Theaetetus.*” *International Philosophical Quarterly* 45 (1): 21–39.

———. 2008. *Plato on the Rhetoric of Philosophers and Sophists.* Cambridge: Cambridge University Press.

———. 2009. “Alcidamas, Isocrates, and Plato on Speech, Writing, and Philosophical Rhetoric.” *Ancient Philosophy* 29 (2): 45–66.

McDowell, J. 1982. “Falsehood and Not-Being in Plato’s *Sophist.*” In *Language and Logos,* edited by M. Schofield and M. Nussbaum, 115–34. Cambridge: Cambridge University Press.

McKeon, Richard. 1951. “Literary Criticism and the Concept of Imitation in Antiquity.” In *Critics and Criticism: Ancient and Modern,* edited by R. S. Crane, 147–75. Chicago: University of Chicago Press.

McLuhan, Marshall. 2003. *Understanding Media: The Extensions of Man.* Corte Madera, CA: Gingko Press.

McNeill, David N. 2001. *An Image of the Soul in Speech: Plato and the Problem of Socrates.* University Park, PA: Pennsylvania State University Press.

Mei, Todd S. 2007. “Justice and the Banning of the Poets: The Way of Hermeneutics in Plato’s *Republic.*” *Review of Metaphysics* 60 (4): 755–78.

Meinwald, Constance. 2011. “Reason v. Literature in Plato’s *Republic*: Does the Dialogue Rule Itself Out?” *Ancient Philosophy* 31:25–45.

Michaelides, Constantine. 1975. “The Concept of Not-Being in Plato.” *Diotima* 3:19–26.

Miller, Mitchell. 1999. “Platonic *Mimesis.*” In *Contextualizing Classics: Ideology, Performance, Dialogue: Essays in Honor of John J. Peradotto,* edited by Thomas M. Falkner, Nancy Felson, and David Konstan, 253–66. Lanham, MD: Rowman and Littlefield.

Mitscherling, Jeff. 2009. *The Image of a Second Sun: Plato on Poetry, Rhetoric, and the Technê of Mimêsis.* Amherst, NY: Humanity Books.

Moes, Mark Matthew. 2011. “Dialectical Rhetoric and Socrates’ Treatment of Mimetic Poetry in Book 10 of the *Republic.*” *Philosophy Study* 1 (1): 1–21.

Mondolfo, Rodolfo. 1954. “El problema de Cratilo y la interpretación de Heráclito.” *Anales de filología clásica* 6:157–74.

Monoson, Sara. 2000. *Plato’s Democratic Entanglements: Athenian Politics and the Practice of Philosophy.* Princeton, NJ: Princeton University Press.

Moravcsik, Julius. 1973. “The Anatomy of Plato’s Divisions.” In *Exegesis and Argument.* (Festschrift for Gregory Vlastos), *Phronesis* suppl. vol., edited by E. N. Lee, A. P. D. Mourelatos, and R. M. Rorty, 1:324–48. New York: Humanities Press.

———. 1982. "Noetic Aspiration and Artistic Inspiration." In *Plato on Beauty, Wisdom, and the Arts*, edited by Julius Moravcsik and Philip Temko, 29–46. Totowa, NJ: Rowman & Littlefield.

Moss, Jean. 1996. "Commonplaces and Commonplace Books." *Encyclopedia of Rhetoric and Composition: Communication from Ancient Times to the Information Age*, edited by Theresa Enos, 119–24. New York: Garland.

Most, Glenn W. 1989. "The Challenge of the Context: Simonides' 'Scopas' in Plato's *Protagoras*" in "The 90th General Meeting of the Archaeological Institute of America and the First Joint Archaeological Congress." *American Journal of Archaeology* 93 (2): 243–84. Lille: Presses Universitaires du Septentrion.

———. 2004. "Les Grecs de Heidegger." *Philosophie antique: Problèmes, renaissances, usages*, edited by André Laks and Michel Narcy, 4:169–84. Lille: Presses Universitaires du Septentrion.

Moysan-Lapointe, Héloïse. 2010. "La vérité chez Protagoras." *Laval théologique et philosophique* 66 (3): 529–45.

Mulhern, J. J. 1971. "Two Interpretive Fallacies." *Systematics* 9:168–72.

Murray, James S. 1988. "Disputation, Deception, and Dialectic: Plato on the True Rhetoric (*Phaedrus* 261–266)." *Philosophy and Rhetoric* 21:279–89.

Murray, Penelope. 1992. "Inspiration and Mimesis in Plato" *Apeiron* 25 (4): 27–46.

———. 1999. "What Is a *Muthos* for Plato?" In *From Myth to Reason: Studies in the Development of Greek Thought*, edited by Richard Buxton, 251–62. Oxford: Oxford University Press.

Nails, Debra. 1995. *Agora, Academy, and the Conduct of Philosophy*. Dordrecht, Netherlands: Kluwer.

———. 2002. *The People of Plato: A Prosopography of Plato and Other Socratics*. Indianapolis: Hackett.

Nehamas, Alexander. 1982. "Plato on Imitation and Poetry in *Republic* 10." In *Plato on Beauty, Wisdom, and the Arts*, edited by Julius Moravcsik and Philip Temko, 47–78. Totowa, NJ: Rowman & Littlefield.

Nehamas, Alexander, and Paul Woodruff. 1999. *Plato*: Phaedrus. Princeton, NJ: Princeton University Press.

Nehring, Alfons. 1945. "Plato and the Theory of Language." *Traditio* 3:13–48.

North, Helen. 1952. "The Use of Poetry in the Training of the Ancient Orator." *Traditio* 8:1–33.

Nightingale, Andrea Wilson. 2004. *Spectacles of Truth in Classical Greek Philosophy: Theoria in Its Cultural Context*. Cambridge: Cambridge University Press.

Nussbaum, Martha. 1984. "Plato on Commensurability and Desire." *Proceedings of the Aristotelian Society* suppl. vol. 58 (1): 55–96.

———. 1986. *The Fragility of Goodness: Luck and Ethics in Greek Tragedy and Philosophy*. Cambridge: Cambridge University Press.

O'Brien, Michael J., trans. 1972. "Protagoras." In *The Older Sophists*, edited by Rosamond Kent Sprague, 3–28. Columbia: University of South Carolina Press.

O'Neill, William, trans. 1972a. "Name and Notation." In *The Older Sophists*, edited by Rosamond Kent Sprague, 1–2. Columbia: University of South Carolina Press.

——, trans. 1972b. "Xeniades." In *The Older Sophists*, edited by Rosamond Kent Sprague, 29. Columbia: University of South Carolina Press.

——, trans. 1972c. "Lycophron." In *The Older Sophists*, edited by Rosamond Kent Sprague, 68–69. Columbia: University of South Carolina Press.

Olympiodorus. 1998. *Commentary on Plato's* Gorgias. Translated by Robin Jackson, Kimon Lycos, and Harold Tarrant. Leiden, Netherlands: Brill.

Ong, Walter. 1982. *Orality and Literacy*. New York: Routledge.

Osborne, Catherine. 1987. "The Repudiation of Representation in Plato's *Republic* and Its Repercussions." *Proceedings of the Cambridge Philological Society* 33:53–73.

——. 1999. "'No' Means 'Yes': The Seduction of the Word in Plato's *Phaedrus*." *Proceedings of the Boston Area Colloquium in Ancient Philosophy* 15:263–81.

Ovid. 1961. *Metamorphoses*. Translated by Sir Samuel Garth, John Dryden, Alexander Pope, Samuel Croxall, Joseph Addison, and William Congreve. New York: Heritage.

Owen, G. E. L. 1971. "Plato on Not-Being." In *Plato I: A Collection of Critical Essays, Metaphysics and Epistemology*, edited by Gregory Vlastos, 223–67. Garden City, NY: Anchor Books.

Papillon, Terry L. 2017. "Unity, Dissociation, and Schismogenesis in Isocrates." In *Logos without Rhetoric: The Arts of Language before Plato*, edited by Robin Reames, 11–18. Columbia: University of South Carolina Press.

Pappas, Nicholas. 1975. "Plato's Concept of *Mimesis*." *British Journal of Aesthetics* 15:118–31.

——. 1989. "Socrates' Charitable Treatment of Poetry." *Philosophy and Literature* 13 (2): 248–61.

——. 1999. "*Mimêsis* in Aristophanes and Plato." *Philosophical Inquiry: International Quarterly* 21 (3–4): 61–78.

——. 2012. "Plato on Poetry: Imitation or Inspiration?" *Philosophy Compass* 7 (10): 669–78.

Parry, Hugh. 1965. "An Interpretation of Simonides 4 (Diehl)." *Transactions and Proceedings of the American Philological Association* 96:297–320.

Partee, M. H. 1970. "Plato's Banishment of Poetry." *Journal of Aesthetics and Art Criticism* 29 (2): 209–22.

——. 1974. "Plato on the Rhetoric of Poetry." *Journal of Aesthetics and Art Criticism* 33 (2): 203–12.

Peck, A. 1962. "Plato versus Parmenides." *Philosophical Review* 71:159–84.

Pelletier, Francis Jeffry. 1990. *Parmenides, Plato, and the Semantics of Non-being*. Chicago: University of Chicago Press.

Perelman, Chaïm, and Lucie Olbrechts-Tyteca. 1969. *The New Rhetoric: A Treatise on Argumentation*. South Bend, IN: Notre Dame University Press.

Pfeiffer, W. M. 1972. "True and False Speech in Plato's *Cratylus*." *Canadian Journal of Philosophy* 2:87–104.

Phillip, J. A. 1961. "Mimesis in the *Sophistês* of Plato." *Transactions of the American Philological Association* 92:453–68.

——. 1968. "False Statement in the *Sophistes*." *Transactions and Proceedings of the American Philological Society* 99:315–27.

Plass, Paul. 1968. "The Unity of the *Phaedrus*." *Symbolae Osloenses* 43:7–38. Reprinted 1979 in *Plato: True and Sophistic Rhetoric*, edited by K.V. Erickson, 193–221. Amsterdam: Editions Rodopi.

Plessner, Helmuth. 1970. *Philosophische Anthropolotie*. Frankfurt am Main.

Plochmann, George Kimball, and Franklin E. Robinson. 1988. *A Friendly Companion to Plato's* Gorgias. Carbondale: Southern Illinois University Press.

Popper, Karl. 1963. *The Open Society and Its Enemies Volume 1, The Spell of Plato*. Princeton, NJ: Princeton University Press.

Poster, Carol. 2017. "Gorgias' 'On Non-being': Genre, Purpose, and Testimonia." In *Logos without Rhetoric: The Arts of Language before Plato*, edited by Robin Reames, 30–46. Columbia: University of South Carolina Press.

Poulakos, John. 1995. *Sophistical Rhetoric in Classical Greece*. Columbia: University of South Carolina Press.

Press, Gerald A., ed. 2000. *Who Speaks for Plato? Studies in Plato's Anonymity*. Lanham, MD: Rowman and Littlefield.

Prior, W. J. 1985. *Unity and Development in Plato's Metaphysics*. LaSalle, IL: Open Court.

Quimby, Rollin W. 1974. "The Growth of Plato's Perception of Rhetoric." *Philosophy and Rhetoric* 7 (2): 71–79.

Rabel, Robert J. 1996. "Σχῆμα in Plato's Definition of Imitation." *Ancient Philosophy* 16 (2): 365–75.

Ramsey, Eric. 1998–99. "A Hybrid *Techne* of the Soul." *Rhetoric Review* 17 (2): 247–62.

Raven, J. E. 1965. *Plato's Thought in the Making: A Study in the Development of his Metaphysics*. Cambridge: Cambridge University Press.

Rawlinson, George, trans. 1928. *Herodotus: The History*. New York: Tudor.

Reale, Giovanni. 1987. *Per una nuova interpretazione di Platone: Rilettura della metafisica dei grandi dialoghi alla luce delle "Dottrine non scritte."* Milan: Vita e Pensiero.

Reames, Robin. 2012. "The *Mythos* of Pernicious Rhetoric: The Platonic Possibilities of Logos in Aristotle's *Rhetoric*." *Rhetorica* 30 (2): 134–152.

———. 2013. "The *Logos* Paradox: Heraclitus, Material Language, and Rhetoric." *Philosophy and Rhetoric* 46 (3): 328–50.

———. 2016. "Seeming and Being in the 'Cosmetics' of Sophistry: The Infamous Analogy of Plato's *Gorgias*." *Philosophy and Rhetoric* 49 (1): 74–97.

———. 2017. "Heraclitus' Doublespeak: The Paradoxical Origins of Rhetorical *Logos*." In *Logos without Rhetoric: The Arts of Language before Plato*, edited by Reames, 63–78. Columbia: University of South Carolina Press.

Richardson, Henry S. 1990. "Measurement, Pleasure, and Practical Science in Plato's *Protagoras*." *Journal of the History of Philosophy* 28 (1): 7–32.

Ricoeur, Paul. 1990. *Time and Narrative*. 3 vols. Translated by Kathleen McLaughlin and David Pelauer. Chicago: University of Chicago Press.

Risser, James. 2013. "On the Threefold Sense of 'Mimesis' in Plato's *Republic*." *Epoché: A Journal for the History of Philosophy* 17 (2): 249–56.

Robinson, John M. 1973. "On Gorgias." In *Exegesis and Argument*, edited by E. N. Lee, A. P. D Mourelatos, and R. M. Rorty, 49–60. Assen, Netherlands: Van Gorgum.

Robinson, Richard. 1953. *Plato's Earlier Dialectic*. Oxford: Oxford Universty Press.

———. 1969. *Essays in Greek Philosophy*. Oxford: Oxford University Press.

———. 1984. *Plato's Earlier Dialectic*, 2nd ed. Oxford: Clarendon Press.

Robinson, Thomas M. 2003. "Protagoras, the *Protagoras* and the *Dissoi Logoi*." In *Plato's* Protagoras: *Proceedings of the Third Symposium Platonicum Pragense*, edited by Aleš Havlíček and Filip Karfík, 233–46. Prague: Oikoymenh.

Rohdich, Hermann. 1979. "Das Verspottete Jenseits." *Rheinisches Museum für Philologie* 122 (2): 119–30.

Roochnik, David. 1995. "Socrates' Rhetorical Attack on Rhetoric." In *The Third Way: New Directions in Platonic Studies*, edited by Francisco J. Gonzalez, 81–94. Lanham, MD: Rowman & Littlefield.

Rouse, W. H. D., trans. 1961. *Euthydemus*. In *Plato: The Collected Dialogues*, edited by Edith Hamilton and Huntington Cairns, 385–420. Princeton, NJ: Princeton University Press.

Rowe, Christopher J. 1989. "The Unity of the *Phaedrus*: A Reply to Heath." *Oxford Studies in Ancient Philosophy* 7:175–88.

———. 2009. "The Charioteer and His Horses." *Plato's Myths*, edited by Catalin Partenie, 134–47. Cambridge: Cambridge University Press.

Rutherford, Richard B. 1995. *The Art of Plato: Ten Essays in Platonic Interpretation*. Cambridge, MA: Harvard University Press.

Ryan, Eugene E. 1979. "Plato's *Gorgias* and *Phaedrus* and Aristotle's Theory of Rhetoric: A Speculative Account." *Athenaeum* 57:452–61.

Ryan, Paul. 2012. *Plato's Phaedrus: A Commentary for Greek Readers*. Norman: University of Oklahoma Press.

Sallis, John. 1986. *Being and Logos: The Way of Platonic Dialogue*, 2nd ed. Atlantic Highlands, NJ: Humanities Press International.

Sandbach, F. H. 1969. *Fragments*. Vol. 15 of *Plutarch's "Moralia."* Cambridge, MA: Harvard University Press.

Saxonhouse, Arlene. 1983. "An Unspoken Theme in in Plato's *Gorgias*: War." *Interpretation* 11:139–69.

———. 1992. *Fear of Diversity: The Birth of Political Science in Ancient Greek Thought*. Chicago: Chicago University Press.

———. 1996. *Athenian Democracy: Modern Mythmakers and Ancient Theorists*. South Bend, IN: University of Notre Dame Press.

Sayre, Kenneth. 1993. "Review of Krämer's *Plato and the Foundations of Metaphysics*." *Ancient Philosophy* 13:167–84.

Schiappa, Edward. 1990. "Did Plato Coin *Rhêtorikê*?" *American Journal of Philology* 111 (4): 457–470.

———. 1999. *The Beginnings of Rhetorical Theory in Classical Greece*. New Haven, CT: Yale University Press.

———. 2003. *Protagoras and Logos: A Study in Greek Philosophy and Rhetoric*. Columbia: University of South Carolina Press.

Schiappa, Edward, and Stacey Hoffman. 1994. "Intertextual Argument in Gorgias's *On What Is Not*: A Formalization of Sextus, *Adv. Math.* 7. 77–80." *Philosophy and Rhetoric* 27 (2): 156–61.

Schleiermacher, Friedrich. 1836. *Introductions to the Dialogues of Plato*. Translated by William Dobson. London: Pitt Press.

Schofield, Malcolm. 1982. "The Dénouement of the *Cratylus*." In *Language and Logos*, edited by M. Schofield and M. Nussbaum, 61–81. Cambridge: Cambridge University Press.

———. 1992. "Socrates versus Protagoras." In *Socratic Questions: New Essays on the Philosophy of Socrates and Its Significance*, edited by Barry S. Gower and Michael C. Stokes, 122–36. New York: Routledge.

Scodel, Ruth. 1986. "Literary Interpretation in Plato's *Protagoras*." *Ancient Philosophy* 6:25–37.

Sedley, David. 2003. "The Nomothetês in Plato's *Cratylus*." *Studiea Philonica Annual* 15:5–16.

Segal, Charles P. 1962. "Gorgias and the Psychology of the Logos." *Harvard Studies in Classical Philology* 66:99–155.

———. 1970. "Protagoras' Orthoepeia in Aristophanes' 'Battle of the Prologues.'" *Rheinisches Museum für Philologie* 113 (2/3): 158–62.

———. 1978. "'The Myth Was Saved': Reflections on Homer and the Mythology of Plato's *Republic*." *Hermes* 106:315–36.

Sevic, Heda. 2006. "Homer in Plato's *Protagoras*." *Classical Philology* 101 (3): 247–62.

Sidwell, Keith. 2005. "Some Thoughts on the Sophist in Bed." *Hermathena* 179:67–76.

Slaveva-Griffin, Svetla. 2003. "Of Gods, Philosophers, and Charioteers." *Transactions of the American Philological Association* 133 (2): 227–53.

Smith, Andrew. 2007. "Plotinus and the Myth of Love." In *Texts and Culture in Late Antiquity: Inheritance, Authority, and Change*, edited by John Scourfield, 233–45. Swansea: Classical Press of Wales.

Smith, Nicholas D. 1996. "Plato's Divided Line." *Ancient Philosophy* 16:25–46.

Soares, Lucas. 2011. "Crítica y empleo platónico de la exégesis sofística de los mitos y poemas tradicionales." *Nova Tellus* 29 (1): 21–39.

Solmsen, Felix. 1901. "Zwei Nominalbildungen Auf–μμ." *Rheinisches Museum für Philologie* 56:497–507.

Solmsen, Friedrich. 1966. "Review: *Preface to Plato* by Eric Havelock." *American Journal of Philology* 87 (1): 99–105.

Sörbom, G. 1966. *Mimesis and Art: Studies in the Origin and Early Development of an Aesthetic Vocabulary*. Uppsala: Appelbergs.

Sprague, Rosamond Kent. 1971. "A Reply to Dr. Levinson." *Essays in Ancient Greek Philosophy*, edited by John P. Anton with George L. Kustas, 367–71. Albany: State University of New York Press.

———, ed. 1972. *The Older Sophists: A Complete Translation by Several Hands of the Fragments in "Die Fragmente der vorsokratiker," Edited by Diels-Krantz, with a New Edition of "Antiphon" and of "Euthydemus."* Columbia: University of South Carolina Press.

Stanford, W. B. 1973. "Onomatopoetic Mimesis in Plato, *Republic* 396b–397c." *Journal of Hellenic Studies* 93:185–91.

Stauffer, Devin. 2006. *The Unity of Plato's* Gorgias: *Rhetoric, Justice, and the Philosophic Life*. Cambridge: Cambridge University Press.

Stern-Gillet, Suzanne. 2004. "On (Mis)interpreting Plato's *Ion*." *Phronesis* 49 (2): 169–201.

Steven, R. G. 1933. "Plato and the Art of His Time." *Classical Quarterly* 27:149–55.

Stewart, Douglas J. 1965. "Man and Myth in Plato's Universe." *Bucknell Review* 13 (1): 72–90.

——, trans. 1972. "Prodicus." In *The Older Sophists*, edited by Rosamond Kent Sprague, 70–85. Columbia: University of South Carolina Press.

Stoeber, Michael. 1992. "Phaedrus of the *Phaedrus*: The Impassioned Soul." *Philosophy and Rhetoric* 25 (3): 271–80.

Stokes, Michael C. 1986. *Plato's Socratic Conversations: Drama and Dialectic in Three Dialogues.* London: Bloomsbury.

Strauss, Leo. 1964. *The City and Man.* Chicago: Chicago University Press.

Street, Brian V. 1984. *Literacy in Theory and Practice.* Cambridge: Cambridge University Press.

Sullivan, J. P. 1961. "The Hedonism in Plato's *Protagoras*." *Phronesis* 6:10–28.

Szlezák, Thomas. 1996. *Reading Plato.* Translated by Graham Zanker. London: Routledge. First published 1993 as *Platon lessen* (Stuttgart: Verlag frommann-holzboog).

Tarnopolsky, Christina. 2010. *Prudes, Perverts, and Tyrants: Plato's* Gorgias *and the Politics of Shame.* Princeton, NJ: Princeton University Press.

Taylor, A. E. 1926. *Plato: The Man and His Work.* London: Methuen.

Taylor, C. C. W., trans. and comm. (1976) 1991. *Protagoras.* Oxford: Clarendon Press.

Taylor, Thomas, trans. 1985. *Proclus.* Vol. 1 of Platonic Theology, edited by Harris R. Baine. Kew Gardens, NY: Selene Books.

Tell, Håkan. 2011. *Plato's Counterfeit Sophists.* Cambridge, MA: Center for Hellenic Studies.

Thesleff, Holger. 1982. *Studies in Platonic Chronology.* Vol. 70 of Commentationes Humanarum Litterarum. Helsinki: Societas Scientiarum Fennica.

——. 1989. "Platonic Chronology." *Phronesis* 34:1–26.

Thompson, William Hepworth, ed. (1871) 1973. *Plato: Gorgias.* New York: Arno Press.

Thornton, M. T. 1970. "Knowledge and Flux in Plato's *Cratylus*." *Dialogue: Canadian Philosophical Review* 8:581–91.

Tigerstedt, E. N. 1977. *Interpreting Plato.* Stockholm: Almqvist and Wiksell.

Timmerman, David, and Edward Schiappa. 2010. *Classical Greek Rhetorical Theory and the Disciplining of Discourse.* Cambridge: Cambridge University Press.

Tindale, Christopher. 2010. *Reason's Dark Champions: Constructive Strategies of Sophistic Argument.* Columbia: University of South Carolina Press.

Todd, O. J., trans. 2006. *Xenophon: Symposium.* Cambridge, MA. Harvard University Press.

Treanor, Brian. 2001. "The Overqualified Artist: The Regulation of 'Mimesis' in Plato's *Republic*." *Auslegung: A Journal of Philosophy* 24 (2): 163–83.

Tredennick, Hugh, trans. 1961. *Socrates' Defense* (*Apology*). In *Plato: The Collected Dialogues*, edited by Edith Hamilton and Huntington Cairns, 3–26. Princeton, NJ: Princeton University Press.

Trivigno, Franco V. 2013. "Childish Nonsense? The Value of Interpretation in Plato's *Protagoras*." *Journal of the History of Philosophy* 51 (4): 509–43.

Untersteiner, Mario. 1954. *The Sophists*. Translated by Kathleen Freeman. Oxford: Blackwell.

Urmson, James O. 1982. "Plato and the Poets." In *Plato on Beauty, Wisdom, and the Arts*, edited by Julius Moravcsik and Philip Temko, 125–136. Totowa, NJ: Rowman & Littlefield.

———. 1997. "Plato and the Poets." In *Plato's Republic: Critical Essays*, edited by Richard Kraut, 223–34. Lanham, MD: Rowman and Littlefield.

Van den Berg, R. M. 1997. "Proclus: The Myth of the Winged Charioteer." *Syllecta Classica* 8:149–62.

Van Eck, Job. 2009. "Moving like a Stream: Protagoras' Heracliteanism in Plato's *Theaetetus*." *Oxford Studies in Ancient Philosophy* 36 (Summer):199–248.

Van Groningen, B. A. 1958. *La composition littéraire archaique grecque: Procédé et réalisations*. Amsterdam: N.V. Noord-Hollandsche Uitgevers Maatschappij.

Verdenius, W. J. 1949. *Mimesis: Plato's Doctrine of Imitation and Its Meaning to Us*. Leiden, Netherlands: Brill.

Versenyi, Laszlo. 1962. "Protagoras' Man-Measure Fragment." *American Journal of Philology* 83 (2): 178–84.

Vickers, Brian. 1988. *In Defence of Rhetoric*. Oxford: Clarendon Press.

Vlastos, Gregory. 1956. *Plato's Protagoras*. New York: Liberal Arts Press.

———, ed. 1970. *Plato: A Collection of Critical Essays, II: Ethics, Politics, and Philosophy of Art and Religion*. Garden City, NY: Anchor Books/ Doubleday.

———. 1991. *Socrates: Ironist and Moral Philosopher*. Ithaca, NY: Cornell University Press.

Voliotis, N. 1977. "Isocrates and Plato: An Effort to Interpret *Phaedrus* 278e–279b." *Platon* 29:145–51.

Von Reden, Sitta. 1995. "Deceptive Readings: Poetry and Its Value Reconsidered." *Classical Quarterly* 45 (1): 30–50.

Wardy, Robert. 1996. *The Birth of Rhetoric: Gorgias, Plato, and Their Successors*. London: Routledge.

Waterfield, Robin, trans. 1994. *Plato: Gorgias*. Oxford: Oxford University Press

———, trans. 2002. *Plato: Phaedrus*. Oxford: Oxford University Press.

———, trans. 2008. *Plato: Republic*. Oxford: Oxford University Press.

Waterlow, Sarah. 1977. "Protagoras and Inconsistency." *Arhiv für Geschichte der Philosophie* 14:19–36.

Werner, Daniel. 2012. *Myth and Philosophy in Plato's "Phaedrus."* Cambridge: Cambridge University Press.

West, Elinor J. M. 1995. "Plato's Audiences, or How Plato Replies to the Fifth-Century Intellectual Mistrust of Letters." In *The Third Way: New Directions in Platonic Studies*, edited by Francisco J. Gonzalez, 41–60. Lanham, MD: Rowman & Littlefield.

West, M. L. 1992. *Iambi et elegi Graeci*. Oxford: Clarendon Press.

White, David A. 1993. *Rhetoric and Reality in Plato's "Phaedrus."* Albany: State University of New York Press.

White, Nicholas P. 1976. *Plato on Knowledge and Reality*. Indianapolis: Hackett.

———. 1979. *A Companion to Plato's "Republic."* Indianapolis: Hackett.

———, trans. 1993. *Plato: Sophist.* Indianapolis: Hackett.

Wiegmann, Hermann. 1990. "Plato's Critique of the Poets and the Misunderstanding of His Epistemological Argumentation." *Philosophy and Rhetoric* 23 (2): 109–24.

Wiitala, Michael. 2010. "Negating the Image: the Apophatic Character of Philosophy in Plato's *Phaedrus*." *Kinesis: Graduate Journal in Philosophy*. 37(1): 56–65.

Wilamowitz-Moellendorff, Ulrich von. 1898. "Das Skolion des Simonides an Skopas." In *Nachrichten von der Königlichen Gesellschaft der Wissenschaften zu Göttingen* 2:204–236.

Williams, Bernard. 1982. "Cratylus' Theory of Names and Its Refutation." In *Language and Logos*, edited by M. Schofield and M. Nussbaum, 83–93. Cambridge: Cambridge University Press.

Woodbury, Leonard. 1953. "Simonides on Ἀρετή." *Transactions and Proceedings of the American Philological Association* 84:135–63.

———. 1971. "Parmenides on Names." In *Essays in Ancient Greek Philosophy*, edited by John P. Anton with George L. Kustas, 145–62. Albany: State University of New York Press.

Woodruff, Paul. 1982. "What Could Go Wrong with Inspiration? Why Plato's Poets Fail." *Plato on Beauty, Wisdom, and the Arts*, edited by Julius Moravcsik and Philip Temko, 137–50. Totowa, NJ: Rowman & Littlefield.

———. 1999. "Rhetoric and Relativism: Protagoras and Gorgias." In *The Cambridge Companion to Early Greek Philosophy*, edited by A. A. Long, 290–310. Cambridge: Cambridge University Press.

Woolf, Raphael. 1999. "The Written Word in Plato's *Protagoras*." *Ancient Philosophy* 19 (1): 21–30.

Wyller, Egil A. 1991. "Plato's Concept of Rhetoric in the *Phaedrus* and Its Tradition in Antiquity." *Symbolae Osloenem* 66:51–69.

Yunis, Harvey. 2007. "The Protreptic Rhetoric of the *Republic*." In *The Cambridge Companion to Plato's Republic*, edited by G. R. F. Ferrari, 1–26.

Zeyl, Donald J. 1980. "Socrates and Hedonism: *Protagoras* 351b–358d." *Phronesis* 25:250–69.

Zilioli, Ugo. 2007. *Protagoras and the Challenge of Relativism: Plato's Subtlest Enemy*. Aldershot: Ashgate.

Zuckert, Catherine H. 2000. "Who's a Philosopher? Who's a Sophist? The Stranger v. Socrates." *Review of Metaphysics* 54 (1): 65–97.

Index

Note: An *italicized* page number indicates a diagram.

allegory of the cave, 126–27, 138–39, 143–47, 200n26. *See also* analogies

analogies: to gymnastic, *22*, 36–37; and language, 153, 156, 159; to mathematics, 97; and metaphysics, 126–27, 138–46, 199nn19–23; to mirrors, 136–37; to painting, 156, 196n9; and *poiêsis*, 135–36; and rhetoric, 16, 21–28, *22*, 32, 38, 43–44, 178–79nn2–4, 180n12; and underworld, 121–22; to weaving, 153. *See also* allegory of the cave; divided line; simile of sun

antilogic: definition of, 101; *diakritikê* versus, 188n12; and Presocratic thought, 94, 149–54, 188n16; Socrates's use of, 90, 99–100, 104, 111–21; sophistic use of, 58–59, 74–75, 78–79, 94, 149–54. *See also* contradiction; dialectic; *dissoi logoi*; eristic

apodeixis: poetry versus, 61, 65–66, 183n11; and sophistic speech, 49, 54–56, 73–74

Asianism, 30–31

assertion, 1–2, 19–20, 148, 150, 155, 166–72, 203n20

bacchanalia. *See* corybantism

Bassett, Louis, 150, 154–57, 160, 188n14, 201n8, 202n9

being: and becoming, 8–9, 80–81, 88–91, 95–96, 114–15, 141, 145, 190n25, 199n22; chain of, 124; and *logos*, 78, 86, 122, 123, 167–68; and metaphysics, 8–11, 20, 145–48, 176n8; and nonbeing, 93–96, 161–62, 186n3, 187n8, 190nn24–25, 203n18; and seeming, 1–2, 16–17, 21–24, 44–45, 89, 137–38, 169, 179n5, 180n12, 199n21; and sophistic thought, 14; and *to on*, 157–58, 161. *See also* Heidegger, Martin; ontology; *phusis*

Cole, Thomas, 5–7, 18, 69, 100, 103, 126–33, 191n6

contradiction: impossibility of, 18, 78, 86, 92–97, 99, 154, 186n3, 190n25; in Plato's dialogues, 11–12, 198n14; in Plato's views of rhetoric, 26, 38, 49–52; Protagorean, 85–86, 92–97, 112–15, 117, 119, 127–28, 149–50, 166–67, 186n3, 190n25; Socratic, 25; sophistic, 101–2, 151, 153–55, 157, 162, 202n14. *See also* antilogic; eristic; *dissoi logoi*; Protagoras of Abdera
corybantism, 49, 60, 64–66, 70, 73
cosmetics. See *kommôtikê*
Cratylus, 82–85, 96–97, 188n10, 188n13

Dasein. *See* being
Deleuze, Gilles: on Heraclitus and sophists in Plato, 123; on Plato's metaphysics, 125–26, 137, 147–48, 176n10, 196n5; on Plato's use of myth, 44–45, 57
Derrida, Jacques: on *Phaedrus*, 52, 71–72, 183n9, 196n5; on Plato's metaphysics, 125–26, 176n10; and signification, 171
developmentalism. *See* interpretation, schools of
dialectic: Greek terms for, 191n3; in *Phaedrus*, 183n9; and rhetoric, 2, 17, 49, 75, 103, 118–22; Socrates's preference for, 108–111, 118–22, 145, 193n15; and sophistry, 18, 78–79, 99–104, 111, 113, 116, 118–22
dialegesthai. *See* dialectic
diakritikê, 83, 152–53, 188n12
diêgêsis, 129, 131–32, 196n8, 197n11
dissoi logoi, 14, 18, 77, 78, 85, 186n2, 193n15. *See also* contradiction; Protagoras of Abdera
divided line, 138–39, 141–46, *142*, 199n23. *See also* analogies

enthusiasm, religious. *See* corybantism; inspiration, divine; possession, divine
epic: and palinode, 55–67, 185n23, 186n29; and *poiêsis*, 198n17; and sophistry, 49, 54, 73–74, 183n11. *See also* poetry
eristic, 18, 78–79, 93, 99–104, 109, 111–22, 150, 154, 203n15
eroticism, 18, 45, 48–49, 64–67, 72, 73, 169, 186n26, 186n27
esotericism. *See* interpretation, schools of
etymology: in *Cratylus*, 82–84, 96–97, 157–58, 195n29; Heidegger and, 7–8, 176n6; of *kommotîkê*, 30–35, 37–38, 78, 181n21, 181n26; of *onoma* and *rhêma*, 150, 154–58; scholiast, 32–33, 181n21

flux: Heraclitean doctrine of, 1, 81–82, 96–97, 139, 167–68, 188n13; and Protagoras's thought, 18, 80–90, 102, 149–62, 188n16. *See also* being; Heraclitus
Foucault, Michel, 1, 171–72, 176n10

Gorgias of Leontini: ambassadorial visit to Athens, 40–43; and Athenian politics, 35–36, 41–42, 120–22, 124, 185n20, 193n17; *Encomium of Helen*, 179n3, 185n20; *On Nature*, 179n5, 186n3; Plato's treatment of, 14–15, 25, 27, 71, 77, 169, 178n1, 183n8; and rhetoric definition, 25–26, 28, 39
gums (*kommi*), 23–24, 32, 33–34, 37, 181n21

hairstyling, 23–24, 29–30, 30–31, 181n21
Havelock, Eric: on Greek epic, 17, 65–66, 128, 186n27, 186n28; on literacy, 3–4, 70, 175n3; on Plato's view of poetry, 124, 196n4; on sophistry, 103
Heidegger, Martin, 3, 7–11, 23, 168, 170–73, 176nn6–11, 196n5, 201n6, 203n20
Heraclitus: and being, 9, 190n26; and etymologies of *Cratylus*, 82–84, 157–58, 188n10, 188n13; flux doctrine of, 18, 81–85, 139, 155, 160–62, 167–68; and language, 19–20, 167–68, 170; and Protagoras's thought 18–20, 79–93, 95–97, 99, 123, 149–53, 186n3, 188n16, 190n27. *See also* being; Cratylus; flux; ontology
Herodotus, 33–34
Hesiod, 17, 48, 60–66, 128
Homer: and medieval scholiasts, 33; and Neoplatonism, 57; and *onoma*, 201n7; and oral tradition, 3–4, 66; and palinode, 17, 48, 59–67, 185n23, 186n29;

and Plato's critiques of poetry, 19, 118, 123, 126, 128–33, 135–36, 147, 169, 191n6, 197n11, 197n12
horses: and Athenian displays of wealth, 30–31, 40; as epic symbols, 63, 186n29; as erotic symbols, 60, 64–67; and myth of charioteer, 48, 56, 61, 65–66, 70

imitation. See *mimêsis*
inoculation, 48–49, 71–74. See also *pharmakon*
inspiration, divine: and epic tradition, 48–49, 198n13; and Socrates's palinode, 17, 55–56, 65–66, 68, 71, 182n1, 184n14, 185n22. *See also* corybantism; madness, divine; possession, divine
interpretation, schools of: developmentalist, 12, 176n12, 177n15; esotericist, 12, 177n13; literary-dramatic, 3, 11–13, 15, 175n3, 177n14, 177n16; Neoplatonist, 11, 29, 52, 57–58, 74; unitarian, 11–12

kommi (gums), 23–24, 32, 33–34, 37, 181n21
kommôtikê: and analogy to sophistry, 16, 22–29, 43–44; and cosmetics, 16, 22–23; etymology of, 23–24, 29–35, 37–38, 78, 179n6, 180n14, 180n15, 181n20, 181n21; and perfume, 24, 34–38. *See also* analogies; gums (*kommi*)

literacy, 3–7, 58, 175n3. *See also* orality, theory of
logos: as assertion, 20, 155, 163, 167–68, 170, 175n1; and Heraclitean ontology, 19–20, 80–86, 88, 96–97, 150, 167–68, 169–70, 172, 187n7; and metaphysics, 145, 168, 170; and *mimêsis*, 163–67; Plato's theory of, 10, 19–20, 78, 97–98, 99–100, 118, 120, 122–23, 126, 149–50, 154–58, 160–63, 167–68, 169–73, 190n27, 202n14; Protagoras's theory of, 78, 80–82, 85, 86, 88, 93, 96–98, 116; and truth, 82, 85, 96–98, 99–100, 119, 123, 126, 127, 137, 147, 149–50, 166–68, 170, 187n8; and writing, 48, 72
Lysias: and perfume testimony, 35, 181n22; and Phaedrus's written speech, 17, 48–49, 54–56, 59, 60, 64–70, 74, 182n2, 184n12, 184n13, 191n6, 194n18; and speechwriting, 48, 184n19

madness, divine, 53, 65–67, 70, 74, 184n14, 185n22. *See also* corybantism; eroticism; inspiration, divine; possession, divine
man-measure doctrine (Protagoras of Abdera): definition of, 79, 95–96; and Socrates, 78–79, 83, 85–93, 97–98, 149, 188n15, 189nn17–21, 190n22; and two-*logoi* doctrine, 18, 77–78, 85–86, 93, 96–98, 101, 116, 154, 186n2, 193n15. *See also* Protagoras of Abdera
mathematics, 97–98, 199n25
metaphysics, Western: and charioteer myth 56–58, 60–61; and Christianity, 10, 58; critiques of, 3, 7–11, 125, 170–71, 196n5; *mimêsis* and structure of, 125–26, 138; Platonist, 16–17, 44–45, 56–58, 89, 125–27, 147–48, 168, 169–71, 176n8, 176n10; *Republic* and, 137–47. *See also* being; ontology
mimêsis: and *diêgêsis*, 129, 131; and falseness, 126–27, 133–34, 136–37, 138, 148; and imitation, 19, 130–32, 136, 196n9; and language, 19–20, 126–29, 133–34, 137, 148, 200n29; and literary theory, 124–25; and poetic performance, 19, 130–32, 134, 137, 198n13, 200n29; and *poiêsis*, 135–37; and rhetorical theory, 3, 10, 19, 103, 125–28, 131, 133, 147–48, 149–50, 155–56, 158–60, 163, 167–68, 170, 195n1; and sophists, 147–48, 149–50, 163–66; and Western metaphysics, 125–26, 133, 137–48, 176n10, 196n5, 199n25. *See also* rhetorical theory
myth: of afterlife, 25, 44–45, 124; of Boreas and Oreithuia, 54, 72–74; of charioteer, 25, 48, 52–54, 56–58, 60–67, 183n10, 184n18, 185n21; of cicadas, 72; Plato's use of, 44–45, 56–57, 74; of Prometheus, 107–8, 120; of Theuth, 48, 71–72

Neoplatonism. *See* interpretation, schools of; palinode
nonbeing. *See* being

Ong, Walter J., 4, 58–59, 172
onoma: archaic uses of, 155–56, 201nn6–7; and assertion, 19, 163, 166–68, 170; correctness of, 82–86, 96–97; etymology of, 150, 154–63, 188n14, 200n4, 201n8, 202n9; and reference, 20, 151, 154, 156–58, 160, 162–63, 170, 175n1, 190n24, 200n2, 202n10, 203n15; and rhetorical theory, 2, 10, 103, 123, 126, 138, 149–51, 154–63, 170, 195n29, 202n14. *See also* Bassett, Louis; *rhêma*
ontology: Heraclitean, 18, 79, 157–58, 161, 188n13; Parmenidean, 79, 95; pre-Socratic, 3–4, 8, 18, 72–73, 78–79, 95, 149–50, 168, 178n18; Protagorean, 80–82, 86–88, 99, 153, 187n6. *See also* being; *phusis*
orality, theory of, 3–7. *See also* Cole, Thomas; epic; Ong, Walter J.; poetry
orthoepeia, 85, 102, 114–15, 194n20

palinode: Neoplatonist interpretation of, 57–58, 74; and references to epic tradition, 55, 58–67, 72; and rhetoric, 48–49, 52–54, 70–74, 194n18; and Socratic irony, 182n1; standard interpretation of, 47–48, 52, 56–57, 74; and unity of *Phaedrus*, 183nn9–10
Parmenides: and *logos*, 170; and nonbeing, 9, 79, 93–96, 190n26; and Protagoras, 95–96, 190n25; and Socrates's palinode, 61–62; and sophistic movement, 186n3
Peloponnesian War, 24, 31, 38–43, 78, 104, 107, 122, 124. *See also* Thucydides
perfume: and aristocratic Athenian profligacy, 24, 30, 34–39, 43, 105, 181nn23–24; Athenaeus's testimony regarding, 35, 181n22; and Egyptian commerce, 16, 24, 33–34. *See also* gums (*kommi*)
pharmakon, 18, 45, 71–72, 134, 179n3. *See also* Derrida, Jacques; inoculation
phusis: Heraclitean, 1, 19, 80–90, 96–97, 150, 167–68, 170, 187n7; and language, 19–20, 81–86, 95–97, 102, 150, 157–62, 167–68, 169–72, 187n7, 188n11, 200n2, 202n14; and *mimêsis*, 137, 159; and *nomos*, 187n9, 195n2; Parmenidean, 94–96, 170. *See also* flux; ontology
poetry: dithyrambic, 55; and Greek oral culture, 58–61, 65–67, 74–75, 186nn27–28; literary analysis of, 100, 104, 111–19, 129–32, 194n18, 194n20; and *mimêsis*, 124, 127, 129–32, 133–34, 144, 146, 164, 196n9; Plato's critique of, 124–25, 127–30, 132–33, 134, 147, 195n3, 196n4, 196n7, 198n13, 200n29; and *poiêsis*, 133–37, 198n17; and rhetorical theory, 19, 54, 73–75, 194n18; and sophistry, 9–10, 17, 19, 45, 49, 54, 73, 77–78, 103–4, 115–16, 133, 135–36, 147, 164, 169, 194n20, 195n3, 196n4, 200n29. *See also* epic; inspiration, divine; palinode
possession, divine, 17, 55, 62–65, 183n9, 184n14, 185n22. *See also* corybantism; inspiration, divine; madness, divine
pre-Socratics. *See* Heraclitus; ontology; Parmenides; sophists
Proclus, 57–58, 184nn17–18
Prometheus. *See* myth
Protagoras of Abdera: apology of, 90–93; and Athenian politics, 120–22; charging fees, 36, 105–6; and Heraclitus, 79–86, 88, 95–97, 150, 152, 186n3, 188n16, 190n27; major doctrines, 18, 78–80, 99; oratorical power of, 18–19, 104, 107–8, 113; and Parmenides, 94–96; and Simonides's poem, 111–13, 194n18; and Socrates, 102–3, 109–11, 114–22, 169, 186n1, 191n7, 193n15, 195n23; testimony about, 77; two-*logoi* doctrine, 18, 77–78, 85–86, 93, 96–98, 101, 116, 154, 186n2, 193n15. *See also* contradiction; *dissoi logoi*; sophists

religion. *See* corybantism; metaphysics, Western
rhêma: and assertion, 150, 163, 167, 203n15;

etymology of, 150, 154–58, 202n9; as phrase, 155–58, 160, 162–63; Plato's use of, 19–20, 149, 155, 201n6, 201n8; rhetorical theory of, 2, 10, 103, 123, 126, 138, 150, 154, 167–70; as verb, 155, 175n1, 200n4
rhetorical theory: definition of, 5–7, 14, 103–4, 177n17; Plato's use of, 8–10, 18–20, 74, 78, 97, 100, 122, 123–24, 127, 157, 167–68, 170–72, 195n24. See also *logos*; *mimêsis*; *onoma*; *rhêma*

Schiappa, Edward, 5–7, 18, 28, 79, 85, 95, 101–2, 116, 178n18
seeming. *See* being
Sextus Empiricus, 80–82, 179n5, 187n5
simile of sun, 126, 138–41, *141*, 143–47. *See also* analogies
Simonides, 18, 100, 103–4, 111–19, 191n7, 193n15, 194n18
sophists; and analogy to *kommôtikê*, 21–24, *22*, 37; common practices of, 101–3, 114–16, 153, 187n9, 188n12, 191n7; definition of, 13–16, 105, 151–52, 177n17; and *mimêsis*, 135–37, 147–48, 163–68, 170, 196n4, 200n29, 203n16; movement of, 14, 77, 79; Plato's critique of, 14–16, 18–19, 41–45, 71, 77–79, 99–100, 105–6, 121–22, 147–48; and Plato's rhetorical theory, 2, 79, 104, 126, 147–48, 151, 155–56, 163–68, 203n18; Plato's victory over, 9–10, 19–20, 170; and poetic tradition, 17–18, 48–49, 59–60, 73–75, 200n29; political influence of, 35–36, 106, 120–22, 183n8; and pre-Socratic thought, 79–98, 186n3, 188n16, 190n25; and speech writing, 53, 59, 68, 72–73, 184n19. *See also* Gorgias of Leontini; Protagoras of Abdera

Thucydides, 24, 31, 40–43, 180n19, 182n29, 201n7. *See also* Peloponnesian War
two-*logoi*. *See* contradiction; *dissoi logoi*; Protagoras of Abdera

unitarianism. *See* interpretation, schools of

writing: Plato's critique of, 17–18, 47–49, 59, 67–74; Plato's use of, 177n13; and rhetorical theory, 4–7, 14, 19, 67–74, 100, 103–4, 112, 122–29, 133, 169–70, 191n6; and speeches, 59, 182n2, 184n19, 186n30. *See also* literacy

Xenophon, 24, 35–37, 105